Getting Started with Oracle Data Integrator 11g: A Hands-On Tutorial

Combine high volume data movement, complex transformations and real-time data integration with the robust capabilities of ODI in this practical guide

Peter C. Boyd-Bowman

Christophe Dupupet

Denis Gray

David Hecksel

Julien Testut

Bernard Wheeler

BIRMINGHAM - MUMBAI

Getting Started with Oracle Data Integrator 11g: A Hands-On Tutorial

First published: May 2012

Production Reference: 1180512

Published by Packt Publishing Ltd.
Livery Place
35 Livery Street
Birmingham B3 2PB, UK.

ISBN 978-1-84968-068-4

www.packtpub.com

Cover Image by David Gutierrez (bilbaorocker@yahoo.co.uk)

Credits

Authors
Peter C. Boyd-Bowman
Christophe Dupupet
Denis Gray
David Hecksel
Julien Testut
Bernard Wheeler

Reviewers
Uli Bethke
Kevin Glenny
Maciej Kocon
Suresh Lakshmanan
Ronald Rood

Acquisition Editor
Stephanie Moss

Lead Technical Editor
Hyacintha D'Souza

Technical Editors
Veronica Fernandes
Joyslita D'Souza

Project Coordinator
Joel Goveya

Proofreader
Katherine Tarr

Indexer
Hemangini Bari

Graphics
Valentina D'silva
Manu Joseph

Production Coordinator
Prachali Bhiwandkar

Cover Work
Prachali Bhiwandkar

Foreword

The May 26, 2011 edition of the Economist magazine cites a report by the the the McKinsey Global Institute (MGI) about data becoming a factor of production, such as physical or human capital. Across the industry, enterprises are investing significant resources in harnessing value from vast amounts of data to innovate, compete, and reduce operational costs.

In light of this global focus on data explosion, data revolution, and data analysis the authors of this book couldn't have possibly chosen a more appropriate time to share their unique insight and broad technical experience in leveraging Oracle Data Integrator (ODI) to deliver key data integration initiatives across global enterprises.

Oracle Data Integrator constitutes a key product in Oracle's Data Integration product portfolio. ODI product architecture is built on high performance ELT, with guiding principles being: ease of use, avoiding expensive mid-tier transformation servers, and flexibility to integrate with heterogeneous platforms.

I am delighted that the authors, six of the foremost experts on Oracle Data Integrator 11g have decided to share their deep knowledge of ODI in an easy to follow manner that covers the subject material both from a conceptual and an implementation aspect. They cover how ODI leverages next generation Extract-Load-Transformation technology to deliver extreme performance in enabling state of the art solutions that help deliver rich analytics and superior business intelligence in modern data warehousing environments. Using an easy-to-follow hands-on approach, the authors guide the reader through successively complex and challenging data integration tasks — from the basic blocking and tackling of creating interfaces using a multitude of source and target technologies, to more advanced ODI topics such as data workflows, management and monitoring, scheduling, impact analysis and interfacing with ODI Web Services. If your goal is to jumpstart your ODI 11g knowledge and productivity to quickly deliver business value, you are on the right track. Dig in, and Integrate.

Alok Pareek
Vice President, Product Management/Data Integration
Oracle Corp

About the Authors

Peter C. Boyd-Bowman is a Technical Consulting Director with the Oracle Corporation. He has over 30 years of software engineering and database management experience, including 12 years of focused interest in data warehousing and business intelligence. Capitalizing on his extensive background in Oracle database technologies dating back to 1985, he has spent recent years specializing in data migration. After many successful project implementations using Oracle Warehouse Builder and shortly after Oracle's acquisition of the Sunopsis Corporation, he switched his area of focus over to Oracle's flagship ETL product: Oracle Data Integrator. He holds a BS degree in Industrial Management and Computer Science from Purdue University and currently resides in North Carolina.

Christophe Dupupet is a Director of Product Management for ODI at Oracle. In this role, he focuses on the Customer Care program where he works closely with strategic customers implementing ODI. Prior to Oracle, he was part of the team that started the operations for Sunopsis in the US (Sunopsis created the ODI product and was acquired by Oracle in 2006).

He holds an Operations Research degree from EISTI in France, a Masters Degree in Operations Research from Florida Tech, and a Certificate in Management from Harvard University.

He writes blogs (mostly technical entries) at `http://blogs.oracle.com/dataintegration` as well as white papers.

> Special thanks to my wife, Viviane, and three children, Quentin, Audrey, and Ines, for their patience and support for the long evenings and weekends spent on this book.

David Hecksel is a Principal Data Integration Architect at Oracle. Residing in Dallas, Texas, he joined Oracle in 2006 as a Pre-sales Architect for Oracle Fusion Middleware. Six months after joining, he volunteered to add pre-sales coverage for a recently acquired product called Oracle Data Integrator and the rest (including the writing of this book) has been a labor of love working with a platform and solution that simultaneously provides phenomenal user productivity and system performance gains to the traditionally separate IT career realms of Data Warehousing, Service Oriented Architects, and Business Intelligence developers. Before joining Oracle, he spent six years with Sun Microsystems in their Sun Java Center and was CTO for four years at Axtive Software, architecting and developing several one-to-one marketing and web personalization platforms such as e.Monogram. In 1997, he also invented, architected, developed, and marketed the award-winning JCertify product online—the industry's first electronic delivery of study content and exam simulation for the Certified Java Programmer exam. Prior to Axtive Software, he was with IBM for 12 years as a Software Developer working on operating system, storage management, and networking software products. He holds a B.S. in Computer Science from the University of Wisconsin-Madison and a Masters of Business Administration from Duke University.

Julien Testut is a Product Manager in the Oracle Data Integration group focusing on Oracle Data Integrator. He has an extensive background in Data Integration and Data Quality technologies and solutions. Prior to joining Oracle, he was an Applications Engineer at Sunopsis which was then acquired by Oracle. He holds a Masters degree in Software Engineering.

I would like to thank my wife Emilie for her support and patience while I was working on this book. A special thanks to my family and friends as well.

I also want to thank Christophe Dupupet for driving all the way across France on a summer day to meet me and give me the opportunity to join Sunopsis. Thanks also to my colleagues who work and have worked on Oracle Data Integrator at Oracle and Sunopsis!

Bernard Wheeler is a Customer Solutions Director at Oracle in the UK, where he focuses on Information Management. He has been at Oracle since 2005, working in pre-sales technical roles covering Business Process Management, SOA, and Data Integration technologies and solutions. Before joining Oracle, he held various pre-sales, consulting, and marketing positions with vendors such as Sun Microsystems, Forte Software, Borland, and Sybase as well as worked for a number of systems integrators. He holds an Engineering degree from Cambridge University.

About the Reviewers

Uli Bethke has more than 12 years of experience in various areas of data management such as data analysis, data architecture, data modeling, data migration and integration, ETL, data quality, data cleansing, business intelligence, database administration, data mining, and enterprise data warehousing. He has worked in finance, the pharmaceutical industry, education, and retail.

He has more than three years of experience in ODI 10*g* and 11*g*.

He is an independent Data Warehouse Consultant based in Dublin, Ireland. He has implemented business intelligence solutions for various blue chip organizations in Europe and North America. He runs an ODI blog at www.bi-q.ie.

> I would like to thank Helen for her patience with me. Your place in heaven is guaranteed. I would also like to thank my little baby boy Ruairí. You are a gas man.

Kevin Glenny has international software engineering experience, which includes work for European Grid Infrastructure (EGI), interconnecting 140K CPU cores and 25 petabytes of disk storage. He is a highly rated Oracle Consultant, with four years of experience in international consulting for blue chip enterprises. He specializes in the area of scalable OLAP and OLTP systems, building on his Grid computing background. He is also the author of numerous technical articles and his industry insights can be found on his company's blog at www.BigDataMatters.com.

GridwiseTech, as Oracle Partner of the Year 2011, is the independent specialist on scalability and large data. The company delivers robust IT architectures for significant data and processing loads. GridwiseTech operates globally and serves clients ranging from Fortune Global 500 companies to government and academia.

Maciej Kocon has been in the IT industry for 10 years. He began his career as a Database Application Programmer and quickly developed a passion for the SQL language, data processing, and analysis.

He entered the realm of BI and data warehousing and has specialized in the design of EL-T frameworks for integration of high data volumes. His experience covers the full data warehouse lifecycle in various sectors including financial services, retail, public sector, telecommunications, and clinical research.

To relax, he enjoys nothing more than taking his camera outdoors for a photo session.

He can be reached at his personal blog `http://artofdi.com`.

Suresh Lakshmanan is currently working as Senior Consultant at Keane Inc., providing technical and architectural solutions for its clients in Oracle products space. He has seven years of technical expertise with high availability Oracle Databases/Applications.

Prior to joining Keane Inc., he worked as a Consultant for Sun Microsystems in Clustered Oracle E-Business Suite implementations for the TSO team. He also worked with Oracle India Pvt Ltd for EFOPS DBA team specializing in Oracle Databases, Oracle E-Business Suite, Oracle Application servers, and Oracle Demantra. Before joining Oracle India, he worked as a Consultant for GE Energy specializing in the core technologies of Oracle.

His key areas of interests include high availability/high performance system design and disaster recovery solution design for Oracle products. He holds an MBA Degree in Computer Systems from Madurai Kamaraj University, Madurai, India. He has done his Bachelor of Engineering in Computer Science from PSG College of Technology, Coimbatore, India. He has written many Oracle related articles in his blog which can be found at `http://applicationsdba.blogspot.com` and can be reached at `meet.lsuresh@gmail.com`.

First and foremost I would like to thank Sri Krishna, for continually guiding me and giving me strength, courage, and support in every endeavor that I undertake. I would like to thank my parents Lakshmanan and Kalavathi for their blessings and encouragements though I live 9,000 miles away from them. Words cannot express the amount of sacrifice, pain, and endurance they have undergone to raise and educate my brother, sister, and me. Hats off to you both for your contributions in our lives. I would like to thank my brother Srinivasan and my sister Suganthi. I could not have done anything without your love, support, and patience. There is nothing more important in my life than my family. And that is a priority that will never change. I would like to thank authors David Hecksel and Bernard Wheeler for giving me a chance to review this book. And my special thanks to Reshma, Poorvi, and Joel for their patience while awaiting a response from me during my reviews.

Ronald Rood is an innovating Oracle DBA with over 20 years of IT experience. He has built and managed cluster databases on about each and every platform that Oracle has ever supported, right from the famous OPS databases in version 7 until the latest RAC releases, the current release being 11*g*. He is constantly looking for ways to get the most value out of the database to make the investment for his customers even more valuable. He knows how to handle the power of the rich Unix environment very well and this is what makes him a first-class troubleshooter and solution architect. Apart from the spoken languages such as Dutch, English, German, and French, he also writes fluently in many scripting languages.

Currently, he is a Principal Consultant working for Ciber in The Netherlands where he cooperates in many complex projects for large companies where downtime is not an option. Ciber (CBR) is an Oracle Platinum Partner and committed to the limit.

He often replies in the oracle forums, writes his own blog called *From errors we learn...* (`http://ronr.blogspot.com`), writes for various Oracle-related magazines, and also wrote a book, *Mastering Oracle Scheduler in Oracle 11g Databases* where he fills the gap between the Oracle documentation and customers' questions. He also was part of the technical reviewing teams for *Oracle 11g R1/R2 Real Application Clusters Essentials* and *Oracle Information Integration, Migration, and Consolidation*, both published by *Packt Publishing*.

He has many certifications to his credit, some of them are Oracle Certified Master, Oracle Certified Professional, Oracle Database 11*g* Tuning Specialist, Oracle Database 11*g* Data Warehouse Certified Implementation Specialist.

He fills his time with Oracle, his family, sky-diving, radio controlled model airplane flying, running a scouting group, and having lot of fun.

He believes "A problem is merely a challenge that might take a little time so solve".

www.PacktPub.com

Support files, eBooks, discount offers and more

You might want to visit www.PacktPub.com for support files and downloads related to your book.

Did you know that Packt offers eBook versions of every book published, with PDF and ePub files available? You can upgrade to the eBook version at www.PacktPub.com and as a print book customer, you are entitled to a discount on the eBook copy. Get in touch with us at service@packtpub.com for more details.

At www.PacktPub.com, you can also read a collection of free technical articles, sign up for a range of free newsletters and receive exclusive discounts and offers on Packt books and eBooks.

http://PacktLib.PacktPub.com

Do you need instant solutions to your IT questions? PacktLib is Packt's online digital book library. Here, you can access, read and search across Packt's entire library of books.

Why Subscribe?

- Fully searchable across every book published by Packt
- Copy and paste, print and bookmark content
- On demand and accessible via web browser

Free Access for Packt account holders

If you have an account with Packt at www.PacktPub.com, you can use this to access PacktLib today and view nine entirely free books. Simply use your login credentials for immediate access.

Instant Updates on New Packt Books

Get notified! Find out when new books are published by following @PacktEnterprise on Twitter, or the *Packt Enterprise* Facebook page.

Table of Contents

Preface

Oracle Data Integrator—background and history

Oracle has been a leading provider of database, data warehousing, and other data management technologies for over 30 years. More recently it has also become a leading provider of standards-based integration, Service-oriented architecture (SOA) and Business Process Automation technologies (also known as Middleware), Big Data, and Cloud solutions. Data integration technologies are at the heart of all these solutions. Beyond the technical solutions, adopting and using ODI allows IT to cross the chasm between business requirements and data integration challenges.

In July 2010, the 11gR1 release of Oracle Data Integrator was made available to the marketplace. Oracle Data Integrator 11g (referred to in the rest of this book as ODI) is Oracle's strategic data integration platform. Having roots from the Oracle acquisition of Sunopsis in October 2006, ODI is a market leading data integration solution with capabilities across heterogeneous IT systems. Oracle has quickly and aggressively invested in ODI to provide an easy-to-use and comprehensive approach for satisfying data integration requirements within Oracle software products. As a result, there are dozens of Oracle products such as Hyperion Essbase, Agile PLM, AIA Process Integration Packs, and Business Activity Monitor (BAM) that are creating an explosive increase in the use of ODI within IT organizations. If you are using Oracle software products and have not heard of or used ODI yet, one thing is sure—you soon will!

This book is not meant to be used as a reference book — it is a means to accelerate your learning of ODI 11*g*. When designing the book, the following top-level objectives were kept in mind:

- To highlight the key capabilities of the product in relation to data integration tasks (loading, enrichment, quality, and transformation) and the productivity achieved by being able to do so much work with heterogeneous datatypes while writing so little SQL

- To select a sample scenario that was varied enough to do something useful and cover the types of data sources and targets customers are using most frequently (multiple flavors of relational database, flat files, and XML data) while keeping it small enough to provide an ODI accelerated learning experience

- To ensure that where possible within our examples, we examine the new features and functionality introduced with version 11*g* — the first version of ODI architected, designed, and implemented as part of Oracle

Data integration usage scenarios

As seen in the following figure, no matter what aspect of IT you work on, all have a common element among them, that is, **Data Integration**. Everyone wants their information accessible, up-to-date, consistent, and trusted.

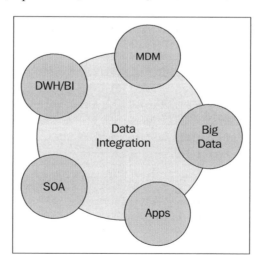

Data warehouses and BI

Before you can put together the advanced reporting metrics required by the different entities of your enterprise, you will have to consolidate, rationalize, and organize the data. Operational systems are too busy serving their customers to be overloaded by additional reporting queries. In addition, they are optimized to serve their applications—not for the purposes of analytics and reporting.

Data warehouses are often time-designed to support reporting requirements. Integrating data from operational systems into data warehouses has traditionally been the prime rationale for investing in integration technologies: disparate and heterogeneous systems hold critical data that must be consolidated; data structures have to be transposed and reorganized. Data Integrator is no exception to the rule and definitely plays a major role in such initiatives.

Throughout this book, we will cover data integration cases that are typical of integration requirements found in a data warehousing environment.

Service-oriented architecture (SOA)

Service-oriented architecture encourages the concept of service virtualization. As a consequence, the actual physical location of where data requests are resolved is of less concern to consumers of SOA-based services. The SOA implementations rely on large amounts of data being processed so that the services built on top of the data can serve the appropriate information. ODI plays a crucial role in many SOA deployments as it seamlessly integrates with web services. We are not focusing on the specifics of web services in this book, but all the logic of data movement and transformations that ODI would perform when working in a SOA environment would remain the same as the ones described in this book.

Applications

More and more applications have their own requirements in terms of data integration. As such, more and more applications utilize a data integration tool to perform all these operations: the generated flows perform better, are easier to design and to maintain. It should be no surprise then that ODI is used under the covers by dozens of applications. In some cases, the ODI code is visible and can be modified by the users of the applications. In other cases, the code is operating "behind the scenes" and does not become visible.

In all cases though, the same development best practices, and design rules are applied. For the most part, application developers will use the same techniques and best practices when using ODI. And if you have to customize these applications, the lessons learned from this book will be equally useful.

Master Data Management

The rationale for **Master Data Management (MDM)** solutions is to normalize data definitions. Take the example of customer references in an enterprise for instance. The sales application has a definition for customers. The support application has its own definition, so do the finance application, and the shipping application. The objective of MDM solutions is to provide a single definition of the information, so that all entities reference the same data (versus each having their own definition). But the exchange and transformation of data from one environment to the next can only be done with a tool like ODI.

Big Data

The explosion of data in the information age is offering new challenges to IT organizations, often referenced as Big Data. The solutions for Big Data often rely on distributed processing to reduce the complexity of processing gigantic volumes of data. Delegating and distributing processing is what ODI does with its ELT architecture. As new implementation designs are conceived, ODI is ready to endorse these new infrastructures. We will not look into Big Data implementations with ODI in this book, but you have to know that ODI is ready for Big Data integration as of its 11.1.1.6 release.

What this book covers

The number one goal of this book is to get you familiar, comfortable, and successful with using Oracle Data Integrator 11gR1. To achieve this, the largest part of the book is a set of hands-on step-by-step tutorials that build a non-trivial Order Processing solution that you can run, test, monitor, and manage.

Chapter 1, Product Overview, gets you up to speed quickly with the ODI 11g product and terminology by examining the ODI 11g product architecture and concepts.

Chapter 2, Product Installation, provides the necessary instructions for the successful download, installation, and configuration of ODI 11g.

Chapter 3, Using Variables, is a chapter that can be read out of sequence. It covers variables in ODI, a concept that will allow to have very dynamic code. We will mention variables in the subsequent chapters, so having this reference early can help.

Chapter 4, ODI Sources, Targets, and Knowledge Modules, is a general introduction to the key features of ODI Studio. It will also explain how they map onto core concepts and activities of data integration tasks, such as sources, targets and how data flows between them.

Chapter 5, Working with Databases, is the first chapter that will show how to use ODI Studio to work with databases: how to connect to the databases, how to reverse-engineer metadata, how to design transformations, and how to review the executions. This chapter will specifically concentrate on connecting to Oracle databases, and will be a baseline for chapters 6 to 9.

Chapter 6, Working with MySQL, will introduce the requirements of working with a different technology: MySQL. We will expand on the techniques covered in the previous chapter with a description of how to incorporate joins, lookups, and aggregations in the transformations.

Chapter 7, Working with Microsoft SQL Server, will expand the examples with use of yet another database, this time Microsoft SQL Server. It will focus on possible alteration to transformations: Is the code executed on the source, staging area, or target? When making these choices, where is the code generated in the Operator? We will also detail how to leverage the ODI Expression editor to write the transformations, and how to have ODI create a temporary index to further improve integration performance.

Chapter 8, Integrating File Data, will introduce the notion of flat files and will focus on the differences between flat files and databases.

Chapter 9, Working with XML Files, will focus on a specific type of file, that is XML files. This chapter will show how easy it is with ODI to parse XML files with standard SQL queries.

Chapter 10, Creating Workflows – Packages and Load Plans, will show you how to orchestrate your work and go beyond the basics of integration.

Chapter 11, Error Management, will explore in depth the subject of error management: data error versus process errors, how to trap them, and how to handle them.

Chapter 12, Managing and Monitoring ODI Components, will conclude with the management aspect of the processes, particularly with regard to to scheduling of the jobs designed with ODI.

If it is not obvious by the time you finish reading this book, we *really like* ODI 11gR1. Those feelings have been earned by rock solid architecture choices and an investment level that allows innovation to flourish—from new agent clustering and manageability features to integrating with any size of system, including the largest data warehouses using Oracle, Exadata, Teradata, and others from files to in-memory data caches.

What you need for this book

If you want to follow the examples in your own environment, you'll need:
- Oracle Data Integrator 11g
- Oracle database (10g or 11g)
- Microsoft SQL Server (2005 or 2008)
- MySQL 5 and higher
- RCU (Oracle Repository Creation Utility) and Java 1.6 (needed for the Oracle Universal Installer that installs ODI)

Who this book is for

This book is intended for those who are interested in, or responsible for, the content, freshness, movement, access to, or integration with data. Job roles that are a likely match include ETL developers, Data Warehouse Specialists, Business Intelligence Analysts, Database Administrators, Database Programmers, Enterprise, or Data Architect, among others.

Those interested in, or responsible for, data warehouses, data marts, operational data stores, reporting and analytic servers, bulk data load/movement/transformation, real-time Business Intelligence, and/or MDM will find this material of particular interest.

No prior knowledge or experience with Oracle Data Integrator is required or assumed. However, people with experience in programming with SQL or developing ETL processes with other products will better understand how to achieve the same tasks—hopefully being more productive and with better performance.

Who this book is not for

This book is not for someone looking for a tutorial on SQL and/or relational database concepts. It is not a book on advanced features of ODI, or advanced integration techniques using ODI.

Conventions

In this book, you will find a number of styles of text that distinguish between different kinds of information. Here are some examples of these styles, and an explanation of their meaning.

Code words in text are shown as follows: "We'll be integrating data into the PURCHASE_ORDER table in the data mart".

A block of code is set as follows:

```
<?xml version="1.0" encoding="UTF-8"?>
<Building>
   <StreetAddr>32 Lincoln Road</StreetAddr>
   <Locality>Olton</Locality>
   <City>Birmingham</City>
   <StateOrProv>West Midlands</StateOrProv>
   <PostCode>B27 6PA</PostCode>
   <CountryCode>44</CountryCode>
</Building>
```

Any command-line input or output is written as follows:

```
OdiFileCopy -FILE=c:/po/input/order_20001.xml
 -TOFILE=c:/po/input/single_po.xml -CASESENS=yes
```

New terms and **important words** are shown in bold. Words that you see on the screen, in menus or dialog boxes for example, appear in the text like this: "Next we click on the browse icon to the right of the **JDBC Url** field to open the **URL examples** dialog".

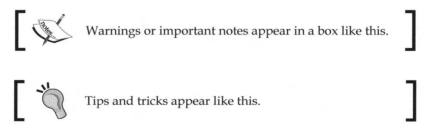

Warnings or important notes appear in a box like this.

Tips and tricks appear like this.

Reader feedback

Feedback from our readers is always welcome. Let us know what you think about this book—what you liked or may have disliked. Reader feedback is important for us to develop titles that you really get the most out of.

To send us general feedback, simply send an e-mail to feedback@packtpub.com, and mention the book title through the subject of your message.

If there is a topic that you have expertise in and you are interested in either writing or contributing to a book, see our author guide on www.packtpub.com/authors.

Customer support

Now that you are the proud owner of a Packt book, we have a number of things to help you to get the most from your purchase.

Errata

Although we have taken every care to ensure the accuracy of our content, mistakes do happen. If you find a mistake in one of our books—maybe a mistake in the text or the code—we would be grateful if you would report this to us. By doing so, you can save other readers from frustration and help us improve subsequent versions of this book. If you find any errata, please report them by visiting http://www.packtpub.com/support, selecting your book, clicking on the **errata submission form** link, and entering the details of your errata. Once your errata are verified, your submission will be accepted and the errata will be uploaded to our website, or added to any list of existing errata, under the Errata section of that title.

Piracy

Piracy of copyright material on the Internet is an ongoing problem across all media. At Packt, we take the protection of our copyright and licenses very seriously. If you come across any illegal copies of our works, in any form, on the Internet, please provide us with the location address or website name immediately so that we can pursue a remedy.

Please contact us at `copyright@packtpub.com` with a link to the suspected pirated material.

We appreciate your help in protecting our authors, and our ability to bring you valuable content.

Questions

You can contact us at `questions@packtpub.com` if you are having a problem with any aspect of the book, and we will do our best to address it.

1
Product Overview

The purpose of ETL (Extract, Load, Transform) tools is to help with the consolidation of data that is dispersed throughout the information system. Data is stored in disparate applications, databases, files, operating systems, and in incompatible formats. The consequences of such a dispersal of the information can be dire, for example, different business units operating on different data will show conflicting results and information cannot be shared across different entities of the same business.

Imagine the marketing department reporting on the success of their latest campaign while the finance department complains about its lack of efficiency. Both have numbers to back up their assertions, but the numbers do not match!

What could be worse than a shipping department that struggles to understand customer orders, or a support department that cannot confirm whether a customer is current with his/her payment and should indeed receive support? The examples are endless.

The only way to have a centralized view of the information is to consolidate the data—whether it is in a data warehouse, a series of data marts, or by normalizing the data across applications with master data management (MDM) solutions. ETL tools usually come into play when a large volume of data has to be exchanged (as opposed to Service-Oriented Architecture infrastructures for instance, which would be more transaction based).

In the early days of ETL, databases had very weak transformation functions. Apart from using an insert or a select statement, SQL was a relatively limited language. To perform heavy duty, complex transformations, vendors put together transformation platforms—the ETL tools.

Over time, the SQL language has evolved to include more and more transformation capabilities. You can now go as far as handling hierarchies, manipulating XML formats, using analytical functions, and so on. It is not by chance that 50 percent of the ETL implementations in existence today are done in plain SQL scripts — SQL makes it possible.

This is where the ODI ELT architecture (Extract-Load-Transform — the inversion in the acronym is not a mistake) comes into play. The concept with ELT is that instead of extracting the data from a source, transforming it with a dedicated platform, and then loading into the target database, you will extract from the source, load into the target, then transform into the target database, leveraging SQL for the transformations.

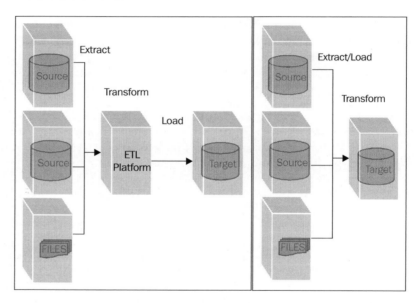

To some extent, ETL and ELT are marketing acronyms. When you look at ODI for instance, it can perform transformations on the source side as well as on the target side. You can also dedicate some database or schema for the staging and transformation of your data, and can have something more similar to an ETL architecture. Similarly, some ETL tools all have the ability to generate SQL code and to push some transformations at the database level.

The key differences then for a true ELT architecture are as follows:

- The ability to dynamically manage a staging area (location, content, automatic management of table alterations)

- The ability to generate code on source and target systems alike, in the same transformation

- The ability to generate native SQL for any database on the market — most ETL tools will generate code for their own engines, and then translate that code for the databases — hence limiting their generation capacities to their ability to convert proprietary concepts

- The ability to generate DML and DDL, and to orchestrate sequences of operations on the heterogeneous systems

In a way, the purpose of an ELT tool is to provide the comfort of a graphical interface with all the functionality of traditional ETL tools, to keep the efficiency of SQL coding with set-based processing of data in the database, and limiting the overhead of moving data from place to place.

In this chapter we will focus on the architecture of Oracle Data Integrator 11*g*, as well as the key concepts of the product. The topics we will cover are as follows:

- The elements of the architecture, namely, the repository, the Studio, the Agents, the Console, and integration into Oracle Enterprise Manager

- An introduction to key concepts, namely, Execution Contexts, Knowledge Modules, Models, Interfaces, Packages, Scenarios, and Load Plans

ODI product architecture

Since ODI is an ELT tool, it requires no other platform than the source and target systems. But there still are ODI components to be deployed: we will see in this section what these components are and where they should be installed.

The components of the ODI architecture are as follows:

- **Repository**: This is where all the information handled by ODI is stored, namely, connectivity details, metadata, transformation rules and scenarios, generated code, execution logs, and statistics.

- **Studio**: The Studio is the graphical interface of ODI. It is used by administrators, developers, and operators.

- **Agents**: The Agents can be seen as orchestrators for the data movement and transformations. They are very lightweight java components that do not require their own server—we will see in detail where they can be installed.

- **Console**: The Console is a web tool that lets users browse the ODI repository, but it is not a tool used to develop new transformations. It can be used by operators though to review code execution, and start or restart processes as needed.

- The **Oracle Enterprise Manager** plugin for ODI integrates the monitoring of ODI components directly into OEM so that administrators can consolidate the monitoring of all their Oracle products in one single graphical interface.

At a high level, here is how the different components of the architecture interact with one another. The administrators, developers, and operators typically work with the ODI Studio on their machine (operators also have the ability to use the Console for a more lightweight environment). All Studios typically connect to a shared repository where all the metadata is stored. At run time, the ODI Agent receives execution orders (from the Studio, or any external scheduler, or via a Web Service call). At this point it connects to the repository, retrieves the code to execute, adds last minute parameters where needed (elements like connection strings, schema names where the data resides, and so on), and sends the code to the databases for execution. Once the databases have executed the code, the agent updates the repository with the status of the execution (successful or not, along with any related error message) and the relevant statistics (number of rows, time to process, and so on).

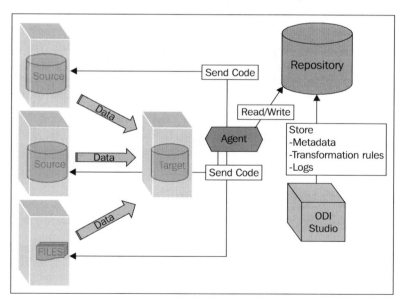

Now let's look into the details of each component.

ODI repository

To store all its information, ODI requires a repository. The repository is by default a pair of schemas (called Master and Work repositories) stored in a database. Unless ODI is running in a near real time fashion, continuously generating SQL code for the databases to execute the code, there is no need to dedicate a database for the ODI repository. Most customers leverage existing database installations, even if they create a dedicated tablespace for ODI.

Repository overview

The only element you will never find in the repository is the actual data processed by ODI. The data will be in the source and target systems, and will be moved directly from source to target. This is a key element of the ELT architecture. All other elements that are handled through ODI are stored into the repository. An easy way to remember this is that everything that is visible in the ODI Studio is stored in the repository (except, of course, for the actual data), and everything that is saved in the ODI Studio is actually saved into the repository (again, except for the actual data).

The repository is made of two entities which can be separated into two separate database schemas, namely, the Master repository and the Work repository.

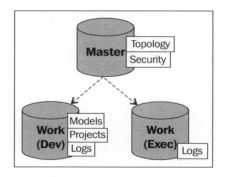

We will look at each one of these in more detail later, but for now you can consider that the Master repository will host sensitive data whereas the Work repository will host project-related data. A limited version of the Work repository can be used in production environments, where the source code is not needed for execution.

Repository location

Before going into the details of the Master and Work repositories, let's first look into where to install the repository.

The repository is usually installed in an existing database, often in a separate tablespace. Even though ODI is an Oracle product, the repository does not have to be stored in an Oracle database (but who would not use the best database in the world?). Generally speaking, the databases supported for the ODI repository are Oracle, Microsoft SQL Server, IBM/DB2 (LUW and iSeries), Hypersonic SQL, and Sybase ASE. Specific versions and platforms for each database are published by Oracle and are available at:

```
http://www.oracle.com/technetwork/middleware/ias/downloads/fusion-
certification-100350.html.
```

It is usual to see the repository share the same system as the target database.

We will now look into the specifics of Master and Work repositories.

Master repository

As stated earlier, the Master repository is where the sensitive data will be stored. This information is of the following types:

- All the information that pertains to ODI users privileges will be saved here. This information is controlled by administrators through the Security Navigator of the ODI Studio. We will learn more about this navigator when we look into the details of the Studio.

- All the information that pertains to connectivity to the different systems (sources and targets), and in particular the requisite usernames and passwords, will be stored here. This information will be managed by administrators through the Topology Navigator.

- In addition, whenever a developer creates several versions of the same object, the subsequent versions of the objects are stored in the Master repository. Versioning is typically accessed from the Designer Navigator.

Work repository

Work repositories will store all the data that is required for the developers to design their data transformations. All the information stored in the Work repository is managed through the Designer Navigator and the Operator Navigator. The Work repository contains the following components:

- The Metadata that represents the source and target tables, files, applications, message buses. These will be organized in Models in the Designer Navigator.

- The transformation rules and data movement rules. These will be organized in Interfaces in the Designer Navigator.

- The workflows designed to orchestrate the transformations and data movement. These are organized in Packages and Load Plans in the Designer Navigator.

- The jobs schedules, if the ODI Agent is used as the scheduler for the integration tasks. These can be defined either in the Designer Navigator or in the Operator Navigator.

- The logs generated by ODI, where the generated code can be reviewed, along with execution statistics and statuses of the different executions (running, done successfully or in error, queued, and so on). The logs are accessed from the Operator Navigator.

Execution repository

In a production environment, most customers do not need to expose the source code for the processes that are running. Modifications to the processes that run in production will have to go through a testing cycle anyway, so why store the source code where one would never access it? For that purpose, ODI proposes an execution repository that only stores the operational metadata, namely, generated code, execution results, and statistics. The type of Work repository (execution or development) is selected at installation time. A Work repository cannot be converted from development to execution or execution to development—a new installation will be required if a conversion is needed.

Lifecycle management and repositories

We now know that there will be different types of repositories. All enterprise application development teams have more than one environment to consider. The code development itself occurs in a development environment, the validation of the quality of the code is typically done in a test environment, and the production environment itself will have to be separate from these two. Some companies will add additional layers in this lifecycle, with code consolidation (if remote developers have to combine code together), user acceptance (making sure that the code conforms to user expectations), and pre-production (making sure that everything works as expected in an environment that perfectly mimics the production environment).

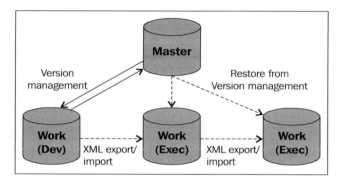

In all cases, each environment will typically have a dedicated Work repository. The Master repository can be a shared resource as long as no network barrier prevents access from Master to Work repository. If the production environment is behind a firewall for instance, then a dedicated Master repository will be required for the production environment.

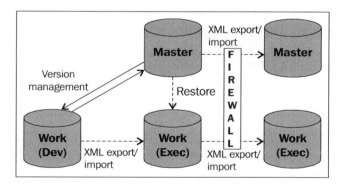

The exchange of metadata between repositories can be done in one of the following ways:

- Metadata can be exchanged through versioning. All different versions of the objects are uploaded to the Master repository automatically by ODI as they are created. These versions can later be restored to a different Work repository attached to the same Master repository.

- All objects can be exported as XML files, and XML files can be used to import the exported objects into the new repository. This will be the only option if a firewall prevents connectivity directly to a central Master repository.

In the graphical representations shown previously, the leftmost repository is obviously our development repository, and the rightmost repository is the production repository. Why are we using an execution for the test environment? There are two rationales for this. They are as follows:

- There is no point in having the source code in the test repository, the source code can always be retrieved from the versioning mechanisms.

- Testing should not be limited to the validation of the artifacts concocted by the developers; the process of migrating to production should also be validated. By having the same setup for our test and production environments, we ensure that the process of going from a development repository to an execution repository has been validated as well.

Studio

The ODI Studio is the graphical interface provided to all users to interact with ODI.

People who need to use the Studio usually install the software on their own machine and connect to a shared repository. The only exception would be when the repository is not on the same LAN as the Studio. In that case, most customers use Remote Terminal Service technologies to ensure that the Studio is local to the repository (same LAN). Only the actual display is then sent over the WAN.

The Studio includes four navigators that are typically used by different users who can share the same objects and the same repository. Some users may not have access to some navigators, depending on their security profiles. The navigators are as follows:

- **Security Navigator**: This navigator is typically used by system administrators, security administrators, and DBAs. Through this interface, they can assign roles and privileges to the different users, making sure that they can only view and modify objects that they are allowed to handle.

- **Topology Navigator**: This navigator is usually restricted to DBAs and System administrators. Through this interface, they declare the systems where the data resides (sources, targets, references, and so on), along with the credentials that ODI will use to connect to these systems. Developers and operators will leverage the information stored in the repository, but will not necessarily have the right to modify, or even view that information. They will be provided with a name for the connections and this is all they will need. We will see this in more detail when we address logical schemas.

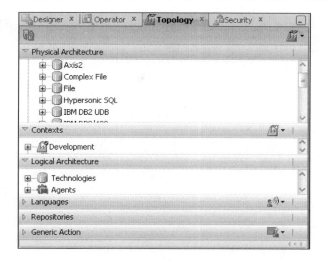

- **Designer Navigator**: This navigator is used by developers and data custodians alike. Metadata are imported and enriched through this navigator. The metadata is then used to define the transformations in objects called Interfaces. The Interfaces are finally orchestrated in workflows called Packages.

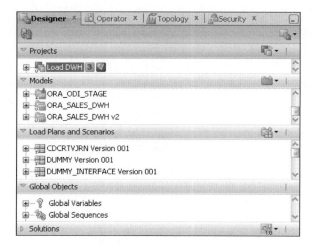

- **Operator Navigator**: This navigator is used by developers and operators. In a development environment, developers will use the **Operator** views to check on the code generated by ODI, to debug their transformations, and to validate and understand performance of their developments. In a production environment, operators use this same navigator to view which processes are running, to check whether processes are successful or not, and to check on the performance of the processes that are running.

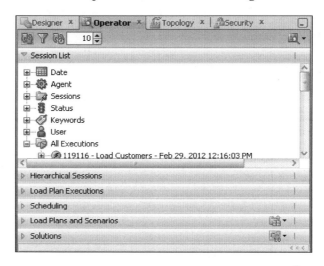

Agent

The ODI Agent is the component that will orchestrate all the operations. If SQL code must be executed by a database (source or target), the agent will connect to that database and will send the code (DDL and DML, as needed) for that database to perform the transformations. If utilities must be used as part of the transformations (or, more likely, as part of the data transfer) then the agent will generate whatever configuration files or parameter files are required for the utility, and will invoke this utility with the appropriate parameters—SQL Loader, BCP, Multiload, and NZload are just a small list of such utilities.

There are two types of ODI Agent, namely, the standalone agent (available in all releases of ODI) and the JEE agent (available with ODI 11*g* and after) that runs on top of WebLogic Server. Each type has its own benefits, and both types of agents can co-exist in the same environment:

- The JEE agent will take advantage of Weblogic in terms of high availability and pooling of the connections.

- The standalone agents are very lightweight and can easily be installed on any platform. They are small Java applications that do not require a server.

A common configuration is to use the JEE agent as a "Master" agent, whose sole purpose it is to distribute execution requests across several child agents. These children can very well be standalone agents. The master agent will know at all times which children are up or down. The master agent will also balance the load across all child agents.

In a pure standalone environment, the Agent is often installed on the target server. Agents are also often installed on file servers, where they can leverage database loading utilities to bulk load data into the target systems. Load balancing can also be done with a standalone master agent. Multiple standalone agents can run on the same server, as long as they each have a dedicated port. This port number is defined in the Topology navigator, where the agent is defined.

The Agent can receive execution orders from different origins as follows:

- **Execution from the Studio**: When a user executes a process from the Studio, he/she is prompted for the name of the agent that will be in charge of the execution.

- **Execution from the Console**: Similarly to the Studio execution, the person requesting a process execution will have to choose the Agent in charge.

- **Execution from a command line**: In this case, ODI will start a dedicated session of the agent, limited to the execution of the process that is passed as a parameter. The script to be used to start a process from a command line is `startscen.bat` on Windows or `startscen.sh` on Unix. This script can be found under the `/bin` directory under the agent installation path.

- **Execution from a web service**: ODI 10*g* offered this feature but required a dedicated setup. ODI 11*g* offers this feature as part of the agent deployment. All agents support web services to start processes. For a standalone agent, connect to the agent via HTTP to view the associated WSDL. For instance, if the agent is running on server odi_dev on port 20910, the wsdl can be found on this very machine at `http://odi_dev:20910/oraclediagent/OdiInvoke?wsdl`.

  The application name for a standalone agent will always be `oraclediagent`. Customers using a JEE agent will use the application name for the ODI Agent.

- **ODI Schedules**: If ODI processes are scheduled from within ODI (from the Operator navigator or the Designer navigator) then the schedule itself is associated with an agent. Either the schedules will be uploaded to the agent by an administrator, or the agent will refresh its list of schedules when it is restarted.

Console

The Console is an HTML interface to the repository. The Console is installed on a WebLogic Server (other application servers will be supported with later releases of the product).

The Console can be used to browse the repository, but no new developments can be created through this interface.

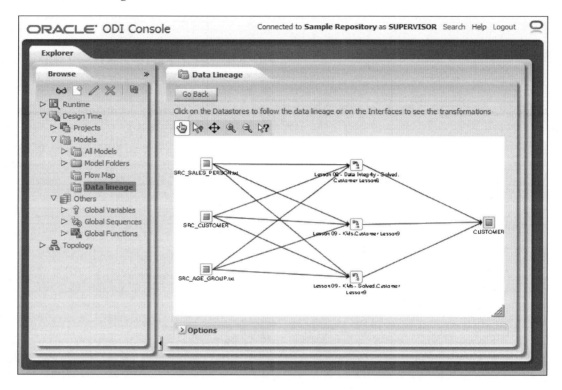

The Console is useful for viewing lineage and impact analysis without having the full Studio installed on a machine. Operators can also perform most of the tasks they would perform with the Studio, including starting or restarting processes.

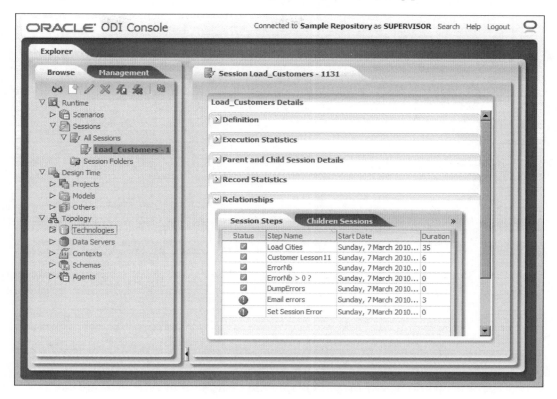

The exact information that is available in the Operator Navigator of the Studio will be found in the matching view of the Console: generated code, execution statistics, and statuses of executed processes are all available.

Oracle Enterprise Manager

As part of the consolidation of features across all Oracle product lines, ODI now integrates with WebLogic Enterprise Manager.

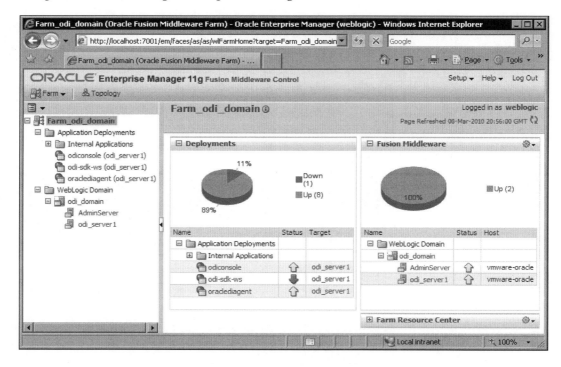

Administrators can now use one single tool (OEM) to monitor the overall health of their environment, including ODI Agents and ODI processes.

ODI key concepts

Understanding key concepts in ODI will help developers take advantage of the graphical interface and further improve their productivity. In no specific order, we will now review the notions of Execution Contexts, Knowledge Modules, Models, Interfaces, Packages, and Scenarios.

Execution Contexts

Everyone encounters the same issue. The parameters used to connect to the development server are different from the parameters used in the QA or production servers and there could be more than these few environments. Some companies add environments such as user acceptance, code consolidation, and pre-production; you name it and it is there! Maintaining the connection parameters is a cumbersome activity. Beyond the maintenance itself, there is a risk if these parameters are modified in the code after the code has been validated by the QA team. Ideally, connection parameters and environment-specific parameters should be maintained independently of the code. This is what ODI provides with the notion of Execution Contexts.

To make sure that developers are independent of the physical location of the different systems, ODI enforces the use of Logical Schemas. Logical Schemas are labels or aliases that represent the connections for the developers. At execution time, the agent will translate these logical names into physical ones based on the information stored in the repository. This way, the maintenance of the connection parameters, location of the databases, and schema names is entirely independent of the code itself.

In addition, whenever an ODI process is executed, a Context must be selected. The structure of the metadata will always be the same from one environment to the next (say for instance, development, QA, and production) but the connection information will be different. By selecting an execution context, the agent will know which connection definition to use when completing the code.

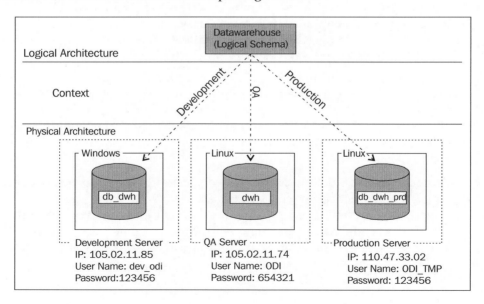

In the previous figure, the logical name **Datawarehouse** is actually pointing to the physical schema **db_dwh** in the development server as long as we execute the transformations in the development context. It will automatically point to the **dwh** schema in the QA server for the QA context.

The physical details are maintained in the **Physical Architecture** of the Topology Navigator and the logical names that point to the physical implementations are defined in the **Logical Architecture** of the Topology Navigator. The **Context** accordion lets administrators define as many contexts as needed. At run time, the selection of a Context will define which physical implementation to use for each logical name used in the code.

The physical architecture will contain the details for ODI to log in to the database, the IP address or name of the server on which the database runs, the port numbers to connect to the database, as well as the name of the actual schemas, catalogs, libraries, and other objects found in these databases.

Knowledge Modules

A Knowledge Module (KM) is a template of code that defines what types of SQL queries (insert, select, and so on) and what scripts need to be generated to complete the data extraction, loading, and transformation operations.

There were several objectives behind the inception of these KMs. Some of them are as follows:

- **Improve productivity**: Integration tasks are very repetitive in nature. Once the extract/load techniques have been defined for a given project, they will be reused over and over again. Consolidating these practices in reusable templates helps improve developers' productivity.

- **Encapsulate integration best practices**: Even if a team agrees on integration best practices, there is usually no guarantee that all developers will implement what has been decided. In other cases, only the best developers will come up with the best integration strategies. By encapsulating the integration strategies in a template, all developers can share the same quality of code.

- **Allow for further customizations**: Oracle is doing its best to encapsulate industry best practices in all KMs no matter what database you are using—but your environment is unique, and at times only you can further optimize the code that will be generated. Again, to make sure that all developers will benefit from the ultimate optimizations, customized KMs will be shared by all developers.

Typically, an ETL developer will be able to use a Knowledge Module without any need to understand the underlying requirements (creation of staging tables, location of these tables, intermediate operations on these tables, cleanup of these tables, and so on).

The developer will control what code will be generated by setting yes/no options to insert records, perform updates, create the target table, and so on.

There are six types of Knowledge Modules that will enable various steps in the data integration process:

- **Loading Knowledge Modules (LKM)**: These modules determine how to extract and load data across two heterogeneous technologies. Different Knowledge Modules will offer different connection strategies such as JDBC connection, and database load/unload utilities.

- **Integration Knowledge Modules (IKM)**: These modules define the strategy used to integrate the data into the target. The different strategies include inserts only, update and inserts, slowly changing dimension, and so on.

- **Check Knowledge Modules (CKM)**: These modules implement in-line data quality control before insertion into the target such as validate business rules, control the uniqueness of primary keys, and validate the existence of parent records for foreign keys.

- **Reverse-engineering Knowledge Modules (RKM)**: These modules import the metadata for a given technology into the ODI repository. These KMs are usually used for enterprise applications rather than databases. Most reverse-engineering operations will not require any KM since the JDBC drivers leveraged by ODI usually support reverse-engineering operations.

- **Journalizing Knowledge Module (JKM)**: This module manages the ODI journals and necessary CDC mechanisms to provide automatic Changed Data Capture (CDC) functionality.

- **Service Knowledge Modules (SKM)**: These modules automatically generate the code and expose the database table operations as web services. Insert, update, delete, select, or consumption of data changes can then be performed by using these web services.

Knowledge Modules are named after the specific database for which they have been optimized, the utilities that they leverage, and the technique that they implement. For instance, an IKM Teradata to File (TTU) will move data from Teradata into a flat file, and leverage the TTU utilities for that operation, or an LKM File to Oracle (EXTERNAL TABLE) will expose a flat file as an external table for Oracle. Similarly, an IKM Oracle Slowly Changing Dimension will generate code optimized for the Oracle database which implements a Slowly Changing Dimension (Type 2) type of integration.

Most developers will only use out of the box KMs—only the most advanced developers will modify the code templates. For that reason, we will keep KM modifications outside the scope of this book. But the examples we will go through in the rest of this book will help you understand how best to select a KM for the task at hand.

Models

Models in ODI are used to store the metadata imported from the databases. When developers (or data custodian) create a model, they have the choice of importing only the relevant metadata (you may not want to import the definition of all tables and views in your environment). As we have seen earlier with Knowledge Modules for reverse-engineering, metadata can also be imported from applications, where objects can be a business representation of the data rather than an actual physical table.

Once the metadata has been imported, it can be organized and enhanced—Models can be grouped in folders. Submodels can be created within Models to organize tables in logical units.

When submodels are created, the users can define how tables will be organized; either they will be manually moved into the appropriate subfolders, or their location will be determined automatically by ODI based on their names.

Metadata can be enhanced by adding more constraints (such as referential integrity, check constraints) that would not exist in the database.

Metadata can also be directly created in ODI. Each model has a `Diagrams` folder. Diagrams let users graphically design their table structures. More importantly, they can drag-and-drop object definitions from other technologies, and ODI will automatically translate the datatypes from one technology to the next.

If tables are derived from another technology, they can still be manually modified (by changing the column names, datatypes, adding or removing columns, and constraints). The hidden benefit of the use of diagrams to create tables from other Models is the ability to automate the generation of Interfaces.

ODI knows what table was used as a basis for the new one. If you right-click on the model name, and select the menu option **Generate Interfaces IN**, ODI will automatically create an interface with the original table as a source and the new table as a target with all columns properly mapped. You will be prompted to place the interface in the project and folder of your choice. We will take a detailed look at Interfaces in the next section. If you choose to select the menu option **Generate Interfaces OUT**, ODI will generate the reverse interface, with the new table as a source and the original one as a target.

Interfaces

Interfaces are where the transformations are defined. We will spend a lot of time in this book covering the details of Interfaces. Interfaces are created in projects, and the various components are organized in Packages.

There are multiple parts to an interface such as description, mappings, flow, controls, to name a few.

Interface descriptions

Often overlooked, descriptions are the documentation of the objects. Because the descriptions are stored with the objects in the repository, all documentation generated by ODI will contain the descriptions. It may sound trivial, but the descriptions are key to the success of your projects.

Interface mappings

ODI adheres to a concept called "declarative design". The definition of the transformation logic is isolated from the definition of the data movement and integration logic for two reasons which are as follows:

- **Change to one should not alter the other**: If I decide to add or remove columns in my mappings, it should have no impact on the type of technology I use (external tables, bulk load, JDBC, and so on) or the type of integration strategy I use (inserts only, updates, and so on). Similarly if I decide to change technology or integration strategy, this should have no impact on my transformations.

- **Productivity can be greatly improved**: Mappings are often unique and must be handled one column at a time. Integration strategies and technologies can be selected once for a complete project with minimal changes and reviews. Separating the two allows developers to focus more on the moving parts (the transformations) than on the stable parts (the integration strategy).

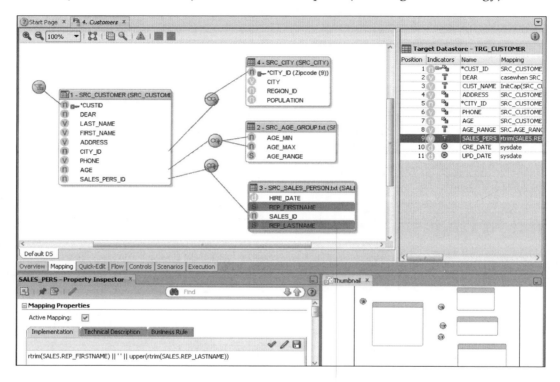

Mappings are where the transformation logic is defined.

Interface flow tab

The flow tab of the interfaces is where the integration strategies are selected. The Loading Knowledge Modules (LKM) will define which techniques must be used to extract data from remote source systems and how to load the data in the target system. The Integration Knowledge Module (IKM) will define which integration strategy will be used to integrate the data in the target system.

Interfaces will only list the KMs that have been imported into the project where they are created (and starting with ODI 11.1.1.6, the Global KMs that are shared across projects). One key benefit is that it is possible to control which strategies will be used for a given project, hence limiting the choices of the developers to the choices made by the team.

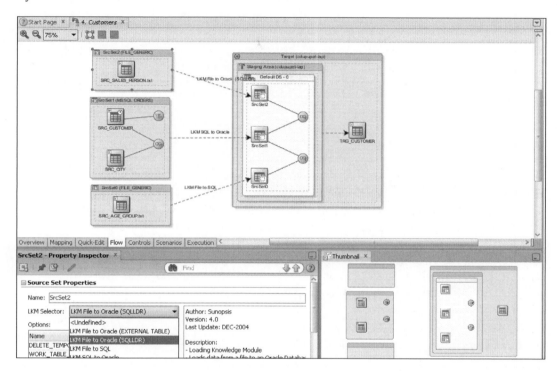

This will ensure the following:

- All developers implement the same best practice
- If changes are required later in the project, they can be done extremely efficiently by changing the standard for a given project
- Ideally, because the choice can be limited, developers know that ODI will always choose the KM they need and do not even have to worry about that step

Interface controls

One option that is available with some IKMs is the ability to control data integrity on the fly. There are two options called Flow Control and Static Control. Flow Control will check for data inconsistencies, remove invalid data from the staging tables, and write them to a separate error table. Static Control will check for inconsistencies in the target table after it has been loaded with all incoming records. Invalid records identified in the target table are then copied to the error table but they are not removed from the target table. When developers decide to activate one or both options in the Flow tab of the interface, they can then refine what will be done—the error table can be recreated automatically. Some constraints can be ignored while others are enforced.

All constraints listed here are defined at the metadata level, under the definition of the tables in the Models.

Packages and Scenarios

Packages are designed to orchestrate the individual objects created by the developers—interfaces, variables, procedures will be sequenced in Packages. If a step fails in a package, it is possible to branch out and immediately take action based on the errors that are detected. For execution purposes, Packages are compiled into Scenarios. Scenarios execution can then be organized with Load Plans. We will see all these concepts in more detail in a dedicated chapter.

Summary

In this chapter we started by exploring the core concepts behind ODI architecture and components.

In terms of architecture, you should now have a better understanding of what the different elements are, in particular the repository, Studio, and Agents. This will be important as you go into the next chapter where we cover the installation of the product.

In terms of concepts, we have covered the key elements that differentiate ODI from other products, namely, Execution Contexts, Knowledge Modules, Models, Interfaces, Packages and Load Plans. We will now illustrate these concepts with actual examples in the rest of the book, expanding on this quick introduction.

2
Product Installation

This chapter provides instructions for installing and configuring the Oracle Data Integrator product for a development or production environment. After reviewing the prerequisites for the product installation, we will cover the installation and configuration of the ODI repository, the Studio (graphical interface), and the Standalone Agent.

As a point of reference, Oracle maintains a list of prerequisites and step by step installation instructions at `http://www.oracle.com/technetwork/middleware/data-integrator/documentation/index.html`.

Prerequisites

Before installing the product, we have to make sure that all components are available and that the systems where the product will be installed conform to the product requirements. Download the required components as follows:

- The components need to be downloaded from the ODI OTN web page at `http://www.oracle.com/technetwork/middleware/data-integrator/downloads/index.html`. For the purpose of this book, we will assume that the installation is done on a Windows operating system. Download the ODI installation file.

- Download the **Repository Creation Utility (RCU)** tool that will be needed to create the ODI repositories. RCU can be downloaded from the ODI download page on OTN.

Make sure to download the latest release of both products. Note that the ODI file is quite large (close to 2 GB). Depending on the quality of your bandwidth, the download could take quite a while and should be scheduled accordingly.

Prerequisites for the repository

To install the repository, you must have access to a database certified by Oracle as being compatible with ODI. The list of supported databases for the repository can be found in the certification matrix available at at http://www.oracle.com/technetwork/middleware/data-integrator/odi-11gr1certmatrix-163773.xls. For the purpose of this book, we will assume that the database hosting the repository is an Oracle database (10*g* and 11*g* are supported at the time of writing). The Oracle databases can be downloaded from http://www.oracle.com/technetwork/database/enterprise-edition/downloads/index.html.

The database that will host the repository does not have to be on the same hardware as the Studio. Multiple developers will share the same repository when projects are developed, so it is convenient to install the repository in a central location.

Keep in mind that the Studio will make very frequent access to the repository. From that perspective, the Studio and the repository will have to be on the same LAN (and since distance adds to latency, they should preferably be at a reasonable distance—not in a different country or continent for instance).

The repository will use a few gigabytes of disk space to store the metadata, transformation rules, and (mostly) the logs. Make sure that you have enough disk space for the database. A good starting point for the size of the repository is 1 GB each for the Master and Work repository.

Each repository (Master or Work) is typically installed in a dedicated schema. The privileges required by ODI are "Connect" and "Resource" on an Oracle database, but keep in mind that the installation program will have more stringent requirements (the RCU utility will require sysdba privileges to be able to create the repositories).

Prerequisites for the Oracle Universal Installer

Java 1.6 is required for the installer to run. The documentation for the installer indicates that a JDK version is required, but a JRE installation will be sufficient for the installation of ODI.

Prerequisites for the Studio

When the setup program installs ODI, it will also install a copy of Java under the ODI directories, solely for ODI's needs. This will have no impact on other products you may have that use other versions of Java, and will ensure that you always have the proper version of Java for ODI.

The Studio itself will have the following requirements:

- Disk space: 1 GB (in addition to what is required to store the downloads from the Oracle website)
- Memory: 2 GB

Prerequisites for the Standalone Agent

The prerequisites for the ODI Standalone Agent are fairly limited. They are as follows:

- Disk space: 20 MB (but keep in mind that the installation program itself will require some disk space)
- Memory: 1 GB

Installing ODI 11*g*

In this section we will view step-by-step instructions for installing ODI.

Two installation modes

Since the installation involves several components, there are two distinct installation modes for the repositories. They are as follows:

- **Oracle Repository Creation Utility (RCU) installation**: Oracle provides a dedicated program that assists with the creation of repositories. This tool will create repositories for any Oracle tool that requires such an infrastructure, including ODI. This tool makes installation extremely simple, but will necessarily be less flexible than a repository created directly from the ODI Studio.
- **Creation from the ODI Studio**: The installation program will only install the graphical interface and the Agent. The repositories can be created from the Studio graphical interface after it has been properly installed. The Agent will have to be manually configured to connect to the repository in this case. This installation mode may be required when additional repositories are to be created (test, production repositories, and so on). It is worth your while to familiarize yourself with both approaches.

Oracle recommends the use of the RCU tool for repositories creation. We will focus on this recommended approach.

Creating the repository with RCU

If you have not yet downloaded RCU, then download the latest version which is available at `http://www.oracle.com/technetwork/middleware/data-integrator/downloads/index.html`.

Follow these steps:

1. Once you have unzipped the file you have downloaded for RCU, launch RCU by executing the following file `\RCU\rcuHome\BIN\RCU.bat`.

2. RCU will display the welcome screen. Click on **Next,** as seen in the following screenshot, to get RCU started:

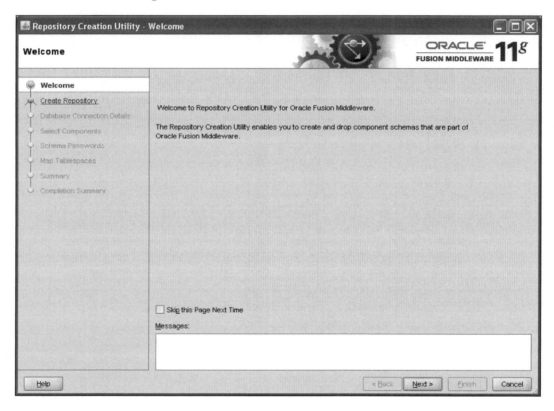

3. Select **Create** to create the ODI repository, as seen in the following screenshot:

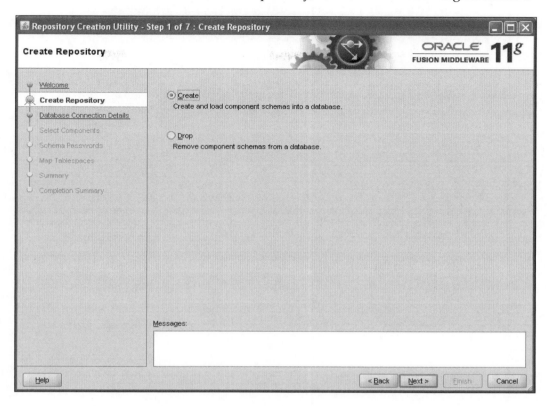

4. The next step will be to enter the appropriate parameters for RCU to connect to the database where the repository will be created. For Oracle, select the Oracle database.

5. Enter the hostname. Try not to use "localhost" for the hostname since the repositories are supposed to be shared by multiple developers and "localhost" will refer to a different machine for each developer. You can use the machine name or the IP address of the machine (unless you are using DHCP, in which case, the IP address could vary on a daily basis).

6. Provide the port number and service name for the database. Then provide a username with dba privileges and select **SYSDBA** for the role. This is because the tool will create a user for the repository and potentially even create a tablespace (depending on the answers you provide on the subsequent screens). Then click on **Next**.

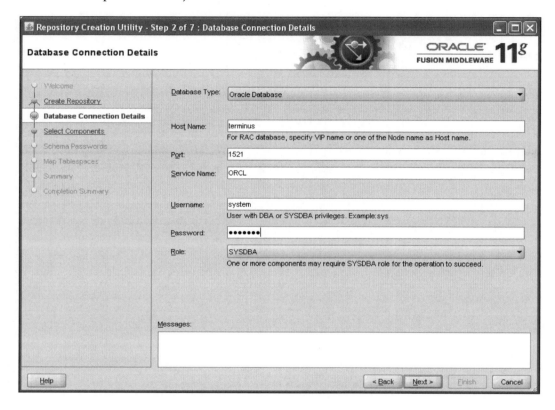

7. RCU will validate the connection parameters. Any connectivity issue (invalid port number or service name, invalid host, not enough privileges for the user, and so on) will be reported in the **Messages** window at the bottom. If you encounter issues, fix them until all prerequisites are validated and click on **OK**:

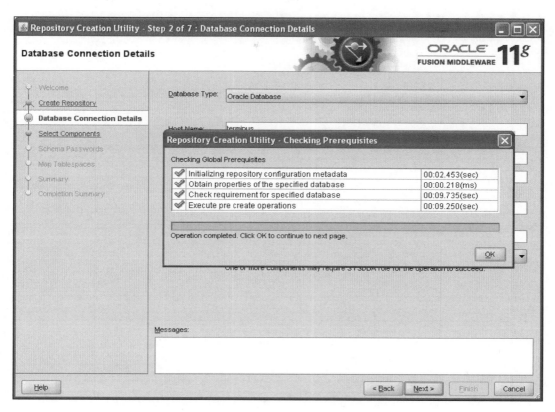

8. Now that we can connect to the database, we can select which repository
    will be created. Select **Oracle Data Integrator**. Note that at this point you
    can rename the schema where the repository will be created (the default
    is DEV_ODI_REPO). Click on **Next**:

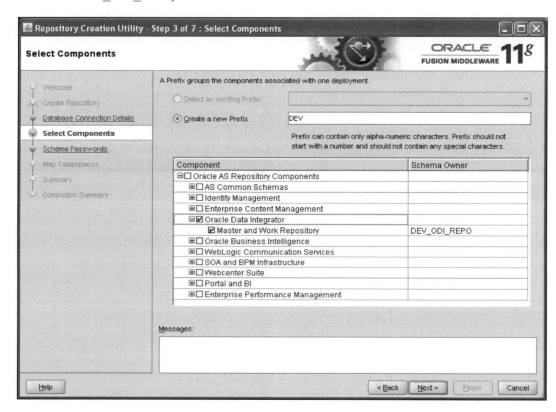

9. RCU will validate the prerequisites that are specific to ODI. Then click on **OK**.

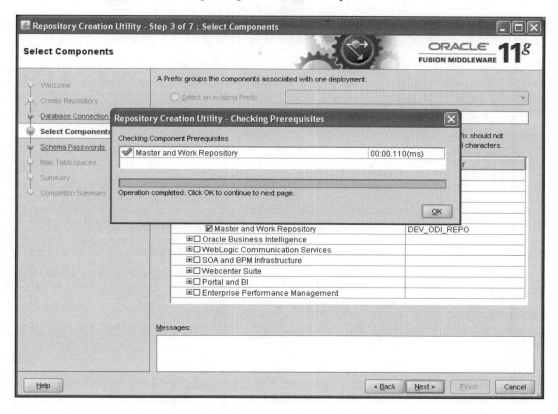

10. You are then prompted for the password for this schema. Enter the password for the ODI repository schema owner, and click on **Next**.

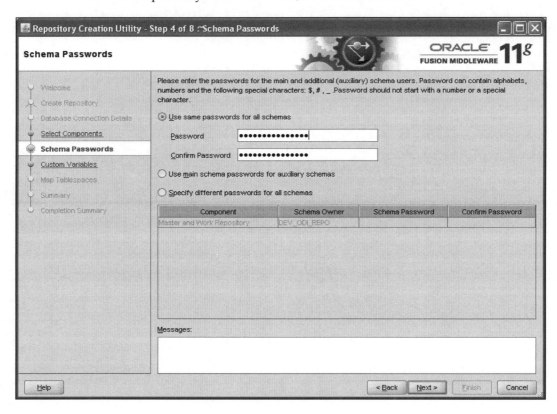

11. At this point, RCU will prompt you for additional security parameters for the creation of the repository. They are as follows:

   ° **Master Repository ID**: This ID should be unique to your environment. If you create more than one Master repository, make sure that each one has a unique ID, even if these repositories are completely independent.

   ° **Supervisor Password**: This will be the password for the ODI user supervisor. You will have to remember this password as you will need it to launch the ODI Studio later on.

- ° **Work Repository Type (Development** or **Execution)**: Execution repositories will not allow any development code. Since this is your first installation, select **D** for development.

- ° **Work Repository ID**: This ID will have to be unique in our environment.

- ° **Work Repository name**: A good practice here is to repeat the repository ID in the repository name.

- ° **Work Repository Password**: Use a password to secure the access to your repository. You will have to remember this value to connect to the repository.

- ° Click on **Next**.

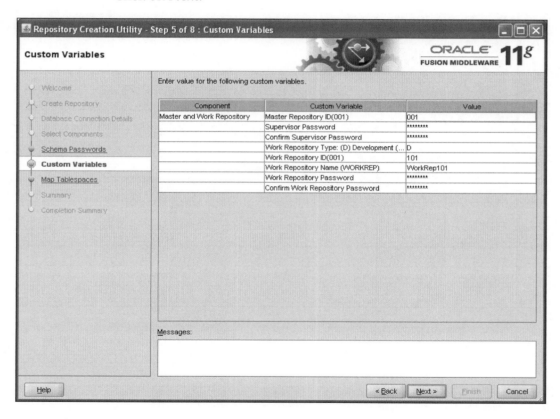

The screenshot shows the Repository Creation Utility - Step 5 of 8 : Custom Variables. The navigation panel lists: Welcome, Create Repository, Database Connection Details, Select Components, Schema Passwords, **Custom Variables**, Map Tablespaces, Summary, Completion Summary.

Enter value for the following custom variables.

Component	Custom Variable	Value
Master and Work Repository	Master Repository ID(001)	001
	Supervisor Password	********
	Confirm Supervisor Password	********
	Work Repository Type: (D) Development (...	D
	Work Repository ID(001)	101
	Work Repository Name (WORKREP)	WorkRep101
	Work Repository Password	********
	Confirm Work Repository Password	********

12. You have the ability to select the tablespace where the repository will be created. You can either keep the default values or set your own values if you have a marked preference. Then click on **Next**.

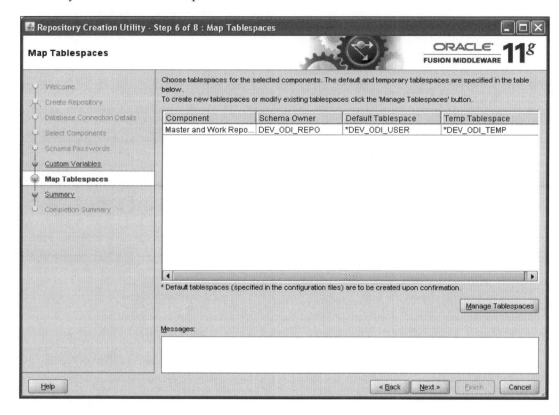

13. If the tablespace does not exist yet, you are prompted to confirm the creation of the tablespace. Click on **OK**.

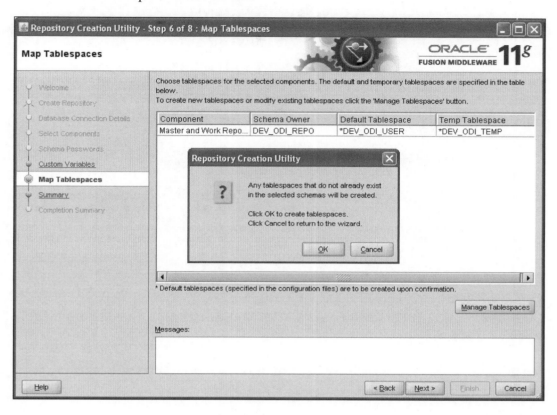

14. The tablespace will then be created. Click on **OK**.

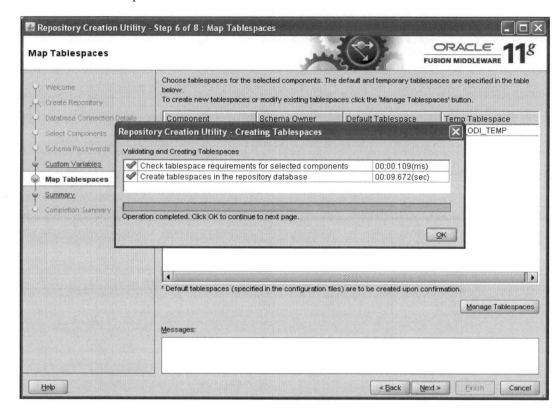

15. RCU will provide a summary of all the selections that were made. Validate your choices and click on **Create**.

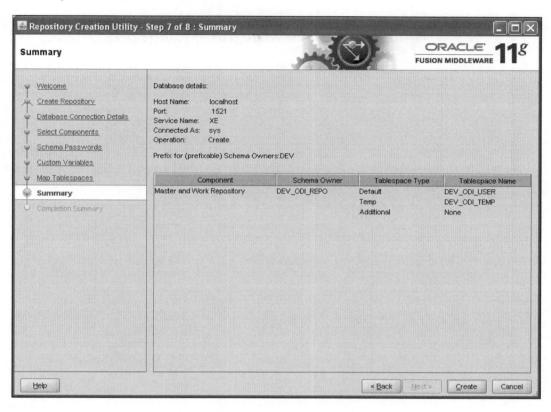

16. Depending on the speed of your processor, the creation of the repositories can take a while (about 15 minutes here on a very slow machine). Click on **Close** when you are done. Your repositories are created.

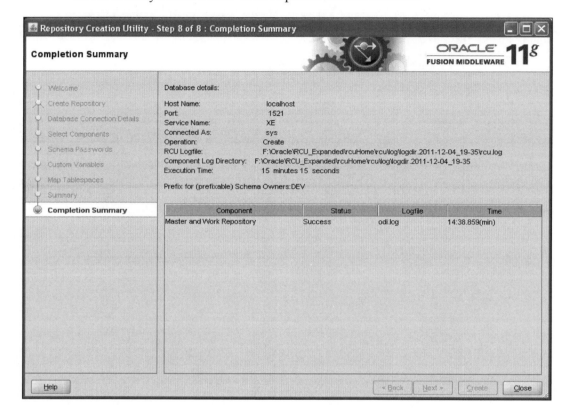

Installing the ODI Studio and the ODI Agent

In this section, we will go through step-by-step instructions to create the ODI repository and install both the ODI Studio and the ODI Agent.

1. The ODI download comes as a single ZIP file. You will first have to unzip the file to access the installation program. Once the file is unzipped, you will see two directories, namely, Disk1 and Disk2. You will find the setup.exe program directly under Disk1.

2. Run the `setup.exe` program either from a command prompt or from the Windows Explorer:

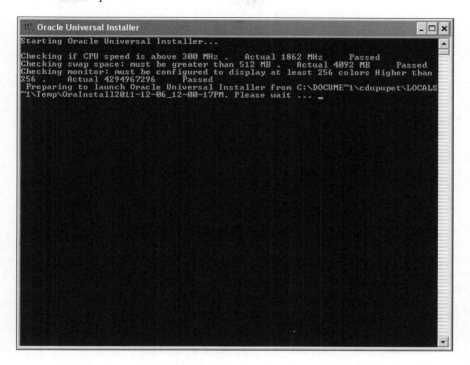

 The installation program will first validate that the environment matches its own requirements (swap space, CPU speed, monitor resolution, and so on). If any of the prerequisites are missing, you will be prompted to continue or abort. If all prerequisites are satisfied, an "ODI installer" screen will be displayed as the installer starts.

If the Oracle Universal Installer window does not appear after the prerequisites have been validated, check the Oracle installer specific documentation that can be found at http://docs.oracle.com/cd/E21764_01/core.1111/e16453/install.htm#CHDJIDFD.

The installer screen is as follows:

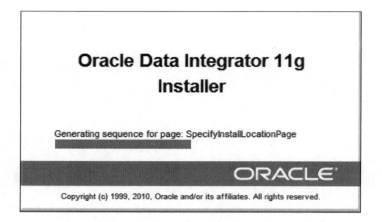

3. After the splash screen disappears, the ODI installation Welcome page appears. From this point on during the installation, online help is available by clicking on the **Help** button at the bottom left at any time. Click on **Next** to proceed.

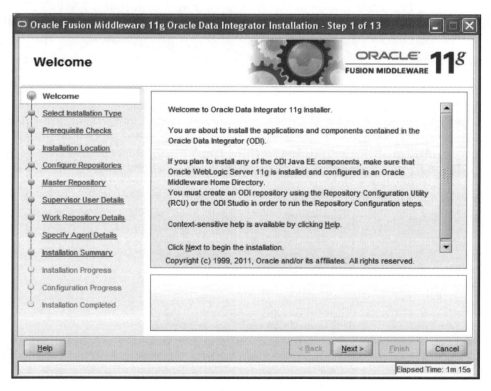

4. The next screen provides the details for the two installation modes, namely, installer driven creation of the repositories (using the Oracle RCU tool), or creation of the repositories from the graphical interface of ODI. Since we have seen how to create the repositories with RCU, we will select the matching option.

5. No action is required on this screen; simply click on **Next**.

6. The installer then asks for the desired installation type the choices are as follows:

   ◦ The **Developer Installation** will install the Studio (the graphical interface used to design ETL processes with ODI). It also gives the option to install the SDK that advanced developers will utilize to use ODI beyond what is available from the Studio. The SDK is not covered in this book, but the complete reference guide for the SDK is available along with the rest of the ODI documentation at http://www.oracle.com/technetwork/middleware/data-integrator/documentation/index.html.

   ◦ The **Standalone Installation** will install the Standalone Agent. You can elect to install the Standalone Agent and the Studio at the same time. The Agent is the component in charge of the execution of the processes in a production environment.

   Note that in a development environment, the Studio acts as an Agent. This is very convenient in the sense that the installation is simplified. However, offloading orchestration of the ETL processes to an Agent as compared to using the Studio for both the design of the processes and their orchestration, is a worthwhile investment in the long run. The additional benefit is that developers collaborating on a project can share the same Agent.

   ◦ The **Java EE Installation** covers all elements that will be installed on a WebLogic server. WebLogic is a prerequisite for the following components (but it will not be covered here):

     • **Java EE Agent**: It is the same module as the Standalone Agent, but this Agent takes advantage of all the features provided by WLS (high availability, pooling of connections, externalization of security, and so on).

     • **ODI Console**: This is a web frontend to access the ODI repository. Most objects will be read-only, but the lineage and impact analysis that are available through this interface will be of particular interest, along with the screens available to operators to monitor processes without having to install the Studio.

- **Public Web Service**: This feature will expose ODI jobs as web services. One single web service will be used and it will take the name of the jobs to be executed as a parameter (along with any other parameters required for the job itself).

7. For the purposes of this book, select the ODI Studio and the Standalone Agent.

8. Click on **Next** to proceed:

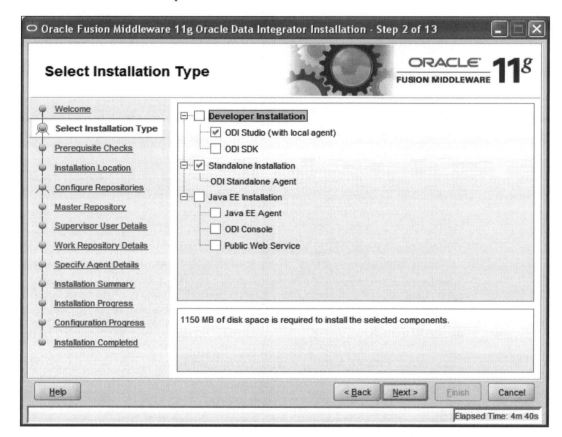

9. The installer will then run several prerequisite checks to ensure the health and viability of downstream installation steps and the overall post-install experience. Click on **Next** to proceed.

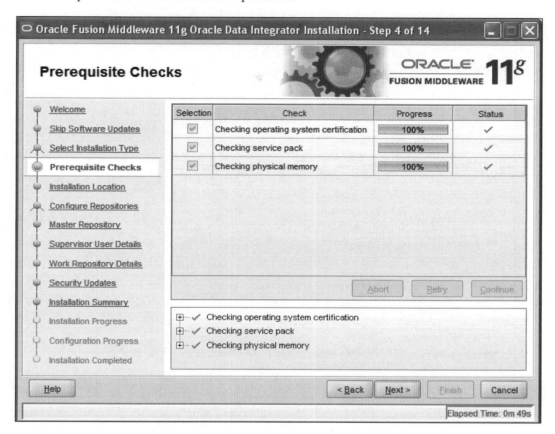

If the prerequisites do not pass, please review the list of hardware and software requirements mentioned earlier in the chapter.

10. You then have to specify the `ODI_Home` directory. As for all Java tools, try to avoid directory names that would contain a space (for that matter, `Program Files` is not a good choice, but you can always use the old MS_DOS equivalent name of `progra~1` or whatever eight character name it is on your platform). Also try to keep the path simple and easy to remember. Click on **Next**.

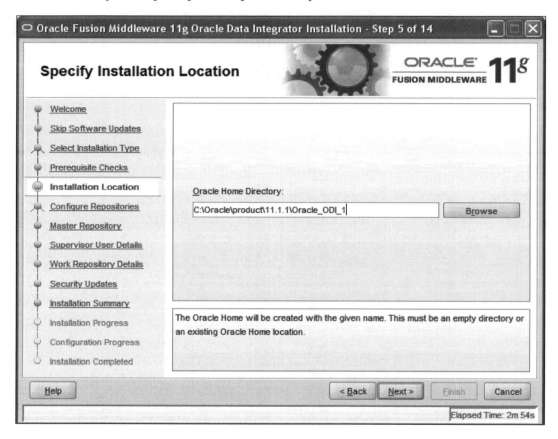

The default installation directory is `c:\oracle\product\11.1.1\Oracle_ODI_1`. This is also known as your `ODI_HOME` directory.

11. You then have to choose whether to configure an existing Master/Work repository pair and items in ODI Studio and Agent that are dependent on the repositories. If you want to manually create the repositories from the Studio, skip the repository configuration. If you did run the RCU tool to create the repositories as described earlier, you want to select the **Configure Repositories** option to make sure that the Studio and the Agent will be automatically configured to connect to these repositories. Select **Configure repositories** and click on **Next** to proceed.

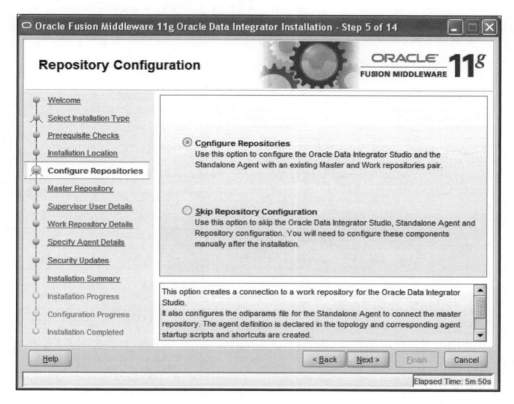

12. When prompted for the connection parameters, enter the same values you selected in the RCU tool. You will have to confirm the parameters for the database connection string and modify them if needed and re-enter the database username for the Master repository. Then click on **Next**.

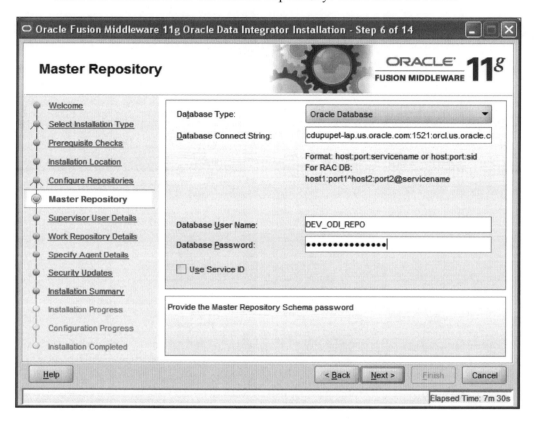

13. You will then have to enter the password that you had entered in RCU for the ODI Supervisor. This password is case-sensitive, so make sure that you type it in exactly the same way that you did in RCU. Click on **Next**.

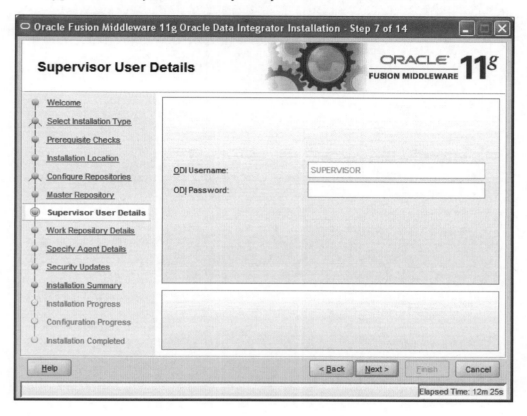

14. You will then be prompted to select your Work repository. If this is your first installation, you only have one repository available. Click on **Next**.

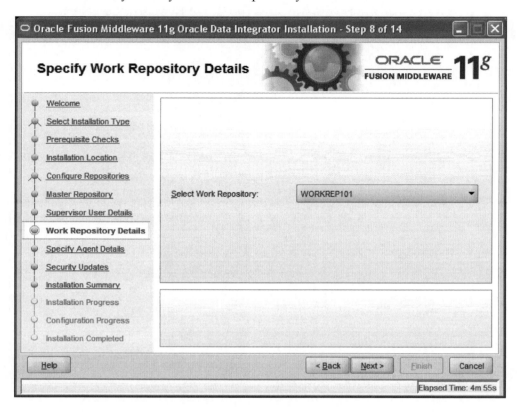

15. It is good practice for the Agent's parameters to name the Agent after the machine on which it is installed. Historically, ODI uses 20910 for the Agent port, but you may want to change this value (particularly if you install more than one Agent on the same machine). After entering your values, click on **Next**.

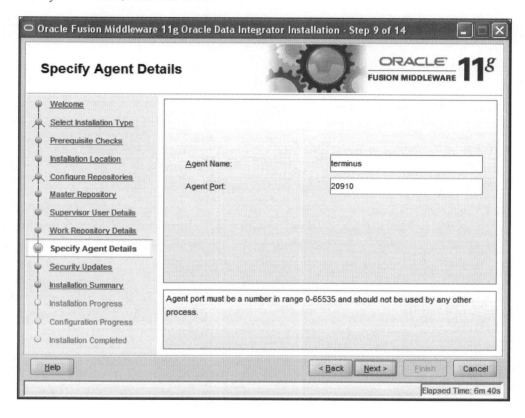

16. You can enter your contact information to be alerted by Oracle if security issues are identified. Click on **Next** to proceed.

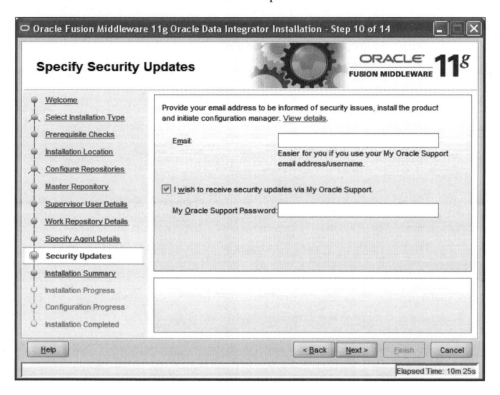

17. If the input fields in the previous step were left blank, a confirmation dialog is presented to validate that notification of critical security issues is not desired. Either click on **Yes** to confirm that critical security issue notification is not desired or **No** to provide your contact information, and then click on **Next**.

18. The **Installation Summary** will allow you to review the components that are about to be installed. Click on **Install** to proceed.

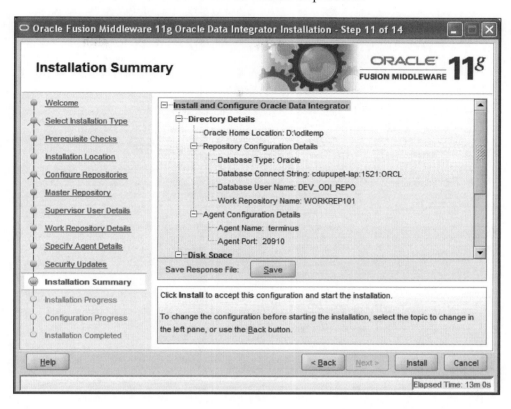

19. The **Installation Progress** displays a progress bar to show the installation progress. An important item on this screen is the location of the log file that is created during execution of the ODI 11*g* installer. The root directory of the installation log file(s) is fixed for a given operating system. If you changed the default installation, the location of the log file does not change. For example, for Windows, the log file root directory location is C:\Program Files\Oracle\Inventory\logs. A log file is created each time the installer is run by appending the date and time information to the string install to form a uniquely named file. Click on **Next** to proceed.

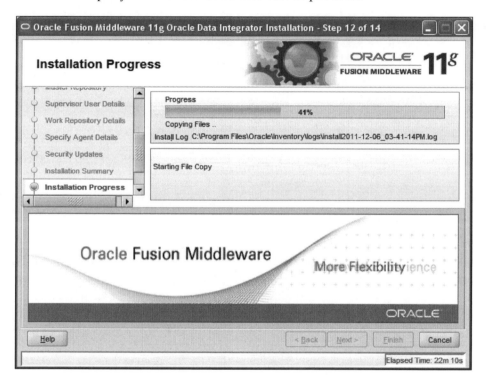

20. After the file installation progress has reached 100 percent and the related configuration steps are completed, a screen reviews the different actions that were performed by the installation program to configure your environment.

21. You are essentially done, however, click on **Next** to proceed.

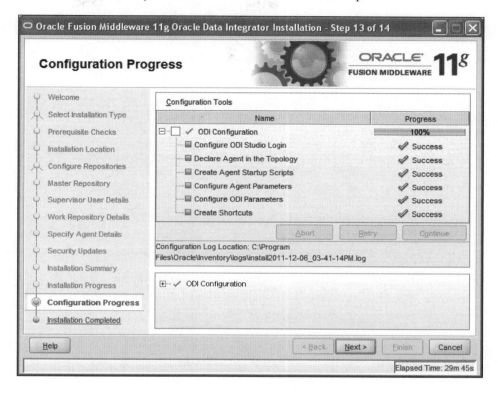

22. Installation Complete! Congratulations. Note that you can click on **Save** to preserve the **Installation Configuration** information.

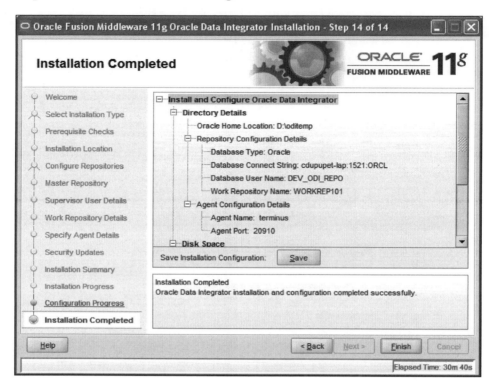

The following screenshot shows a sample of the type of information that will be saved by this operation:

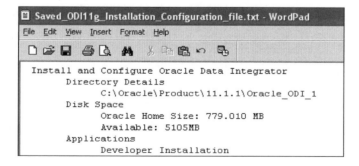

23. Finally, click on **Finish** on the last installation screen.

Starting the ODI Studio for the first time

Follow these steps to start ODI Studio:

1. Launch the newly installed product for the first time from the Windows **Start** menu | **Oracle** | **Oracle Data Integrator.ODI Studio**.

    The installation program has installed JRockit JDK 1.6.0_24 along with ODI so that ODI always has the proper version of Java to work with. You will find this installation of Java under your ODI_Home directory. If you used the default installation directory on Windows then it will be c:\Oracle\ product\11.1.1\Oracle_ODI_1\jrockit-jdk1.6.0_24.

    The ODI Studio and the ODI Agent will be automatically configured to use this version of Java.

2. The ODI splash screen appears as product initialization proceeds prior to the first product screen being presented. Wait for the splash screen to disappear.

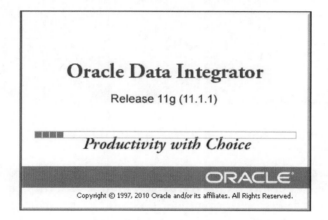

 If the splash screen does not appear, check out the file [ODI_HOME]\oracledi\client\odi\bin\odi.conf and make sure that the SetJavaHome parameter points to the jrockit directory.

3. Congratulations! ODI Studio initialization has completed and presents itself to the user.

4. Click on **Connect To Repository** to record your connection parameters. You will have to name the connection itself (so that you can go back and forth between different connections). In the login screen, click on the **+** icon to create a new connection.

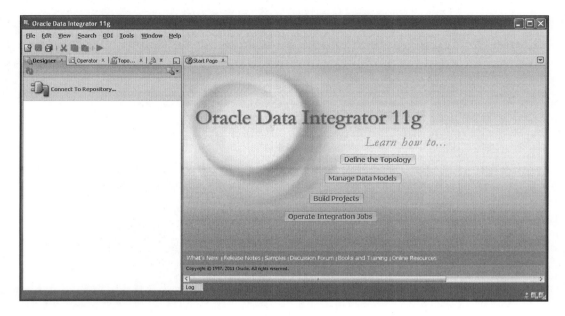

5. Select a name to identify the connection (in this case My First ODI Repository).

6. Then enter the ODI username (SUPERVISOR — you have no other user defined at this point) and the password for this user (the same password that you have entered during the installation process), unless you do not want ODI to remember this password for you.

7. Enter the Master repository username and password, along with the database connection information. Select the appropriate Work repository and if you want to always be prompted with this set of parameters, make this a default connection.

8. Click on **Test** to make sure that all parameters are correct. Then click on **OK**. ODI Studio will connect to your repository. You are now ready to get started with ODI.

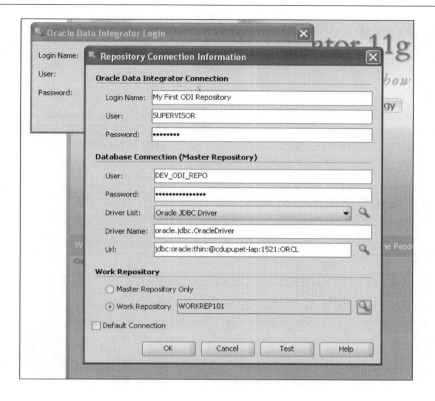

Post installation—parameter files review

The following files are worth looking at:

- For the Studio, you will find under Documents and Settings\<your login name>\Application Data\odi\oracledi\ all the configuration files that contain your login preferences and Studio preferences. If you need to add JDBC drivers for the Studio, you will need to store them into the userlib subdirectory.

- For the Agent, under the agent \bin directory, you will find the odiparams.bat file (the same odiparams.sh will exist on Unix) that defines all the connection parameters for the Agent to connect to the repository. For instance, C:\Oracle\product\11.1.1.5\ODI\oracledi\agent\bin. The installation program has also created an agent_<your_agent_name>.bat file to start the Agent you have defined with the appropriate parameters.

Summary

In this chapter, we have reviewed the environment required for the ODI installation as well as the different steps required to install ODI. If you follow these steps with your installation, ODI will be installed and up and running with properly configured Master and Work repositories.

In the next chapter, we will introduce the notion of variables, how to define them, and how and where to use them. Then we will be ready to go into the actual use of the product.

3
Using Variables

A very important element in all development environments is the ability to leave room for dynamic information. Eventually, you will want to use variables to construct, refresh, and store information as the processes unfold.

This chapter is relatively independent from the others, and can be consulted out of sequence. You will probably want to review some of its content after you have covered more of the following chapters. As variables can be used anywhere in ODI, some of the concepts mentioned here will actually be covered more in depth later. Introducing variables early will allow you to have a better feel for what they are and how and where they can be used. Other chapters will reference variables. Feel free to come back to this chapter for more details on the subject. In this chapter, we will cover the following points:

- How to define variables, and how the different definitions will impact the usability of variables

- How to use variables to process dynamic information, that is variables in models and interfaces

- Using variables to alter the workflows, that is, in Packages and Load Plans

Defining variables

We will now look into defining variables in the following sections.

Variable location and scope

Variables are defined in the **Designer** navigator either under a given project or as global objects.

Project variables can only be used in the project where they are defined. Global variables can be used in any project. We will see later in this chapter that variables can be used to make models more dynamic. When using variables in models, we have to be very careful and make sure that if we use project variables, the model is not used in another project where the variable is not defined. If a model is shared across projects, and if that model must be dynamic, then make sure to use global variables in the model.

The notion of a global variable only means that variables can be used in different projects. It does not necessarily mean that the same value will be shared by all projects. The value of a variable is local to a project and is based on how and when the value is set. From that perspective, multiple processes running in parallel will not share the same values after the processes are started. Each process will operate with its own copy of the values.

Variable definitions

The first element we need to define for a variable is its name. Variable names are case sensitive. In some places (mappings, models, and so on) you will have to reference variables by name, so make sure to follow the same standard for variable names throughout your project. Some conventions that can be used are MyVariableName, myVariableName, my_variable_name, MY_VARIABLE_NAME.

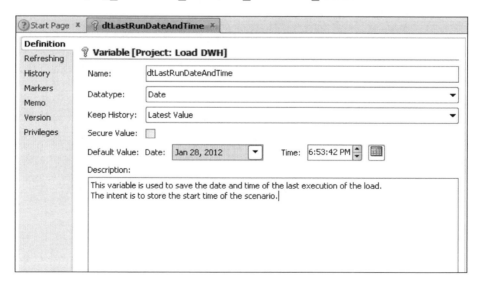

Another important element, as you can see in the previous screenshot, is the variable datatype, namely, **Numeric**, **Date**, **Alphanumeric**, (limited to 255 characters) and **Text** (unlimited length).

Variables can be assigned a **Default Value**, and it is always good practice to describe the purpose of your variables in the **Description** field—there is never too much documentation.

The last field in the definition of the variable allows you to define how much history you want to keep for the values of the variables. You can set it to **No History** (do not remember anything past the execution of the process), **Latest Value** (only remember the last value that was used, and overwrite that value when another value is taken), or **All Values** (save all the values ever taken by the variable).

Version 11.1.1.6 of ODI adds the ability to create **Secure Variables**—variables whose values will never be visible in the generated code (think passwords for instance). These variables will obviously have no history.

Refreshing variables

One key aspect of variables is that they can be associated to an SQL query as long as this query returns a single value (no lists or result sets are allowed). At runtime, it will be possible to **Refresh** the variable to run the associated query and the returned value will automatically be assigned to the variable—all in one operation. We will see this in more detail when we look into the use of variables.

To define the query associated to a variable, select the **Refreshing** tab of the variable, select the name of the logical schema where the query will have to run, and simply type the query as you would in any SQL editor. An example of a query would be:

```
Select sysdate from dual
```

 Note that you have to select a **Logical Schema** in all cases, even in the previous example. The **Logical Schema** will define which server you are connecting to as well as which credentials to use to connect to that server.

Also remember that this query must return a unique value.

The icons you can see on the top right of the query input box will help you build the SQL query. The icons are explained as follows:

- The pencil gives you access to the expression editor, that will guide you with the syntax of the native SQL for the database that hosts your schema

- The green checkmark validates the query with the database (ODI actually sends the query to the database for validation at this point)

- The curved arrows allow you to run the query and store the value of the variable in the history of values for the variable if you chose to keep the history (all values or latest value)

 Even though you can store a value in the history at development time, you have to keep in mind that when you are in a production environment, you will not have the opportunity to preseed the history of your variable. We will see this again later, but whenever you are working with variables, you will have to make sure that they are properly declared and that they are assigned a value before you start using them.

Variable history

Once variables have been used, and if they have been defined to hold either the **Last Value** or **All Values** ever taken, this history will be available in the **History** tab. You can remove elements of the history if you so wish by clicking on the red **X** at the top right of the screen. This view can be extremely helpful for debugging purposes or for analysis purposes.

Using variables for dynamic information

Let's see how we can use variables to process data dynamically.

Assigning a value to a variable

Before we can use a variable, we will have to make sure that a value has been assigned to the variable, as is the case with any programming language. There are multiple ways to assign a value, but in all cases the values will have to be assigned in a **Package**. The package steps defined in this chapter will have to be executed before the interfaces or model operations that make use of the variables.

When you drag-and-drop a variable in a Package, different actions will be available on the variable.

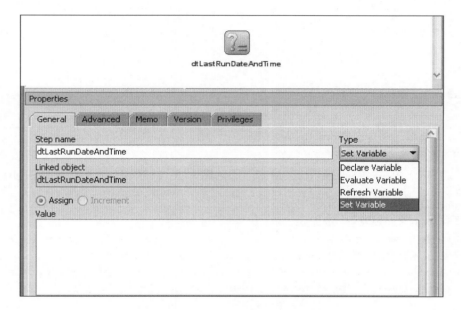

We will review here the different actions (or **Types**, as they are called in the tool) that allow us to get the variable value. As you switch from one type to the other, ODI will change the graphical representation of the variable in the Package so that you know what action is selected without having to look into the details of the step.

Setting a hardcoded value

The **Set Variable** type will allow you to hardcode the value that you want to be assigned to the variable. Remember that this variable may be used in different places, and ODI does not know what you have in mind for this variable. If the variable will only be used in your mappings, and is an alphanumeric for instance, then you are in charge of adding the necessary quotes around the text that you define.

The following values are all valid assignments:

Values	Where and how to use such values
TEXT	If you use this syntax in mappings, remember to add quotes around the variable name
'TEXT'	This variable can be used as-is in the mappings, but cannot be used outside of mappings (models for instance)
2	This is a numeric assignment
'3'	This is a string assignment
'02-JAN-2011'	This is a date assignment (depending on the database you are working with, you may still have to translate this to an actual date with a to_date function or an equivalent)
#GLOBAL.MyVariable	Assign the value stored in the global variable MyVariable
#MYPROJECTCODE.MyVariable	Assign the value of the variable MyVariable located in the current project

We will take a more detailed look at variable referencing a little later in this chapter.

Refresh Variable

The type **Refresh Variable** will simply run the query associated with the variable in its **Refreshing** tab, and will assign the returned value to the variable. If you've asked for any level of history, this step will take care of storing the value for you. These values can be found in the **History** tab of the variable.

Passed as a parameter (Declare Variable)

The type **Declare Variable** will allow you to pass the value of the variable as a parameter to your scenario. The value can be set through the graphical interface—when you run your scenario, ODI will prompt you for the appropriate values. The parameters can also be set from a command-line interface if you decide to execute your processes from an external component. Scenarios can also invoke other scenarios. In that case, the appropriate variables and values would be passed as parameters in the definition of the scenario call. You would need to look into the definition of the ODI tool, OdiStartScen, for more details on this type of approach.

Referencing variables

When you start using variables in your interfaces and models, you will need to reference your variables. Variables are referenced with a # sign, followed by the name of the variable. ODI will first look for a definition of the variable in the project. If the variable is found there, then this variable is used. Otherwise the corresponding GLOBAL variable will be used. If you want to make sure that a global variable is used, you can prefix the variable name with #GLOBAL, for example #GLOBAL.MyVariable.

Similarly, you can prefix the variable name with the project code, which is what ODI will do for you anyway when it generates the code of an interface.

The project code used to prefix variables is different from the name of the project. To check the actual code for a given project, double-click on the project name to edit its definition and read the associated code name. By default, project codes are the uppercase version of the project name, without spaces.

Variables in interfaces

Now that we know how to assign a value to a variable and how to reference it, we can use variables in our interfaces.

You can use a variable in any place where you would be entering code in your interface (for example, mappings, joins, and filters). There are even some Knowledge Module options that can accept variables.

Target Datastore - TRG_CUSTOMER			
Position	Indicators	Name	Mapping
1		*CUST_ID	SRC_CUSTOMER.CUSTID
2		DEAR	SRC_CUSTOMER.DEAR
3		CUST_NAME	SRC_CUSTOMER.FIRST_NAME || ' ' || SRC_CUSTOMER.LAST_NAME
4		ADDRESS	SRC_CUSTOMER.ADDRESS
5		*CITY_ID	SRC_CUSTOMER.CITY_ID
6		PHONE	SRC_CUSTOMER.PHONE
7		AGE	SRC_CUSTOMER.AGE
8		AGE_RANGE	SRC.AGE_RANGE
9		SALES_PERS	RTRIM(SRC1.REP_FIRSTNAME) || ' ' || RTRIM(SRC1.REP_LASTNAME)
10		CRE_DATE	'#dtRunDate'
11		UPD_DATE	'#dtRunDate'

All ODI will do at runtime is to replace the variable name with the current value for that variable. So if the value for your variable `dtLastRunDate` is `29-FEB-2012` and the mapping for your column is:

```
sysdate - '#dtLastRunDate'
```

the code that will be generated is as follows:

```
sysdate - '29-FEB-2012'.
```

Note, that since the variable value did not contain any single quotes, we added them in the previous mapping around the variable name to ensure proper code generation.

> You may have noticed that in this example, we are not using the project code. The first reason is that in an interface we can only use a variable from the current project—so the. project code will be automatically added by ODI. But beyond this convenience, it will allow us to validate directly in the generated code that ODI *did* recognize the variable name. If the project code is not properly added by ODI in the generated code, it means that either the variable is not defined in the project, or it is misspelled—and here pay particular attention to the case sensitivity of variable names.

When you look at the generated code, you will not see the actual variable value, only the variable name will be generated. This name will be substituted dynamically at runtime with whatever value is assigned to the variable at that time.

Version 11.1.1.6 of ODI introduces a new **Log Level, Log Level 6**, for code execution. The only purpose of this log level is to offer the ability to toggle back and forth between variable names and variable values. The toggle button is at the top right corner of the log window.

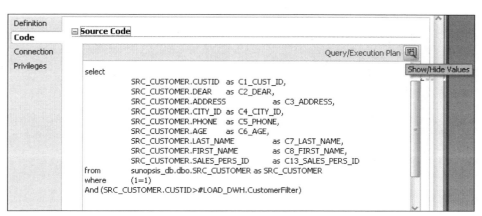

You will only be able to modify the code when the variable name is displayed, but you can always copy the code with the variable value if you want to use it somewhere else.

 Since ODI 11.1.1.6 also introduces Secure Variables, the value for Secure Variables will never be displayed in the operator logs even if you try and toggle from variable name to variable value.

Variables in models

Variables can also be used in models. This will be extremely useful when we start dealing with flat files. It is very common for flat file feeds to be named after the extraction day, the ID of the batch run that generated them, or the server that they came from. In all cases, the same file structure, requiring the exact same processing, will always appear with a different filename. Using a variable for the filename will solve the problem of handling a dynamic name.

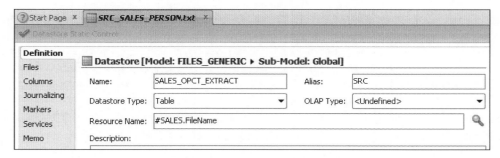

When you edit the definition for a filename, you can use your variable in the **Resource Name**. The **Name** can be set to some meaningful name in your environment, telling you exactly which file type you are referring to. ODI will show both names in the model tree.

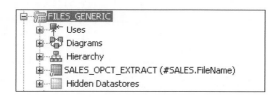

Keep in mind that using variables in the resource name will present some constraints at development time such as you can only process that file if a value has been assigned to the variable. From then on, it becomes more difficult to test the interfaces that use this file (they must be part of a Package where the variable is defined, and can only be executed as part of the Package) and it is not possible to view the content of the file (which file do you want to point to exactly?). For all these reasons, it is actually easier to start working with a predefined filename and once the development work is done and tested, you can look into making your code more dynamic and use a variable for the filename.

> We spoke of using a variable for filenames here because it is the most common case, but you can absolutely use variables for table and view names as well—the product will behave in exactly the same way.

Variables in topology

Just for reference, you should know that it is possible to use variables as part of the **Topology** definition as well. But the use of variables in that part of the tool is a lot more advanced and would require us to cover concepts that are far beyond the scope of this book. Just keep in mind that it is possible though, with enough knowledge and care, to use variables in other areas than the ones we are covering.

Using variables to alter workflows

We will now learn how variables can be used in Packages and Load Plans.

Packages

Variables can be used in Packages for multiple reasons. As we have already seen, variables are assigned different **Types** or actions when they are added to a Package. We have already discussed the ability to **Declare**, **Refresh** or **Set** variables. Another type is to **Evaluate** a variable.

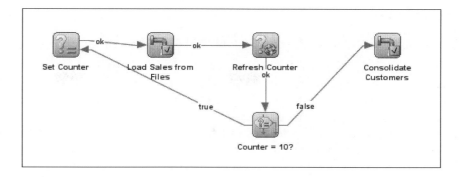

The evaluation of a variable will allow you to choose how you want to proceed — the expression that is evaluated will return **True** or **False**. To continue with the next step of your Package, you will simply use what would otherwise be the **Ok** (which is represented by a green arrow in the ODI Studio) and **Ko** (which is represented by a red arrow in the ODI Studio) arrows — **True** being the green arrow and **False** being the red one. Variables can be compared to literals or to other variables. When comparing variables to one another, pay attention to the variable datatypes, and do not forget to prefix the variable name with the project code.

Using variables, you can easily define loops in your scenarios with the variables being set, refreshed, and/or evaluated to define the values and exit rules for the loops.

You do not want to have infinite loops in the design of your solutions. An infinite loop means that your process would never end, which means that the associated logs will always be "running" and will never be purged. Make sure that you always have an exit in your loops and invoke your scenario if you want it to run again. The next iteration of the scenario will be a new process that will allow administrators to purge the logs of the previous iteration whenever they need to do so.

Load Plans

Load Plans, like Packages, can take advantage of variables.

Load Plans are objects designed for operators to orchestrate their scenarios. Even though it looks like you can add other objects apart from scenarios to your Load Plans (interfaces and variables), behind the scenes ODI generates a scenario for each object that you add to the Load Plan. This is very important for variables—if you modify the definition of a variable after you have added it to a Load Plan, you will have to regenerate the associated scenario for the Load Plan to know about the new definition.

The purpose of the use of variables in Load Plans is to allow for very flexible, multi-choice branching. One of the types of steps you can add to a Load Plan is a **Case** step where a variable will be evaluated. You can then choose what the different cases will be with subsequent **When** steps.

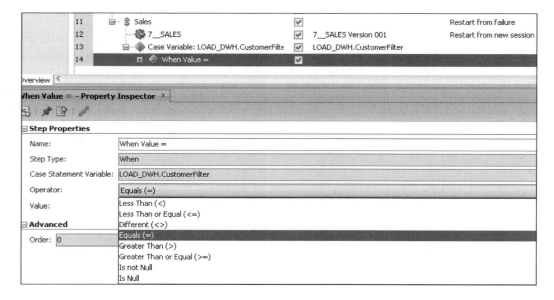

In the previous screenshot, we can see the beginning of a **Case** evaluation at the top portion of the screen, and the bottom portion illustrates the possible choices available for the **When** steps.

Summary

You should now be comfortable with the notions of variables in ODI and how to leverage them to operate in an environment that can be extremely dynamic.

We have seen in detail the following elements:

- How to create variables, and how the different definitions impact the usability of variables

- How to use variables in models and interfaces so that the same code can be used even in a dynamic environment

- How to use variables in Packages and Load Plans as decision points or branching points

We can now look into the different steps required to build your processes, from connectivity to the source and target systems, to the required transformations and loading techniques. As we cover these elements in the following chapters, keep in mind that you can use variables in most places.

4

ODI Sources, Targets, and Knowledge Modules

We know that the primary use of ODI is to move and transform data from one place to another. So in this chapter we'll be delving a bit deeper into the activities and concepts governing the definition and use of source and target datastores and the mechanisms used to move data between them.

First of all we'll take a look at how you define and configure data servers and schemas and how to reverse-engineer them into ODI models to provide sources and targets for interface flows. Then we'll have a look at some simple, but common interface flow examples, and finally we'll revisit Knowledge Modules and the roles they play in data flows. The activities and concepts we'll be covering in this chapter include the following:

- Defining Physical Schemas using the Topology Navigator and linking them to Logical Schema names via Contexts

- Reverse-engineering metadata from database and database-like systems into ODI models using Designer Navigator

- Reverse-engineering data from non-database systems, creating structural metadata from scratch, and enriching existing ODI models and their metadata

- Understanding the main participants and mechanisms in a simple ODI data flow

- Identifying core Knowledge Module types for simple data movement and understanding their involvement in the process

- Choosing and importing specific Knowledge Modules into a data integration project

- Understanding the high-level structure of a Knowledge Module

- Choices available for customizing the behavior of a Knowledge Module

Defining Physical Schemas, Logical Schemas, and Contexts

In order to access or populate data, ODI needs to know where that data resides. The physical locations and connection criteria for servers and the Physical Schemas are defined in the Topology Navigator, under the Physical Architecture. The connection details of the servers and schemas will vary from environment to environment (development environment, testing environment, production environment, and any other environment you have) but the data on these servers will be organized the same way. To shelter developers from these implementation variations, developers will only have to know about one name for all environments, called the Logical Schema (think of it as an alias for all physical connections). A Context will be created for each environment, so that when needed, the Logical Schema can point to the appropriate physical connection. We will now see these elements in more detail.

Defining physical data servers

Once we have connected to the ODI Master and Work repositories, we begin by selecting the Topology Navigator to gain access to the Physical Architecture. Here we will find a list of technologies. Under each technology, data servers will be listed. Data servers will then list their own physical schemas. By default, all supported technologies are listed in both the Physical and Logical Architecture sections. This is helpful when adding the first server of a new technology, but as shown in the following screenshot, the display can be simplified to show only "used" technologies by using the **Hide Unused Technologies** option in the drop-down menu from the tab header of the **Topology** Navigator.

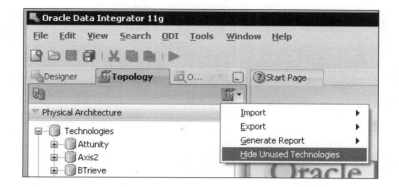

To add a new schema to ODI's Physical Architecture, we would first need to add a **New Data Server** in the **Oracle** technology section where we will define the particular Oracle instance.

> **Pop-up menus and double-clicks in ODI**
>
> Most operations on objects in ODI, whether in the **Topology** Navigator or in the other ODI Studio components (**Designer**, **Operator**, or **Security**) can be accessed via pop-up menus that are activated by a right-click on the object. For many objects the default editor can be opened by double-clicking on the object in the navigator tree view.

The editors in ODI Studio, such as the **Data Server** editor shown in the following screenshot, have a common look and feel, with sidebar tabs on the left and occasionally subtabs across the bottom.

The **Definition** tab of the Data Server editor shows the data server name and the username/password credentials that will be used by ODI Studio and the runtime agents to log on to the server.

Choosing the proper username to log in

It is usually recommended to create a dedicated user to log in. There will be many benefits to this. First, all activity from the tool will be easily monitored by the DBAs since it will all be under one single username. Then from a permissions perspective, you will be able to make sure that the tool has all the necessary privileges, and only the necessary privileges. These can be (and probably will be) different from all existing users' privileges.

This panel also provides the user with the ability to fine-tune the data acquisition performance by adjusting the **Array Fetch Size** and the **Batch Update Size**, which control the number of records acquired per batch and the number of records written when ODI uses JDBC to transfer data from source to target.

It's a good idea to use a naming convention for data server references so that it is easy to tell at a glance which physical data server entry within ODI corresponds to which server in the physical environment. A fairly common naming convention for Oracle data servers uses the Oracle System ID (SID) in conjunction with a hostname, such as ORCL_on_myhost. Alternatively, you might choose to use the construct, <technology>_<purpose>_<environment>, such as ORCL_SALES_DEV.

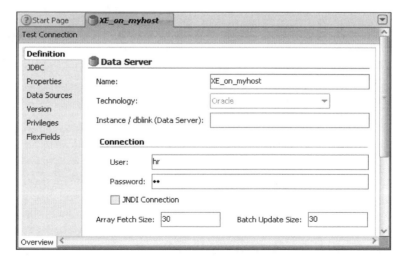

Maximizing and restoring editors

If there is ever a need to maximize an ODI editor to the full extent of ODI Studio's window, we can do this by double-clicking on the editor window's header tab (another double-click on the tab header restores it to its previous size). Don't forget that to close a tab you must hover over the upper-right corner of the tab and click on the **X** that appears.

The **JDBC** tab shows the driver class name and connection URL used to connect to the data server, in conjunction with the credentials on the **Definition** tab.

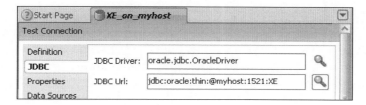

This information can either be typed in directly if known, or can be built using assistants via the search icons which are to the right of the fields (the one next to the **JDBC Url** field in the previous screenshot is highlighted).

Do no use "localhost" in the JDBC URL

Remember that ODI is a central repository-based system and will be used concurrently by any number of developers and/or runtime agents, all running on different hosts. For each of them, the hostname `localhost` will refer to a different machine (the system where they are executed), so a resource which may be local to the person creating its reference in ODI is unlikely to be local to other developers and agents. Therefore, it is always safer to use an explicit hostname or IP address when referring to resource locations, even if it happens to be local at the time of defining that reference.

Once the JDBC driver class and URL information has been entered, we can test the configuration by clicking on the **Test Connection** link in the editor's header bar. After we choose which physical agent will be used to perform the test (the default "no agent" will use ODI Studio as the agent), ODI will then test the connection for the new server.

The **Definition** tab has the option to specify whether the data server's connection details are held in an external LDAP server that ODI can access via JNDI (Java Naming and Directory Interface). If you select the **JNDI** checkbox in the **Definition** tab, then the **JDBC** tab will be changed to **JNDI** so that you can enter the proper connection information for your LDAP server. We won't go into this capability within this book, but it is a mechanism that can be used to avoid maintaining security credentials within the ODI repository.

Defining Physical Schemas

Whenever we create and save a new data server in the ODI Physical Architecture, we are prompted to create a reference to a Physical Schema located on that server, since it is the schemas in a data server that hold the business data of interest. An ODI data server contains one or more Physical Schemas. One of these will be defined as the default schema. The first schema that is created is selected as the default schema if you do not change the selection. It will be important to remember this if you eventually delete this schema, as some tables (error summary for instance) are automatically attached to the default schema.

Data schemas and work schemas

Whenever ODI is performing its data integration work, there will be times (such as when staging some data in a flow or when diverting error records out of the main data flow) when ODI will use temporary "work" tables. To allow these work tables to be managed separately from production business data, ODI introduces the concept of a "Schema" and a "Work Schema" for each Physical Schema. The Schema holds the business data while the Work Schema holds the temporary data tables created and managed by ODI. Temporary tables created by ODI will always have a $ sign in the beginning of their name (for example, E$_xxx, I$_xxx, C$_xxx) This pairing of work and data schemas is specified within the **Physical Schema** panel, as defined within a data server.

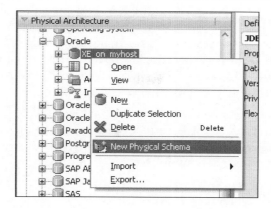

The **Physical Schema** editor shows two drop-down list boxes from which we can select the underlying database schemas that are used to hold the business data (Schema) and to hold any work tables (Work Schema).

 It is quite common for source and target system administrators to insist on the separation of all ODI work artifacts (the $ tables) from the business schema objects. It is for this very reason the ODI provides the ability to specify two distinct schema locations.

ODI will automatically list the available schemas for the servers you are connected to, as long as it is possible to do so. This means that:

- Based on the privileges of the user you have used to connect to the server, you may not see all schemas (and in some cases you may not see any schema at all; this is typical when the user does not have enough privileges).

- Some technologies do not have the necessary "infrastructure" to list the possible entries; flat files would be an example, where the directory names must be entered manually. You can actually type text directly into the drop-down list.

- Some JDBC drivers (luckily there are less and less of these) will not know how to list schemas. If you encounter one of these, you will have to type the schema names directly into the drop-down list.

A few recommendations for schemas and work schemas are as follows:

- Even if you know the schema name, make sure to spell it exactly as it appears in the ODI drop-down. In particular, JDBC is case-sensitive for the schema names, and using the wrong case would prevent you from seeing tables in your database, which would be very inconvenient.

- Always use a dedicated schema for the **Schema (Work Schema)**. One very good practice is to use the schema owned by the dedicated user you have created to connect to the server. Since ODI will create and delete temporary tables, owning the schema will make it easier to assign privileges.

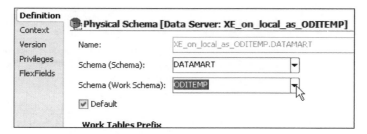

Just below the schema selection are two sections—one shows the prefixes ODI will use when creating its work tables; the other shows the naming conventions ODI will use when accessing local and remote objects (for example when using partitions or database links on an Oracle server). Modifying these values is quite rare and should only be considered if required in your environment for technical reasons (think of environments where $ signs would be problematic for instance).

Defining Logical Schemas and Contexts

A Physical Schema definition needs to be associated with a Logical Schema name (an environment-independent alias or nickname) which will be exclusively used to build ODI models and, subsequently, interfaces and other data integration objects. The association of the physical world to the logical world is achieved via a "Context".

By default ODI delivers a single Context called Global, but we can create as many additional Contexts as needed (for example development, test, staging, and production). In this way we can link our data models and data integration objects to as many similarly configured environments as required for managing the data integration lifecycle and for deploying our data integration solutions with minimal changes as we move from one environment to another.

When you create a new Physical Schema, you can define the Context and Logical Schema that it is associated with in the **Context** tab. Alternatively, you can ignore this tab when you create the Physical Schema, and match your Logical Schema with a Context and Physical Schema either in the definition of the Logical Schema, or in the definition of the Context.

We will see later in this chapter the different views, from a Context or Logical Schema perspective.

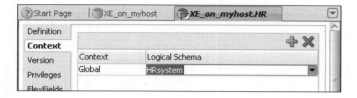

 Entering field values in ODI

It's best to hit the *Enter* key after entering values in ODI data fields to make sure that the newly entered value has been recognized and accepted. This was true of ODI 10*g* and continues with ODI 11*g*. If you ever think that ODI is ignoring any changes or new entries in field values, remind yourself to hit *Enter*.

A new behavior in ODI 11*g* brought in by the use of the JDeveloper IDE framework is that multiple editors can now be opened simultaneously and accessed via different tabs. The current content of each of these tabs can be saved at any time by pressing the appropriate "disk" icon located in the upper left corner of the ODI Studio. Once saved, each of these tabs can safely be closed by clicking on the **X** that appears if you hover the cursor over the right-hand side of the editor's title tab.

The creation of a Physical Schema definition together with the Context-based association to a Logical Schema name completes the basic work necessary within the **Topology** Navigator. We are now able to make use of these schema structures as we build our data models, interfaces, and other ODI objects.

Non-database technologies

Before we leave the **Topology** Navigator, let's take a quick look at two non-database technologies and data servers to see how their definitions and configurations differ from those for a SQL database:

- FILE
- XML

Flat Files

ODI comes pre-configured with a **File** data server called **FILE_GENERIC**. In the Data Server editor for this technology, the **Definition** tab shows the data server name, but the **Host, User,** and **Password** fields are empty. The **JDBC** tab shows that a file accessed by ODI uses a JDBC driver (which is delivered as part of the ODI product).

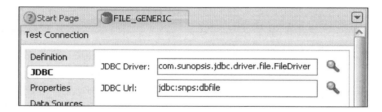

However, the **JDBC Url** field also makes no mention of a hostname or network protocol. This indicates that the ODI file JDBC driver can only access files which are visible by the program using the driver. So by implication, they must be local to the driver itself. If the JDBC driver is used by the ODI Studio, then the file must be visible to the Studio. If the driver is used by the ODI Agent, then the file must be visible to the Agent (either in the form of a local file or files located on a shared-file system). This is something to bear in mind when designing data flows that involve flat files and placements of ODI Agents. ODI 11*g* has several capabilities for transferring and copying files across a network, but when it comes to reading or writing file data, these files have to be accessible to the reader or writer. This will be true whether you decide to load files with JDBC or database native utilities (which ODI can leverage as well)—files must be visible to the loaders and writers.

Using file data servers also means that testing the connection is largely meaningless apart from checking that the ODI file JDBC driver is correctly installed and accessible by ODI Studio.

In the Physical Schema editor for a file data server, we can see that the **Definition** tab has the same **Schema** and **Work Schema** fields as we used before, but this time these fields are *Directory* references, not database schema references. Here we must replace the **<Undefined>** text with the location(s) of our choice, such as **c:/po/input** as shown in the following screenshot:

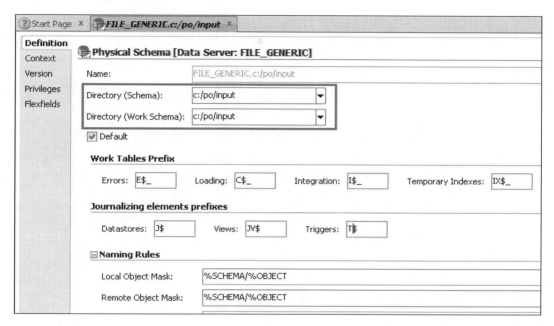

Forward slashes are used as directory separators as these are the platform-portable form in Java—even if the initial c : isn't. A backslash character is treated as an escape character by Java and will create problems if used in the **Directory (Schema)** input field.

Even though an ODI Physical Schema has a slightly different meaning when dealing with filesystems (it's a file directory, not a host or "server" instance), we must still link our Physical Schema to a Logical Schema via the **Context** tab, just as before.

XML files

Next we'll take a quick look at how XML files are handled because these are slightly different from flat files.

Once again the **Host, User**, and **Password** fields in the **Definition** tab of the Data Server editor have no effect and can all be left empty. Similarly to flat files, only XML files that are accessible by the executing agent (including the agent embedded in ODI Studio) can be processed. When we click on the **JDBC** tab, we can click on the search icon next to the **JDBC Driver** field and accept the default driver shown (based upon the technology being used, this driver will be pre-selected to ODI JDBC Driver for XML). The **JDBC** tab indicates that ODI's XML file access will also use a JDBC driver (which of course, is already supplied as part of the ODI product).

When we click on the search icon next to the **JDBC Url** field, we see that an example URL template is provided with a mandatory filename substitution required and a number of optional connection properties that can be added at the end.

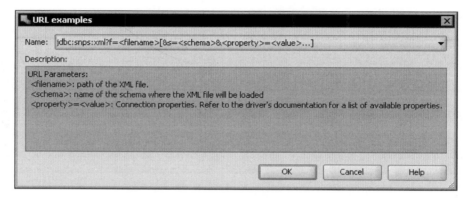

These options set the access behavior, such as whether the file is to be opened as read-only, whether case-sensitivity is to be used, and so on. A full list of URL options is explained in the ODI 11*g* documentation in the *Connectivity and Knowledge Modules Guide for Oracle Data Integrator* (http://download.oracle.com/docs/cd/E23943_01/integrate.1111/e12644/toc.htm).

If we accept the example URL template by clicking on **OK**, it is inserted into the **JDBC Url** field where we can then modify the property values to suit our needs. Two properties that we'll pick out from the dialog box are the values assigned to f and s, but we'll also highlight a third one, namely d. The meaning of these properties is as follows:

- The f value is the full path and name of the XML file which we will be accessing. From this we can see that although most data servers correspond to database instances, servers, or a complete file directory, an XML 'data server' however corresponds to a single XML file. (If you prefer to be more descriptive, the f= assignment can be replaced by file=.) As an example, we could use file=c:/po/input/MarketInc_po_001.xml.

Hardcoding a filename is not always necessary as a variable is often used in more advanced deployments. This makes the driver much more dynamic.

- The s value is the name of the schema into which the XML data will be loaded. (Here again, the s= text is a more explicit alternative of schema=.) In the absence of any other properties being set, this will be a set of in-memory structures that ODI will refer to by this schema name. The schema name must always be uppercase and must not match any XML tag names. It is also highly recommended to keep the schema name short as *all* tables created in the temporary structure will contain this string. So for example, we might choose to use a schema named PO.

- The third property that we'll cover briefly here is the d (or dtd) property. This optional property is used to set the path and filename of a DTD or XSD file which defines the structure of the XML file being accessed. In the absence of this property, ODI will derive a DTD file from what it finds in the XML file. However, it will also designate all discovered fields to be mandatory and will not cater for fields that are optional and missing in the file referenced in the file= property. In the following example, we are setting the value to c:/po/xmlschemas/po.xsd.

If we use these suggested property values, our JDBC settings will look similar to the following screenshot:

There is a **Test Connection** link in the tab header. Unlike flat files, when dealing with XML data server, this test performs a very useful action by checking that the property settings we have specified all work (for example the test would verify that we have an XSD file which accurately describes the structure of our XML file). If we execute the test accepting all default execution settings, we should see a **Successful Connection** message.

To make sure that the connection works, the JDBC driver will attempt to load data from the XML file in its in-memory database schema. Once the data is loaded in memory, the driver will not retrieve data from the file anymore, unless explicitly asked to do so. The driver comes with a large array of commands and configuration parameters that are worth investigating if you want to be serious about XML integration.

When creating a new ODI Physical Schema based on the XML server, we can select our previously specified schema name (PO) for both **Schema** and **Work Schema** using the drop-down lists in the Physical Schema editor. On the **Context** finger-tab, we will add a new association, via the **Global** context, to a Logical Schema name (in the following screenshot that name has been chosen to be **PurchaseOrder**).

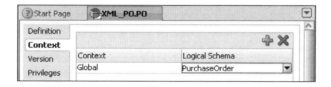

While we still have the **Topology** Navigator open, we can take a look at the Context and Logical Architecture views based on the different examples we have seen so far.

If we expand the **Contexts** pane in the **Topology** Navigator, we can see that we only have one Context defined, namely, **Global**. If we double-click on the Context name to open the Context editor and then choose the **Schemas** tab, we'll see a list of all the logical-to-physical schema mappings within that Context. At the top of the list there are some system-created schemas, but lower down will be any of the schemas that you would create. In the following screenshot these additional schemas have been highlighted with a red box.

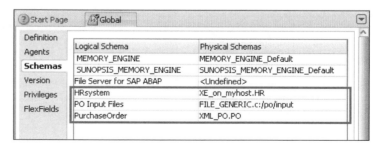

Alternatively, by expanding the **Logical Architecture** view we can see for each technology, all of the Logical Schema names that have been defined so far. (Remember, the **Hide Unused Technologies** option is often useful here.)

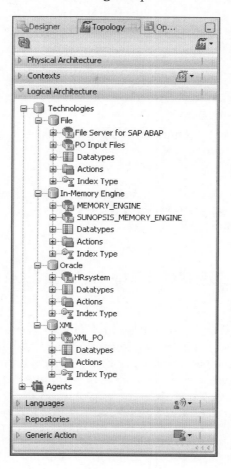

By double-clicking any of these Logical Schemas we can see the associations, by Context, to the various Physical Architectures.

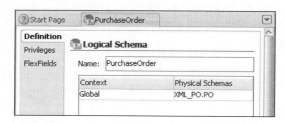

So far we've seen:

- How references to physical servers and schemas are set up
- Some of the key aspects and differences between references for database servers, filesystems, and XML files
- Three different views of the topology information:
  - The Physical Architecture view, which shows the most detail
  - The Context view, which shows all Contexts and all of the logical/physical associations for a given Context
  - The Logical Architecture view, which shows all the Logical Schema names and how each Logical Schema is mapped to Physical Schemas listed by Context name

Next we'll see how all of this topology information is abstracted into ODI models and how individual datastores (tables, files, JMS queues, and so on) are made available for data flow designs.

Reverse-engineering metadata into ODI models

Before we can access and integrate data with ODI Designer, we need to create "models" based on the Logical Schema definitions we have in the topology. ODI models are abstracted to be independent of the physical data server type (database, file, JMS queues and topics, and so on), so they will have a common look and feel despite having dramatically different physical representations. This greatly simplifies their use as sources and targets and is a major benefit of using ODI.

Although we can manually create an ODI model, including its datastore definitions, constraints, and relationships, the normal and recommended method of creating models is by reverse-engineering the structural metadata directly from the databases, files, and other data resources. Sometimes a combination of both activities is used whereby the developer begins with the reverse-engineering process, then augments the captured metadata with additional metadata details (such as referential integrity information that might not be represented within the database).

The term **metadata** is used to refer to data that describes the structure of objects such as tables, columns, views, indexes, constraints, relationships, and so on.

ODI can perform reverse-engineering via several different methods depending on the technology involved and the degree of reverse-engineering required. The following figure shows the three main methods of reverse-engineering, namely, standard, customized, and file-specific.

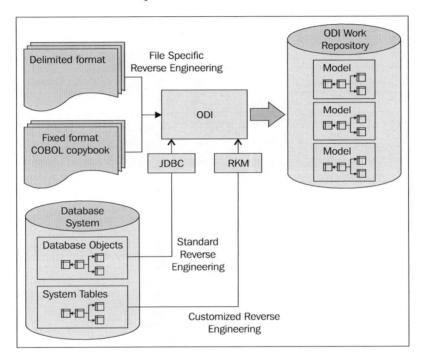

Let's take a brief look at each of the three methods.

Standard reverse-engineering

Standard reverse-engineering is performed by ODI by internally issuing metadata-related JDBC calls to the driver for the specified technology and then processing the responses to build up a metadata picture of the data structures contained within the physical system. This is the most common form of reverse-engineering used with database systems.

As we saw previously, a Logical Schema for a database technology translates to a physical database schema for a given Context. So ODI gives us the choice either to reverse-engineer the entire physical database structure or only selected objects. These choices come in the form of filter checkboxes and individual object checkboxes available in the **Selective Reverse-Engineering** tab.

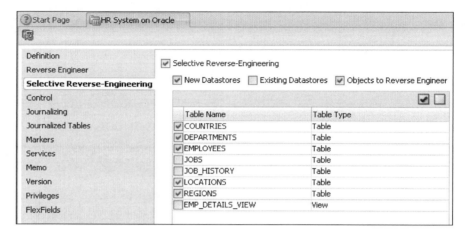

The previous screenshot shows that a reduced set of tables has been selected for reverse-engineering, which can be initiated by clicking on the icon on the left-hand side of the header bar within the model editor tab.

Custom reverse-engineering

There will be cases where JDBC metadata calls will not be sufficient to import metadata from the system you want to reverse-engineer; some JDBC drivers are too limited and do not support this feature. Some systems would be too complex to reverse-engineer solely based on table names (ERPs, for instance, typically have tens of thousands of tables).

For such cases, Reverse-engineering Knowledge Module (RKM) may be needed to directly access the system tables of the underlying system in order to extract the metadata for the ODI model. ODI ships with a series of RKMs for applications (E-Business Suite, PeopleSoft, JD Edwards, SAP, Siebel, and Hyperion) as well as for some databases. As seen in the following screenshot, custom RKMs often include special options that are used to fine-tune the actions of the reverse-engineering process.

File reverse-engineering

The third method for reverse-engineering is limited to flat files. This is because there is no "intelligence" in the file system and the ODI JDBC driver for flat files cannot interrogate any central system on the structures of a group of files in a specified directory. Instead, individual files are reverse-engineered one-by-one. ODI has wizards to assist with this activity and these Wizards do interrogate each file that is being reverse-engineered. We begin by specifying whether a file is fixed format or delimited, what the delimiters or column boundaries are, and whether there are any column header lines at the beginning of the file (and if so, how many). After completing these basic definition steps, the wizard will perform the majority of the metadata creation.

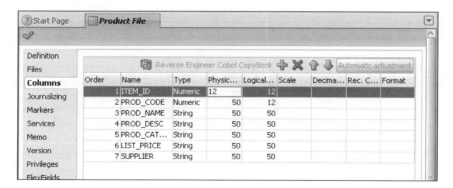

Before closing the file wizards, we also have the opportunity to specify or alter column names, sizes, datatypes, and formatting information (for example, dates) that may have been read or inferred from the file.

> It will be important in particular to review the size of the fields reverse-engineered by the wizards. There is no way for the wizard to ensure that the sizes are accurate for all iterations of the file, and defining column sizes that are smaller than the actual data will result in failing processes. Defining columns that are too large will have no other impact than wasting space.

XML reverse-engineering

Reverse-engineering an XML file is very similar to reverse-engineering a set of related database tables. If the ODI JDBC Driver for XML files is able to use a DTD or XSD file that describes the contents of the XML file (in other words, the DTD or XSD holds the metadata for the XML file), then the XML driver will use that metadata to build a model of datastores linked in the same hierarchy as the tag and attribute nesting within the XML file. If no such DTD or XSD is available, the driver will interrogate the whole XML file and build a new DTD file based on what it discovers. The main difference between a model based on an XML file and one based on database tables is that the ODI XML driver adds additional "columns" to the modeled datastores to enable the nesting hierarchy of tags to be preserved and also to record the order of data entries in the XML file.

> Some technologies, such as JMS do not support any kind of reverse-engineering. This is because the contents of a JMS message (within the envelope and addressing constructs) are not specified by the JMS system, but rather by the sender of that message. In this case we can use either a flat file or XSD file that matches the definition of the structure of the messages. Then copy these definitions in your JMS model.

We now know the high-level basics of how to create ODI models and datastores based on the structures held in database, flat files, and XML files. They are as follows:

- Models are based on Logical Schemas, which must be associated with a Physical Schema for reverse-engineering in order to extract the schema structure.

- There are three main methods of reverse-engineering, namely, simple, customized, (with customizations abstracted into a technology-specific RKM) and file-specific methods.

- We can make a selection from the available tables, views, and other objects in a database to limit what we import into our ODI model, rather than always modeling the complete schema structure.

- Datatype and column name metadata for flat files can be enriched and modified during the reverse-engineering process.

- Not all technologies support reverse-engineering and that manual creation of the model's metadata will be needed in those cases.

- ODI's XML file driver reverse-engineers files using DTD or XSD documents to provide the metadata and creates a hierarchy of linked datastores for each file processed, with a file equating to a Logical Schema. If no DTD or XSD documents are available, the XML driver will derive the structure by scanning the entire XML file.

Examining the anatomy of the interface flow

Once we've created all our definitions and references for the data that we want ODI to transform and transport, we can focus on what precisely it is that we want to take place in terms of data mappings and transformations, that is we can look into creating ODI Interfaces. We have already seen that ODI uses an E-LT approach and architecture, but what does that mean in detail? What actions are performed, where, and at what time during the overall flow, and what components will perform those actions?

In this section we will walk through three very simple yet common ODI data flows to examine and explain these aspects of ODI's operational behavior.

ODI Interfaces are the objects used to transform and transport data from one or more sources to a target, so each of these flow examples will be implemented in a separate interface.

Example 1: Database and file to database

This example forms the foundation of many ETL jobs. It's a simple case of loading data into a data warehouse or data mart to make it ready for other systems such as Enterprise Resource Planning (ERP), business intelligence analysis and reporting, Customer Relationship Management (CRM), Master Data Management (MDM), or archiving.

Here we'll consider taking data from two related source tables in a database, joining them with some additional data from a file, transforming the data and "upserting/ merging" the resulting transformed and enriched data into a single table within our target database. The two source database tables hold **orders** and **orderItem** entries, with the file containing a list of **pricingCorrection** lines by product. The target table, **orderSummary**, is used to hold the total value for each closed order after the pricing corrections have been applied.

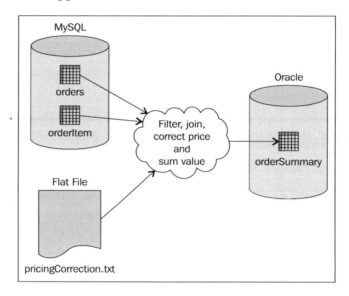

The previous figure shows that information must be extracted from two MySQL tables and the flat file, and then filtered for *closed* orders only. The information from the three data sources must be joined so that order items are associated with the parent order and that any applicable price corrections are applied correctly. The value of each order must then be calculated and the summary values added to the Oracle data mart.

It makes sense to use the power of the MySQL database to perform the filter for closed **orders** and the join of **orderItem** entries to the correct orders: ODI allows exactly that to be done. However there is still a requirement to apply the pricing corrections. We achieve this by joining the pricingCorrection data with the resulting order information, then calculating the summary values by product, and performing any final format transformation needed to add the data into the target **Oracle** data mart table. The work comprising these intermediate steps will be done in an ODI-defined staging area (work schema), co-located on the Oracle server.

As discussed in the *Defining Physical Schemas* section of this chapter, the actual physical location of temporary ODI artifacts will be dependent on how the Physical Schemas were configured. We strongly advocate a separate schema for these staging tables.

So we need "something" that will:

- Issue the join-and-filter query to extract the MySQL data into the staging area in Oracle
- Extract the data from the flat file and upload that into the staging area
- Combine the data in the staging area and upload it from there into the target data schema

In ODI, this "something" comes in the form of Knowledge Modules:

- Loading Knowledge Modules (LKMs) load the source data into the staging area
- Integration Knowledge Module (IKM) will integrate the data from the staging area into the target schema

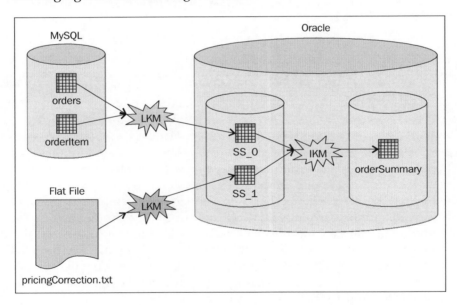

In the previous figure, we see that **SS_0** and **SS_1** (SS literally stands for Source Set) are representations of work tables created by ODI in the staging area to enable the intermediate work of summarizing the data to be performed. These tables will be automatically created by ODI, and deleted when they are not needed anymore.

Knowledge Modules are of different types that relate to the source and target technologies being used and to the methodology chosen to move the data. The choice of which of the available KMs is best often becomes a function of system performance or technology-based advanced features. For instance, loading data using an Oracle Exadata system, selecting a Knowledge Module that leverages "External tables" would be by far more efficient than any other technique. Other databases will have their own utilities that will be leveraged by ODI as well, for example, bcp for Microsoft SQL server or Sybase, nzload for Netezza, and the list of utilities goes on with the list of databases. Using Oracle's MERGE functionality is usually more efficient than using a standard INSERT/UPDATE.

In our example, to filter, join, and load the data from MySQL into the staging area in Oracle, the Loading Knowledge Module (LKM) we choose might be LKM SQL to Oracle. For loading the flat files, our choice might be the generic LKM File to SQL, but it could just as easily be one of the Oracle-specific KMs for loading file data, such as LKM File to Oracle (SQLLDR) or File to Oracle (EXTERNAL TABLE).

The Integration Knowledge Module (IKM) will transfer the data from the staging area into the final target table. In our situation (because the staging area and the target are both in the same Oracle instance), we might choose from one of several suitable KMs such as IKM Oracle Incremental Update and IKM Oracle Incremental Update (MERGE).

Example 2: File and database to second file

ODI requires the staging area location for any data flow to be hosted in an SQL database. This is because it uses SQL processing within the database engine to do the "heavy lifting" of creating, populating, and manipulating work tables within the staging area. This implies that staging areas cannot be located in non-SQL technologies such as filesystems, JMS message stores, or web service systems. Therefore if we are using one of these non-SQL systems as our target, our staging area must be located somewhere other than that target system. Fortunately with ODI, this is very simple to achieve. In this example, the requirements from the sales business unit have changed and now call for the output to be written to a file called orderSummary.csv instead of being sent to the Oracle data mart. The only SQL database server we have in the flow is the MySQL system, so we will locate our ODI staging area there by simply selecting the appropriate Logical Schema from the drop-down list on the interface's definition tab.

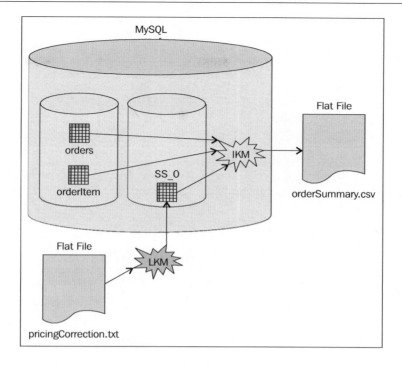

In our current example, there is still a need for the `pricingCorrection` file data
to be loaded using a Loading Knowledge Module (the same `LKM File to SQL`
mentioned before will be sufficient), but there is no longer a need for an LKM for
the MySQL data as the staging area is now located on the same database server as
the source data. Instead, a single Integration Knowledge Module (`IKM SQL to File
Append`) will perform the filtering and joining of information from all three sources
(now that the file information is being loaded into the MySQL server) and integrate
the final results into the output file. Furthermore, because MySQL allows a single
query to span multiple schemas within the same data server (in this case the data
schema and the work schema), the IKM no longer has to create an intermediate work
table to join the `orders` and `orderItem` data (as seen by the absence of an SS_1 icon
in the previous figure).

Example 3: File to Enterprise Application

For the third example, the sales business unit requirements have changed yet again. They now require the resulting flat file data from *Example 2: File and database to second file* section to be integrated with their Enterprise CRM system (Oracle's Siebel CRM).

It's important to remember that although Siebel (and other Enterprise applications) runs on top of a database, they should not be treated as simple database systems themselves. They each have pre-defined integration mechanisms which must always be used when uploading data, in order to ensure that the application's business logic can be properly applied and to keep the underlying data complete and consistent. You will almost always find that administrators of these systems will never allow work not managed by these applications to take place directly inside the primary databases or by using the primary database user identities.

With our Siebel example, one such mechanism is the Enterprise Integration Manager (EIM) and ODI has an IKM that supports and simplifies data integration with Siebel by encapsulating the use of Siebel EIM.

Since we shouldn't treat the Siebel system as a standard SQL database and our input is coming from a flat file (for example, the output file from the previously discussed flow in *Example 2*), we'll need to introduce an SQL database server, (Oracle for instance), into this flow to host our staging area. In this example we are using ODI in a more traditional ETL architecture (rather than an E-LT architecture), due to the strict data integration requirements that the CRM team has imposed on the target Siebel system. Most people will use their datawarehouse for that operation, as it is more likely that additional information will be needed from that database (taking us back to our first example, where information from the file is combined with data from the database).

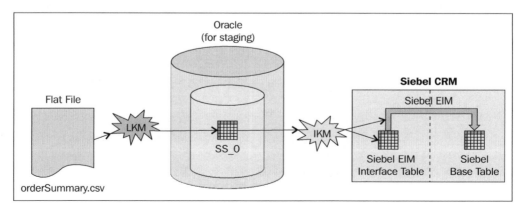

For the `orderSummary.csv` flat file, we can once again use the `LKM File to SQL` KM to load the file data into the staging area located on the Oracle database. For the integration into Siebel, we can use the `IKM SQL to Siebel Append (EIM)`, which not only loads the EIM interface table in Siebel, but also executes the EIM task in Siebel to move the EIM table data into the base tables.

> Oracle's Application Adapters for Data Integration—of which the IKM SQL to Siebel Append (EIM) Knowledge Module is a component—are not licensed as part of the base ODI functionality, so they have an additional license cost attached to their use. Other applications that ODI supports with out of the box Knowledge Modules include, but are not limited to, E-Business Suite, JD Edwards, PeopleSoft, Hyperion, and SAP. Licencing for these KMs will vary.

In this section we've taken a look at three basic and frequently seen requirements-driven data flows and peeked under the covers at some additional details of the core actions and actors in each flow. Lets recap as follows:

- The staging area is co-located with the target for any interface by default, representing ODI's default E-LT architecture. It should be noted that ODI can be easily reconfigured with a few mouse clicks to have the staging data on a separate server, representing a traditional ETL architecture. The staging area can reside on the source or even an intermediate system if required.

- Two types of Knowledge Modules play vital roles in ODI Interfaces as follows:
    - IKMs are used to integrate data into the final target
    - LKMs are used to load the staging area with data located on other source systems

- Some KMs have the capability to issue external commands to finalize the integration of data into the target systems.

- ODI has an agile capability to adapt to changing requirements by leveraging its library of Knowledge Modules that abstract and encapsulate the complexity and details of "the know-how" for integrating with a given technology or application.

Now that we understand the importance of Knowledge Modules and the functionality they deliver, we will look at how we go about selecting which Knowledge Modules we will use and how to bring them into our ODI projects.

Importing and choosing Knowledge Modules

We've now seen that Loading and Integration Knowledge Modules play pivotal roles in performing data integration actions within ODI. So how and when do we choose which KM to use?

The ODI component that actually moves data is called an Interface, and it is located inside the ODI Designer Interface editor where you specify which KM is to be used for source and target data movement behavior. Interfaces are created and organized in folders within a project, but for an interface to be able to leverage a set of KM, the KMs must have been previously imported into this very project.

Choosing Knowledge Modules

Within the six types of Knowledge Modules, let's just focus for a moment on the two types that are central to moving and transforming data namely, LKMs and IKMs.

When a Knowledge Module has been previously imported into the parent project and applied to the interface target and the interface is subsequently executed, it is the steps within the IKM that determine the what, how, and when data is moved into the target data store. Therefore, we can safely say that every interface will need an IKM. But which one?

If we adopt the default E-LT architecture approach and have the staging area residing on the same server as the target, as in our first data flow example, then we need a **single technology** IKM such as like the IKM Oracle Incremental Update mentioned in that example. So the choice of IKM to import into the project and select for use will depend on the following:

- Whether the type of database that you're using for the staging area and target has specific IKMs available (for example, Oracle, Microsoft SQL Server, and many others), or whether you need to use a "generic" SQL flavor (for example for MySQL, PostgreSQL, and so on)

- Whether there is more than one integration technique available for that technology and what method is used by each, such as the Oracle MERGE construct as mentioned in the first flow example

If, as in our second data flow example, the staging area and target are in different servers, then we will need to use a **multi-technology** IKM, such as IKM SQL to File Append suggested in that flow. Indeed, most (but not quite all) of these have IKM SQL to ... names, but all of them will be IKM <something> to <something>, sometimes with a (method) qualifier.

LKMs load data into the staging area from other servers. Therefore all LKMs are multi-technology. If the source data is in the same server as the staging area then you don't need an LKM as can be inferred from the flow path taken by the MySQL data in the second flow example. Without the corrections file data being added in that example, there would have been no need for an LKM at all.

Once again, the choice of LKM is governed by the following:

- The technologies involved at either end of the loading flow and the direction in which data will flow

- The method to be used to move the data, `LKM File to Oracle` (`EXTERNAL TABLE`) and `LKM File to Oracle` (`SQLLDR`) could both be used to load file data but employ very different techniques to achieve that purpose

Having covered IKMs, LKMs, and RKMs earlier in this chapter, let's briefly cover three other types of Knowledge Module used by ODI, as follows:

- **Check Knowledge Modules (CKMs)** are used to check and enforce data integrity through testing conformance to constraints and references, either statically on data tables on source or target systems, or dynamically during the process of a data flow defined in an ODI interface. There are technology-specific CKMs for databases that require specific SQL code. All other databases will use the generic `CKM SQL`.

- **Journalizing Knowledge Modules (JKMs)** are used to manage the journalizing of data for changed data capture. They have a technology flavor (there are no generic SQL JKMs), an approach of either simple or consistent (the latter guaranteeing that no child records are loaded before their parent records), and optionally a method name, such as (Oracle GoldenGate) to differentiate change detection techniques.

- **Service Knowledge Modules (SKMs)** are used for generating fine-grained data web services based on ODI datastores and models based on database technology. There are a few database-specific versions, for example to create web services based on Oracle tables, as well as a generic `SKM SQL`.

Now that we know how to choose between Knowledge Modules and what we will use them for, let's see how we enable that use.

Importing a Knowledge Module

Knowledge Modules are supplied out of the box as XML files and installed as part of the ODI installation process. Rather than having all Knowledge Modules accessible to all projects all the time, a small subset of Knowledge Modules are imported by the ODI Studio user for each project.

 ODI 11.1.1.6 allows for Global Knowledge Modules that can be shared across projects.

So if we have several situations in our overall IT project where we need to transform and upload file data into an Oracle database via External Tables, then we could either develop the necessary interfaces in several projects and import the LKM File to Oracle (External Tables) into each of those ODI projects, or we could create several subfolders in a single ODI project and import the KM just once. How you organize work in ODI is a very subjective topic and there is rarely just one right way to do things.

Importing a single KM—or a set of them—is a very simple exercise. We only have to follow these steps:

1. Expand our project node in the **Projects** section of the Designer Navigator.

2. Right-click on the **Knowledge Modules** node and select **Import Knowledge Modules**.

 If you want to follow along, you will need to create a new project via the menu icon at the right-hand end of the **Projects** section header.

3. A dialog box will appear to allow us to select the KMs to import. When doing it for the first time we'll need to browse to the folder holding the KM files — this is the `oracledi\xml-reference` subfolder below our `ODI_HOME` (where we installed ODI 11*g*).

4. Once we've done this we'll see a list of all the available KMs in that folder. We can scroll through the list selecting which KM(s) we want to import (making multiple selections with *Ctrl+Click*) and then press **OK** to perform the import of the KMs.

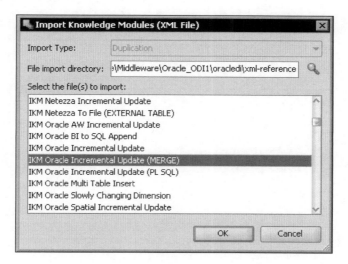

When the import has completed you will see a report of the import process (which can be ignored). Note that all of the imported KMs were automatically organized into their appropriate Knowledge Module subfolders in the ODI project.

KMs—A quick look under the hood

If we drill down within the **Knowledge Modules** node to any given KM and double-click on it, that Knowledge Module will be opened by an editor. On the **Definition** tab we can see the source and/or target technologies for the KM and whether it is the default KM for use with this pairing. If the latter is the case, the KM will automatically be inserted into an interface definition if that technology combination for source and target is used.

We can also see some **Description** text, which often contains very useful information about the use, characteristics, and restrictions for the KM.

Clicking on the **Details** tab shows us an ordered list of the steps included inside the KM, including each step name, whether the steps operate within a transaction and when that transaction is committed, the log detail level for each step, whether each step updates any logged metrics, and so on.

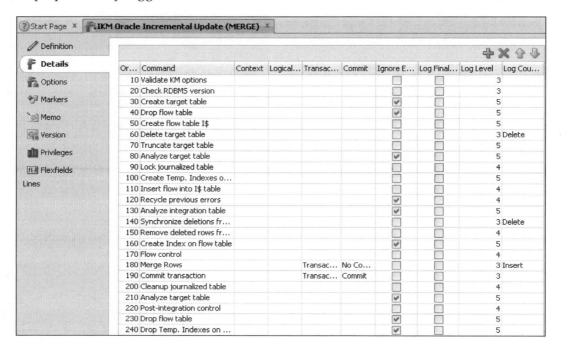

The sequencing of these steps specifies the order in which they will be executed. Later when examining the operator logs generated by our interface, we will see these step names again along with all of the ODI logging information associated with them. These logs will give us a direct link between the code executed, the outcomes of that code, and the source from which the executable code was generated.

If we were to select and double-click on any step name, we would see the actual KM source code for that step. These code blocks usually consist of templates of SQL constructions with various placeholders representing the use of ODI substitution methods. These substitution placeholders will be used by ODI when generating code to insert specific table names, columns, datatypes, where clauses and the like at execution time.

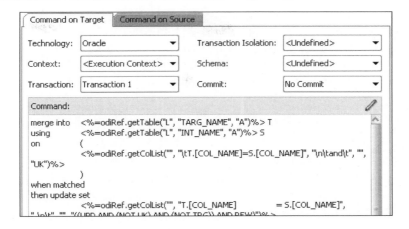

Hopefully by now you will have concluded that we could amend, delete, replace, or otherwise customize the KM code as we desire or require. This is a perfectly acceptable — and not uncommon practice — in ODI, but it falls outside the scope of this book. (For more information on KM development, refer to the *Knowledge Module Developer's Guide for Oracle Data Integrator* manual). Here's a small warning though: if we change the code here, we will be changing only *this* copy of the KM in *this* project in *this* repository. If we want to propagate any of our changes elsewhere, we should do the following:

1. Change a renamed copy of the original KM so it isn't in danger of being overwritten by mistake or by later ODI patches and updates.

2. Export the renamed and amended KM into an XML file.

3. Import the new KM into other ODI projects and repositories as needed.

Configuring behavior with KM options

It would be overly cumbersome if, for every slight change in KM behavior, we had to write, change or otherwise customize a different KM to reflect each of those slight alterations. For example, we may wish to sometimes delete all of the records in a target table before we upload the latest data set, or perhaps we want to control whether a database commit is issued after an interface flow has completed.

The ability to manage behavior in this way can be achieved via KM options. KM options are similar to local parameters with a default value specified. These options can be tested, evaluated, or substituted as values within the KM code and can be represented by one of the three different types—a checkbox (a Boolean true/false value), text, or a specific value (numeric)—as follows:

- The most common type of option used is the **checkbox** type(for example, a checkbox option might be used to decide whether to issue a database transaction commit).

- A **value** typed option is commonly used for Oracle-specific KMs to dynamically alter the code that the KM template will generate when executing against different versions of the Oracle Database (for example 8, 9, 10, and so on.)

- The Oracle-specific IKMs often use a **text** type option (with an empty string as the default value) to provide the ODI interface developer with the ability to specify an optimizer hint when loading the final target table in an interface. This hint text would then be embedded at the appropriate place within the SQL that the KM generates to integrate the data into the target table.

 All objects in an ODI project share the same set of KMs and KM code. Therefore, if during design time you modify or overwrite an existing KM, all design-time objects which use that KM will immediately use the new code. This is something to remember, even if you are just updating KMs from a patch update release of ODI. However, simply setting a KM option value inside an ODI interface only affects the KM's behavior within that one interface.

In this section we learned how to select and import Knowledge Modules ready for use in ODI projects and how to modify their behavior. We took a look at the following points:

- An IKM is always needed in an ODI interface

- An LKM is required when moving data between two different technologies

- The KMs are selected based on:
  - Technology flavors used in the operation
  - The method used to perform the operation

- The ODI-provided KMs are in the `<ODI_HOME>\oracledi\xml-reference` folder and are imported for each project, or as global objects (starting with ODI 11.1.1.6)

- Interfaces can only use KMs that have been imported into their "parent" project or global KMs

- KM steps are individually logged in the execution logs in ODI and they correlate to the interface execution steps presented within the Operator ODI Studio component

- KM code can be customized, but this is not a "Getting started" task

- KM behavior can more easily be modified (within limits) by setting their individual options

- Modifying and/or replacing existing KMs must be treated with great care at design-time

Examining ODI Interfaces

Having had a look at data flows and the roles that KMs play within them, let's now dig a bit deeper into the make-up of the primary data flow component—an **interface**.

The interface component in ODI defines the following data flow properties:

- The destination datastore for the data (the **target**). This will be chosen from an ODI model.

- The datastores that supply the input data (the **sources**). These too will be chosen from ODI models.

- The transformations that are applied to the data during the transition from sources to target (the **mappings**). These are expressed in SQL.

- The physical transfer mechanisms that are used between sources and target (the **flow**). We have already seen that this role is performed by the Knowledge Modules.

The first two of these properties specify *what* we want to achieve in the interface. The flow specifies *how* it will be achieved.

Overview tab

On the **Definition Overview** tab of the Interface editor, we can specify the name of the interface and optionally specify whether we wish to locate the staging area of the flow on the target data server (the default) or somewhere else.

If we have additional Logical Schemas defined that are hosted on other relational database technologies, we could select one of these to be our staging area bearing in mind that ODI will create, populate, update, and delete temporary database objects at runtime within the corresponding Physical Schema.

One such option that is available by default in ODI is the "In-Memory Engine", but this choice can realistically cope with only a few hundred thousand source records and can consume significant memory within the executing ODI agent.

As much as possible, always try to keep the staging area on the target system. In most cases this will provide much better performance (less network hops than staging in a separate server, and a better leverage of the set-based processing that databases have been built for) and a much simpler infrastructure.

The previous screenshot shows a new aspect introduced in the ODI 11*g* Interface editor. There are now tabs along the bottom of the editor as well as the sidebar tabs.

Mapping tab

Clicking on the **Mapping** tab will move us to the main graphical editor used for specifying the interface target, sources, and mappings. It allows us to specify what we want to achieve, where the data is stored initially, where we ultimately want the data, and what transformations we need to perform to store the data in the target system.

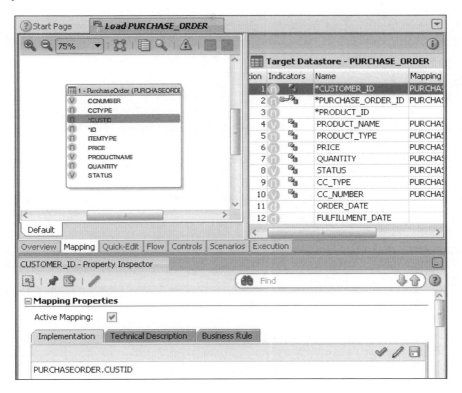

The previous screenshot doesn't show items in the proportion that you'd most likely use them, but it's useful to help explain the main elements. In reality you'd normally expand the editor to full screen (by double-clicking the top tab) when building interfaces.

The top-left pane is the main canvas for adding source datastores, dragging join lines between them, and adding filters to limit the data to be processed by the interface. To the right of the main canvas is the target datastore area, which displays the columns of the target table, a set of indicators for each column, and its mapping text. The bottom section is the Properties Editor where the text and additional configuration information for each mapping, join, and filter can be entered.

We build an interface by dragging-and-dropping a target datastore and all necessary source datastores into their respective screen areas, creating joins and filters in the top-left canvas, and setting all the specific details of those joins, filters, and the mappings by using the Property Editor pane.

Target field mappings can be specified using several different formats, including the following:

- **Source Column**: These are dragged-and-dropped directly into the target column's **Mapping** field from the datastore columns in the source canvas. Each column name is prefixed by the datastore's alias, for example SALES_PERS.LAST_NAME.

- **Fixed Value or Constant**: These must follow SQL formatting rules, so string values are enclosed in single quotes, for example, 'John Doe', whereas numeric values are not, for example, 11.1.

- **DBMS Function**: Any function supported by the platform on which the mapping is to be performed, for example, SYSDATE for execution on Oracle. The location of the mapping's execution is shown by a symbol in the target's Indicators column and also by a radio button in the Property Editor below the textbox that holds the mapping text.

- **DBMS Aggregate**: A simple aggregate of a source column, for example, SUM(ITEM.QUANTITY). ODI will automatically generate a corresponding GROUP BY clause whenever an aggregate function is detected.

> Group-level aggregation functions that correspond to the SQL "having clause" are not implemented here but rather by defining aggregations within an ODI filter.

- **A combination of the previous formats:** As long as the underlying database understands your code, you can build the most complex mappings. A simple example would be. `InitCap(SALES_PERS.FIRST_NAME) || ' ' || InitCap(SALES_PERS.LAST_NAME)`. The location of the mapping's execution will allow you to leverage the database of your choice for the transformations (source, staging area, or target). This choice can be made on a per column basis.

Mappings can also include ODI variables which are covered in the previous chapter.

As you include sources and the target in the interface, the default behavior of ODI is to ask whether you wish to perform an *Automatic Mapping*. Automatic mapping creates straight-through source column to target column mappings where the column names match exactly. There is no capability to add a mapping translation dictionary and underscores *are* significant, so `CUST_ID` is *not* automatically mapped to `CUSTID`. Also, ODI takes no account of column datatypes during this process. If you manually enter or want to amend existing mappings, you can do this directly by changing the text in the **Implementation** textbox, or you can use ODI's Expression Editor which is available via the pencil icon located at the right-hand end of the title bar of the **Implementation** area.

> It is good practice during this step is to validate each SQL expression by clicking on the "check" icon, which is also at the right-hand end of the title bar.

Flow tab

The **Flow** tab on the bottom edge of the top two panes opens the Flow editor for the interface, where we can specify *how* data will be transferred from source to target, and how it will be integrated in the target system—are we just adding new records, replacing existing ones, or maybe we want to have a more advanced type of integration like slowly changing dimensions?

The following screenshot shows the various source datastores, filters, and joins, the intermediate work tables (or source sets) of data, the staging area location, the target datastore, and the Knowledge Modules that ODI will use to implement the flow.

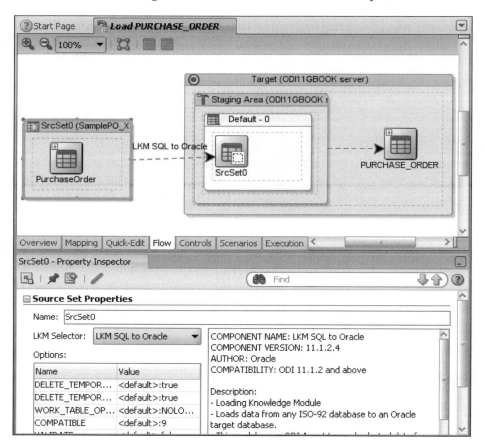

The **Flow** tab also includes a Property editor pane where we can view and select the KM for each flow segment and set configuration options for each KM as our flow requires (for example, turning off work table logging) as depicted in the previous screenshot. Remember, in order for a KM to be included in the drop-down list and available for selection, it must have first been imported into the ODI project containing the interface.

Quick-Edit tab

ODI 11*g* introduces a new view known as the **Quick-Edit** tab. This feature provides a tabular alternative to the normal graphical approach used when building an interface. As opposed to using the normal graphical method, the Quick-Edit tab uses a configuration sheet for setting and editing the target, sources, joins, filters, and mappings. The following screenshot illustrates this new Quick-Edit method. This view is usually more practical for massive edits or cut and paste. For instance, you can change the location of the transformations from staging area to source for multiple columns at once by copying "source" for one column and pasting this in place of multiple "staging area" (select the different lines you want replaced and paste over the multiple selections). Similarly, this view will be very convenient for bulk review of integration options such as which columns are part of the update key, which columns are used for updates/inserts, and so on.

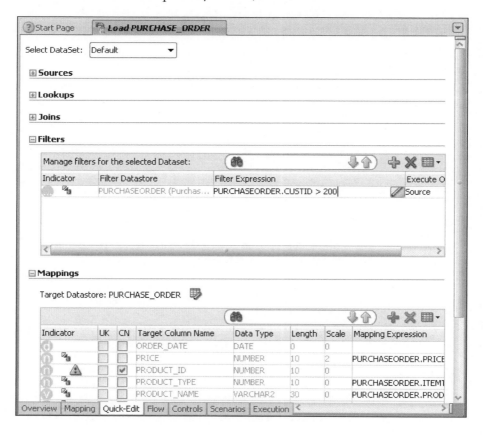

Summary

We've covered a lot in this chapter. We started off by taking a look at how we define physical connections to our data resources, create Logical Schema names to decouple us from any specific operational environment, and link the physical and logical representations via Contexts.

We walked through the high-level concepts of how to reverse-engineer those Logical Schemas to create the ODI models that will become the foundation for our data integration flows.

We examined three simple flow examples that illustrated the use of Knowledge Modules for loading and integrating data, and we learned how to choose and import those Knowledge Modules.

We had a quick look at the internals of a KM, giving us a better understanding of the information that we'll see later in the execution logs of the following chapters.

Finally we had a brief look at Interfaces and the various editor panes used to create them, including the graphical mappings and flow editors and the new configuration sheet oriented Quick-Edit approach. We'll be using these editors a lot in the upcoming chapters.

5
Working with Databases

Databases and database systems hold the vast majority of data processed by ODI around the world, so it's appropriate that we start our Purchase Order example by performing some basic work using databases.

Our overall example scenario involves uploading information concerning Purchase Order processing into a data mart and we'll begin by moving data from a customer data system's database into our data mart. To do this we'll be performing the following tasks:

- Take a quick overview of the physical layout of our source and target systems and the requirements for our first data integration task

- Configure data servers, Physical Schemas, and Logical Schemas for our target and source systems and link them to a Context using the Topology Navigator

- Use the Designer Navigator to create models based on the Logical Schemas and reverse-engineer the metadata from the physical systems in our environment

- Create a new project in the Designer Navigator and import the Knowledge Modules we anticipate we'll use in this task

- Create an interface to integrate data into our data mart from our source customer system, add some transformational mappings, and check if the flow behavior is as required

- Run the interface as a functional test

- Use the Operator Navigator to review the execution tree and examine some of the code generated for the interface we created

This will give us a good first view of the overall sequence of activities normally performed when creating data integration components in ODI 11g and will also give us a solid foundation for expanding our knowledge and expertise in the chapters that follow.

Sample scenario description

During this first example, we'll be moving data from a Customer System database into a data mart. To keep things simple for this stage, we'll deal with just one source table and one target table, and they're both hosted in Oracle databases. However, the structures and formats of these two tables are different, so we'll have to perform some transformations and enrichments along the way. Having accurate and enriched customer data moving from our source Customer System into the data mart will be a key foundational element of being able to process orders within the Purchase Order (PO) processing solution.

It just so happens that in our example environment, both tables are held in schemas managed by the same Oracle server instance and we could probably achieve our integration task with a single SQL statement. However, we're going to simulate having these schemas held on different servers, because in a production system that's far more likely to be the case.

Also, we're not going to be using Oracle database links in this exercise (although ODI can certainly make use of them by choosing an appropriate dblink-based LKM). Our aim here is to use a single heterogeneous tool with a consistent approach for all of our data integration needs, rather than rely on scattered segments of vendor-specific code that need to be knitted together by hand to make the whole integration environment function as it should.

So let's take a look at some of the details of the task we have to complete.

Integration target

The target table we will use is the CUSTOMER table located in the DATAMART schema in an Oracle database and it has the following structure:

Column Name	Data Type	Nullable
CUSTOMER_ID	NUMBER	No
PREFIX	NUMBER	Yes
LAST_NAME	VARCHAR2(30 BYTE)	Yes
FIRST_NAME	VARCHAR2(30 BYTE)	Yes
ADDRESS	VARCHAR2(80 BYTE)	Yes
CITY	VARCHAR2(30 BYTE)	Yes
COUNTRY_ID	NUMBER	Yes
PHONE	VARCHAR2(30 BYTE)	Yes
AGE	NUMBER	Yes
PARTNER_ID	NUMBER	Yes
SALES_PERSON_ID	NUMBER	Yes
CREATE_DATE	DATE	No
LAST_UPDATE	DATE	No

The CUSTOMER table is not the only table in the DATAMART schema, but for now it's the only one that we want to work with. In its initial state, this table is empty, but by completing this chapter's tasks we will populate it with data from the source system.

Integration source

The source table is called CUSTOMER_MASTER and is located in the CUSTSYSTEM schema (to keep things simple, it is the only table in the CUSTSYSTEM Oracle schema). This table has the following structure:

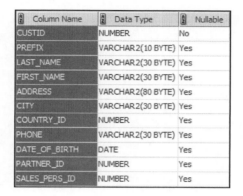

Column Name	Data Type	Nullable
CUSTID	NUMBER	No
PREFIX	VARCHAR2(10 BYTE)	Yes
LAST_NAME	VARCHAR2(30 BYTE)	Yes
FIRST_NAME	VARCHAR2(30 BYTE)	Yes
ADDRESS	VARCHAR2(80 BYTE)	Yes
CITY	VARCHAR2(30 BYTE)	Yes
COUNTRY_ID	NUMBER	Yes
PHONE	VARCHAR2(30 BYTE)	Yes
DATE_OF_BIRTH	DATE	Yes
PARTNER_ID	NUMBER	Yes
SALES_PERS_ID	NUMBER	Yes

Integration mappings

After close examination of the source and target tables, you will see that although the two structures are similar, there are some crucial differences and we'll have to overcome these differences with our mappings. Many of the mappings will be successfully handled by automatic mapping: the column names, types, and lengths are the same in both source and target. However, some mappings have to be done manually:

- The source has a CUSTID column whereas the target column is called CUSTOMER_ID.

- The PREFIX column in our source is a character string, but in the target it's a number. Our Customer System has all the titles normalized to US prefixes, such as Mr, Mrs, Dr, and so on, but we may wish to process the data later to have national-specific titles based on country or residence (such as Hr and Fr for German citizens), so our data mart has all prefixes translated into numeric codes.

- Our target stores an AGE, but our source has a DATE_OF_BIRTH.

- We have another column name difference between SALES_PERS_ID and SALES_PERSON_ID.
- The target has two additional mandatory columns to hold the date when the record was created in the data mart and the date that the record was last changed.

Data flow logistics

We are going to access the source CUSTSYSTEM using the schema owner's username, but in accordance with ODI best practice, our access to the data mart will be via a user called ODITEMP who has its own schema that we will use for the staging area and who has also been given privileges to be able to integrate the incoming data into the DATAMART schema.

The Knowledge Modules (KMs) that we'll be using are LKM SQL to Oracle to load the data from the source into the staging area and then IKM Oracle Incremental Update to integrate the data from the staging area into the final target. At this stage we won't be performing any integrity checks on the data flow, so we won't be using a Check Knowledge Module (CKM) in this task.

So our high-level flow will be something similar to the following figure:

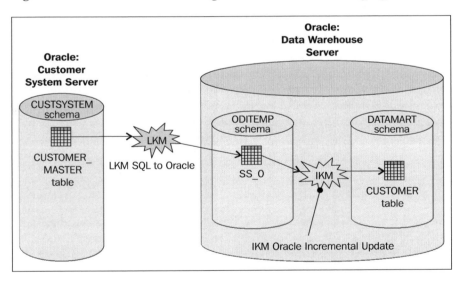

Now that we're armed with all the information, we can get started with the task!

Exercise 1: Building the Load_Customer interface

The rest of this chapter assumes that we have the infrastructure described previously. You can adapt the system names, user names, and table names in your own environment as you see fit.

We'll complete this exercise in a number of sections as follows:

- **Building the topology**: To map the physical data resources and show how to connect to them to the Logical Schemas

- **Reverse-engineering the model metadata**: To translate those physical resources into location-independent representations (Logical Schemas) that will be used in ODI to build data integration objects and workflows

- **Moving the data with an ODI interface**: To construct and execute an interface that will perform the transformation mappings and data flow operations and populate our target table in the data mart

- **Checking the execution with Operator console**: To view the execution status and check the number of rows integrated, together with viewing some of the code generated and run by ODI

Building the topology

In this section we will:

- Create the topology references to our source and target servers and schemas

- Create Logical Schema names for the Physical Schemas, which we will use when we create ODI models based on these schemas

- Associate our Logical and Physical schemas using the default `Global` context, which we will be using throughout this example

Throughout the rest of the example, and especially during setting up the Physical Architecture, there will be times when we will need to enter host name for, say, where a database resource is running. From here on and throughout the rest of the tutorial we'll refer to this host name as `localhost` for simplicity's sake. Remember that if any remote clients were to use this topology information, it will be incorrect and cause errors, but the assumption here is that our whole exercise will run on a single machine.

Setting up the topology

Setting up the topology will require the following steps:

1. If you are following along with your own installation of ODI, then first make sure the Oracle instance that hosts your ODI repositories is up and running. Start ODI Studio (**Oracle | Oracle Data Integrator | Oracle Data Integrator Studio** on the Windows **Start** menu) and connect to your default repository.

2. When we click on the **Topology** tab to switch to the Topology Navigator, we expand the **Technologies** node in the **Physical Architecture** section.

3. If you see a large list of technologies displayed, simplify your view by hiding the unused technologies. To do this, click on the factory icon in the Topology Navigator header bar and select **Hide Unused Technologies**.

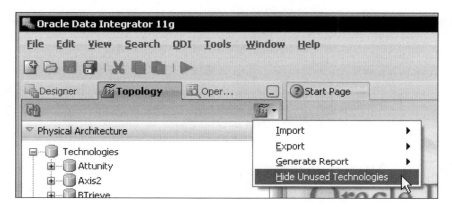

4. We right-click on the **Oracle** node and select **New Data Server**.

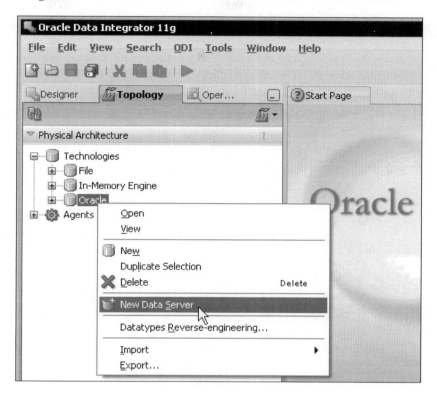

5. An editor creation notification should briefly appear and then the Data Server editor will open. Name the data server as it makes sense in your environment. For our example, we are naming the data server representing the customer data as XE_on_local_as_CUSTSYSTEM and we are setting the user name to be CUSTSYSTEM with a password of welcome1. We leave all other fields as they are. The title tab for the editor will change to the name of the data server.

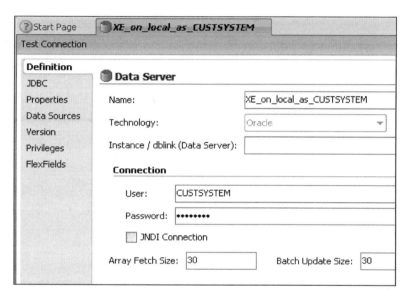

6. On the **JDBC** tab, we click on the magnifying glass icon at the right-hand side of the **JDBC Driver** field to open the selection dialog. The dialog will show the default JDBC driver class for the Oracle technology. This driver is pre-installed with ODI 11*g*.

 If the driver for the database you want is not shown, it is possible to enter it manually into the text field. You will need to refer to the documentation of the driver of your choice to know which class name and which JDBC URL to use. Note also that the driver list may not be sorted alphabetically. We will see how to do this in more detail in the next chapter.

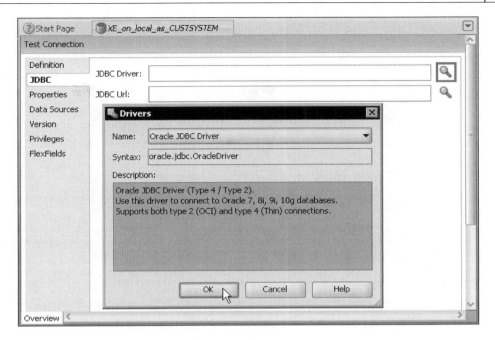

7. We click on **OK** to accept this driver.

8. We click on the magnifier icon next to the **JDBC Url** field and accept the default URL template in the **URL examples** dialog box by clicking on **OK**.

9. We edit the URL template in the **JDBC Url** field to contain the connection details to the actual Customer System Oracle instance, replacing the <host>, <port>, and <sid> sections of the template with appropriate values for our environment.

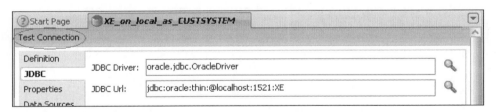

10. We click on the **Test Connection** button (it becomes a button when the mouse moves over it) in the header bar for the editor. When asked if we want to save our data to continue, we click on **Yes** in the **Confirmation** dialog.

11. An informational dialog appears reminding us to create a Physical Schema for this server:

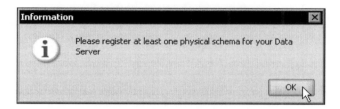

We'll do this later, so we click on **OK** to dismiss this dialog and continue with the test.

12. Another dialog will appear, this one being the actual test execution box (this operation will "ping" the physical connection using the information just provided as a means of validation):

The reference to **Local (No Agent)** in the **Physical Agent** field means that we're going to use the execution agent embedded within ODI Studio, which is precisely what we want to do. So we click on the **Test** button to execute the test.

Testing a remote database connection does not require a remote agent since all the information needed is provided in the URL; this is why we can use the embedded local agent. If we were to run the test with a remote agent, we would be testing the connection from the Studio to the agent, and from the agent to the database.

In your own environment, if all the details have been entered correctly and the database to which you are trying to connect is available, you will see a **Successful Connection** informational message, which can be dismissed by pressing the **OK** button. If the connection fails, check your parameters again, and make sure that your network allows you to connect (firewalls can get in the way!).

13. We close the editor by clicking on the **X** icon that will appear when we move the mouse to the right-hand end of the title tab.

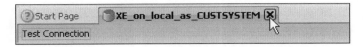

14. We've created our source data server for the Customer System data, but before we create our Physical Schema reference, we'll create another Oracle data server reference, this time for the target data mart server. To do this, we repeat steps 4 to 14, but this time using the following details during the second iteration through step 5 (all other details, including the JDBC Url, will be the same as before):

   ○ **Name**: XE_on_local_as_ODITEMP

   ○ **User**: ODITEMP

   ○ **Password**: welcome1

 As stated earlier, we are simulating two separate servers, even though we only have one. If the different schemas are in the same instance of the database in your environment, you really want to create one single server (connecting with an equivalent of the ODITEMP user) and define all the necessary Physical Schemas underneath that one server.

15. Having created the two servers, we need to create the Topology entries for the Physical Schemas. So we expand the **Oracle** technology node in the **Technologies** list shown in the Topology Navigator's **Physical Architecture** view, we right-click on the data server node for XE_on_local_as_CUSTSYSTEM and we select **New Physical Schema**.

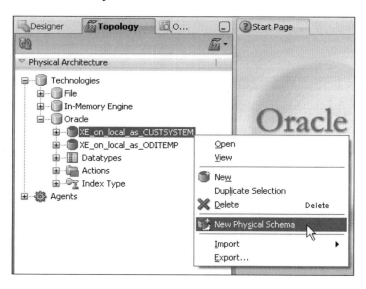

16. On the **Definition** tab of the Physical Schema editor, we use the drop-down lists for the **Schema (Schema)** and **Schema (Work Schema)** fields to select CUSTSYSTEM as the Oracle schema for both

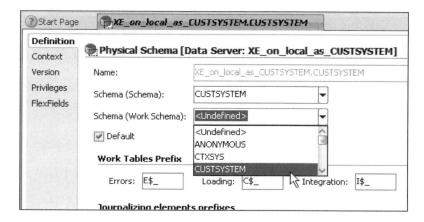

We're only going to be reading data from the CUSTSYSTEM schema and we won't be creating any temporary tables or other artifacts. So in this case, we can safely use the same schema name for both the data and work areas of the ODI Physical Schema definition. In the future however, it is usually considered best practice to isolate ODI artifacts into a separate work schema and to access all other business schemas through this user.

Also remember that we're not actually creating any new database schemas here. We're simply creating new *references* in ODI to *existing* database schemas to give us visibility into the metadata and data they hold.

17. We click on the **Context** finger-tab and on the green + button at the top-right of this pane to add a new context-based mapping to a Logical Schema name.

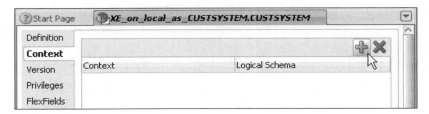

18. We only have one context defined, that is the default one called Global that's created when ODI is installed, so this will appear automatically in the **Context** column. We click in the **Logical Schema** column and replace the **<Undefined>** text with ORACLE_CUSTSYSTEM and then hit the *Enter* key to complete your change.

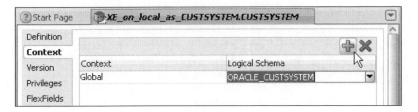

19. We click on the **Save** button (floppy disk icon) on the main ODI toolbar to save the Physical Schema definition and then close the editor pane.

20. We now create another Physical Schema, this time for the XE_on_local_ as_ODITEMP data server and choose DATAMART as the **Schema (Schema)** and ODITEMP as the **Schema (Work Schema)**.

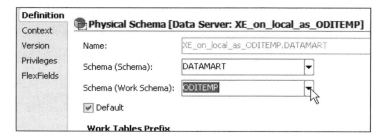

21. We associate the Physical Schema to a Logical Schema called ORACLE_ DATAMART using the Global context, then save our work, and close the editor.

Having created our source and target data servers, the Physical Schemas they hold, and having associated each of those schemas to Logical Schema names using the Global context, we've done all we need to do in the Topology Navigator.

In real-life use of ODI, the creation of a topology is primarily an upfront exercise. Indeed, it is often performed by people other than the majority of ODI developers, as they need to know (or be able to specify, or have access to) the connection credentials that ODI will use to access the various database servers and schemas. That is why there are different navigators in ODI Studio—the Topology Navigator and the Designer Navigator. Topology is usually used by administrators, and Designer is mostly used by developers and data stewards.

Reverse-engineering the model metadata

Next we want to extract the data structure information for our source and target tables from their Oracle databases and create ODI models. So in this section we will:

- Create a model to represent the Customer System we will be using as a data source in our interface and reverse-engineer the metadata from the ORACLE_CUSTSYSTEM Logical Schema into that model.

- Create a second model to represent the data mart we will be using as the target in our interface and perform a selective reverse-engineering operation on the ORACLE_DATAMART Logical Schema to extract only the metadata for the CUSTOMER table.

- View the data in the Customer System to validate that our reverse-engineering of that model has been successful (there is no data in the data mart yet).

Follow the given steps:

1. With ODI Studio still open, we click on the **Designer** Navigator tab in the left-most pane, we expand the **Models** view area, we click on the menu icon in the **Models** view title bar and we select **New Model**.

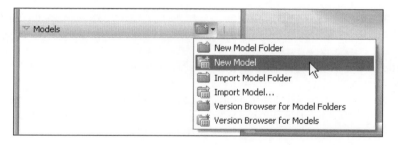

2. Here we chose to name the model Oracle Customer System. Using the drop-down lists, choose Oracle as the technology and ORACLE_CUSTSYSTEM as the logical schema, leaving all the other fields as they are. The **Code** field will automatically be completed as we type the model name.

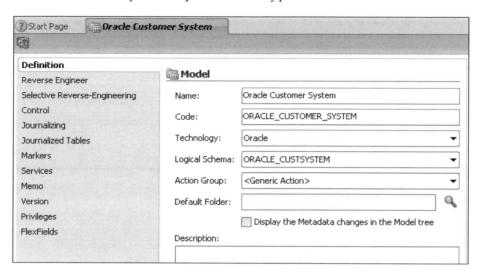

In the previous screenshot, the **Code** for a model is an internal name that ODI uses as a prefix to distinguish between otherwise similarly named datastores. For example, if we had two models that had codes of SRC and TRG, each of which had datastores called CUSTOMER, then ODI would internally (in its code generation) refer to them as SRC.CUSTOMER and TRG.CUSTOMER. The same idea is used for ODI projects as you may notice later. Consequently, if you change the **Code** value after you've started making use of a model's or project's contents, you are at a risk of breaking things.

 Also note that code fields within ODI will standardize the names you use by replacing all blank spaces with underscores and capitalizing all letters.

3. We click on the **Reverse Engineer** tab and we notice that the Global context will be used to translate the Logical Schema name on which the model is based into a physical connection to extract the metadata.

You will also see that we can choose the types of objects whose metadata will be retrieved by type and/or search mask—with % being a wildcard character. We can also influence whether we remove any prefix from the retrieved table names, or whether we need to truncate the table name to a maximum number of characters. These features are primarily used when deriving table *aliases*.

We want to reverse-engineer all the tables from the Customer System (there's only one anyway), so we'll leave all the filter fields with their default settings.

4. We click on the **Reverse Engineer** button at the left-hand side of the Model Editor title bar, then click on **Yes** in the confirmation dialog to save the model and proceed.

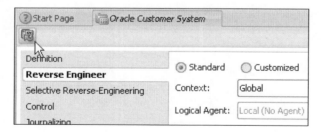

 An alternative way to start the reverse-engineering process would be to use the ODI Studio main menu and select **ODI | Reverse-Engineer**.

5. A progress dialog will appear, tracking progress through the phases of reverse-engineering. Once this process is complete, the dialog will disappear and we can close the Model editor. We will now see the new `Oracle Customer System` model in the **Models** view of the Navigator. When we expand this model node, we see that the `CUSTOMER_MASTER` Oracle table is represented by an ODI datastore with the same name in the newly created ODI model.

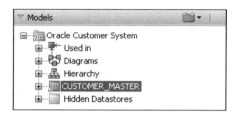

6. Now it's time to create the model for our data mart. We create a new model, this time using the following details on the Definition tab:

- ○ **Name**:   Oracle DataMart
- ○ **Technology**:   Oracle
- ○ **Logical Schema**:   ORACLE_DATAMART

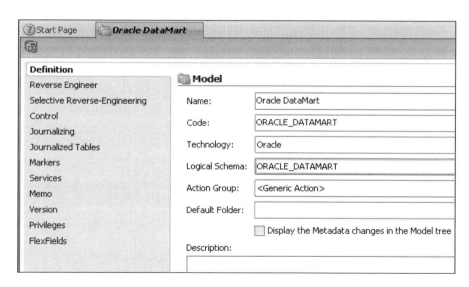

7. If we click on the **Reverse Engineer** tab, we will see that once more the `Global` context will be used by default for the execution of the metadata extraction process.

8. We click straight on the **Selective Reverse-Engineering** tab, as we want to manually select which table definitions to import from the `DATAMART` schema at this stage.

9. On this tab we click on the **Selective Reverse-Engineering** checkbox to enable this option. We then click on **New Datastores** checkbox (we don't have any existing ones in the ODI model that we wish to update, so **Existing Datastores** is left unchecked) and then **Objects to Reverse Engineer** to display a list of all the available tables in the `DATAMART` Oracle database.

> As noted earlier, we could have influenced and refined this list by using the **Types** and **Mask** settings on the **Reverse Engineer** tab if, say, there were a huge number of tables in the database to be reverse-engineered (an ERP system for instance, will have thousands of tables within any given schema).

We clear the selections for all the tables and then recheck the box against the `CUSTOMER` table.

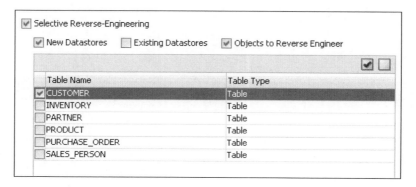

10. We click on the **Reverse Engineer** button once more, saving our model when asked and then close the Model editor. Once again we will be able to see our new model and datastore in the **Models** view.

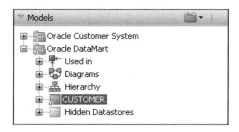

11. Just as a final check, we go back to the source model and right-click on the CUSTOMER_MASTER datastore in the Oracle Customer System model and click on **View Data**:

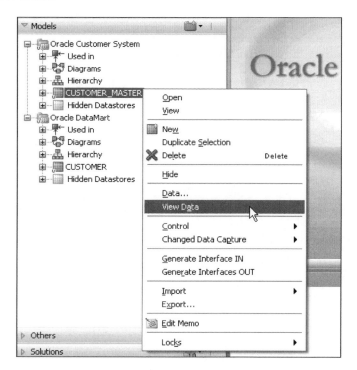

12. A *read-only* data editor opens showing the contents of the CUSTOMER_MASTER table (this data viewing functionality also uses the context defined on the **Reverse Engineering** tab).

 The difference between the **Data...** and **View Data** operations on the datastore is that with **View Data** you cannot alter the data.

Recapping what we've accomplished so far:

- We've now successfully built models and datastores in ODI based on our physical data structures (and tested that at least one is correctly configured).

- We created the Oracle Customer System model based on the ORACLE_CUSTSYSTEM Logical Schema (models are always based on Logical Schemas) and then reverse-engineered the whole of the CUSTSYSTEM database schema—even though it was only one table. This model provides the foundational source of customer data for our PO Processing data mart.

- We created a second model called `Oracle DataMart` and then performed selective reverse-engineering to only create a CUSTOMER datastore.
- In each case, the `Global` context was used to associate the Logical Schema on which each model is based with a real Physical Schema that could be interrogated for its structure.

> It's important to stress that although ODI models and datastores are associated with a specific technology (per the Definition tab), they contain no information about physical locations, server names, user credentials, and so on.
>
> Also note that the context specified in the Model editor pages is *only* used at the point of reverse-engineering and for viewing the data within Designer Navigator. The context specifying which physical environment will be accessed during execution will be determined at a different place/time.

Having configured our ODI representations of our data objects, it's time to build an interface to move and transform the data from our Customer System into our data mart.

Moving the data using an ODI interface

In this section we are going to:

- Create a new ODI project in which to organize our work
- Import the Knowledge Modules that we anticipate we'll need for our task
- Create an interface to load data from the CUSTOMER_MASTER datastore in the `Oracle Customer System` model into the CUSTOMER datastore in the `Oracle Data Mart` model
- Adjust the mappings in the interface to meet our task and overall PO processing requirements outlined at the start of this chapter
- Check the data flow generated by ODI and adjust the configuration options of the KMs to meet our requirements
- Execute the interface and examine the results to ensure that the CUSTOMER datastore in our data mart now has valid customer data consistent with our PO processing requirements

To create our very first interface, we will follow these steps:

1. With Designer Navigator still open, we click on the project menu icon on the title bar of the **Projects** view and select **New Project**.

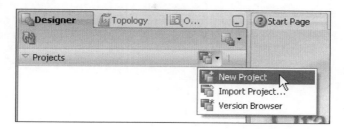

2. We call the project Chapter 5, save our work, and close the editor.

3. In the Projects view, we expand the Chapter 5 project node and the **First Folder** node beneath that to see the general layout of a project's organization.

4. We right-click on the **Knowledge Modules** node and select **Import Knowledge Modules...**.

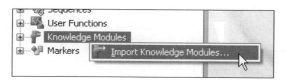

5. The very first time you import a Knowledge Module (KM) you'll need to set the directory from which the import takes place, so we click on the search icon which is to the right of the **File import directory** field.

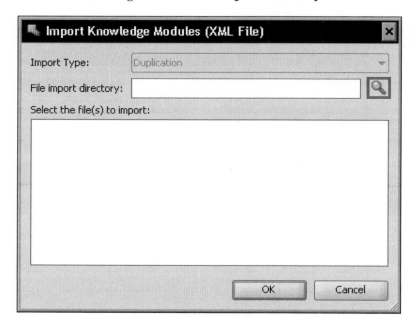

6. We browse to our `<ODI_HOME>\oracledi\xml-reference` directory, where `<ODI_HOME>` is the root folder in which we installed ODI 11*g* in *Chapter 2, Product Installation*. As we followed all the defaults for our installation on Windows, this is `C:\Oracle\Middleware\Oracle_ODI1\oracledi\xml-reference`. Once we've browsed to the correct location, we click on **Open** to return to the KM import dialog.

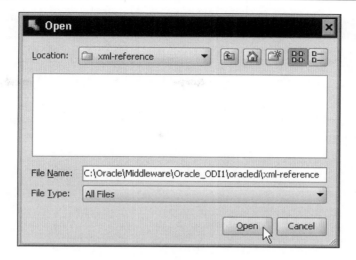

7. The KM import dialog now shows a list of all the Knowledge Modules
    located in the import directory that we have specified. Using the normal
    Windows method of multiple-select (*Ctrl+Click*), we select both IKM Oracle
    Incremental Update and LKM SQL to Oracle and click on **OK** to perform the
    import. (You can also import each KM separately—it makes no difference.)

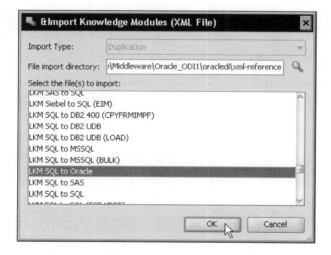

8. We see an ODI action progress dialog for a short while and then an **Import report** window is displayed. The contents of this report (new in ODI 11*g*) are not important here, so we can just close the report window. If you expand the **Knowledge Modules** node in the Chapter 5 project and then expand the loading and integration sub-nodes there, you'll see your newly imported KMs ready for use.

9. In **First Folder**, we right-click on the **Interfaces** node and select **New Interface**.

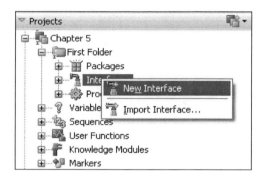

10. On the opening page of the Interface editor, we call the interface Load CUSTOMER and click on the **Mapping** tab at the bottom of the pane to invoke the graphical Mapping editor.

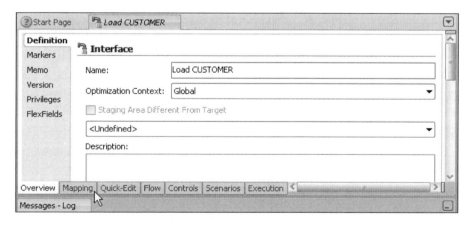

11. The editor starts for the first time with the **Messages, Property Inspector,** and **Thumbnail** sheets along the bottom in three separate panes.

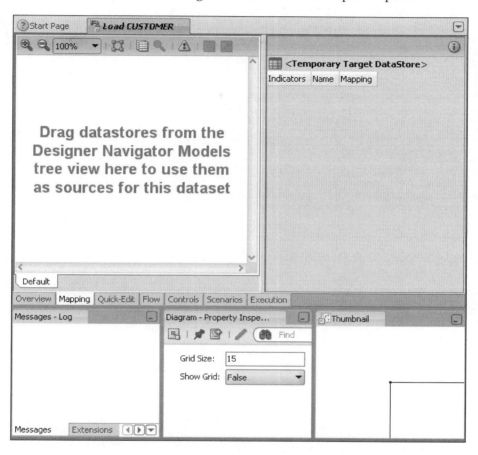

The editor is much easier and productive to use if you overlay these three panes into one tabbed collection. To do this, click on one of the header tabs (say the **Diagram** to start) and drag (keeping the mouse button held down) the tab into the center of an adjacent pane (similar to the **Messages** one). When you see a small message box appear entirely in the center of that adjacent pane (as seen in the following screenshot), then you can release the mouse button to dock the two panes together, and then repeat for the third pane.

You should end up with a combined tab set that looks similar to the following screenshot:

The **Diagram – Property Inspector** view is the most used view during the creation of mappings, so click on that tab to bring its view to the front.

12. We can now start building the Load CUSTOMER mappings. We begin by specifying the target for the interface. We expand the Oracle DataMart node in the **Models** view of the Designer Navigator, and drag-and-drop the CUSTOMER datastore into the top-right pane of the Mapping editor. When we 'drop' the CUSTOMER datastore there, it expands to show its column names, their datatype categories, and the datastore's primary key field. Datatypes are indicated by the letters that precede the column names as shown in the following screenshot:

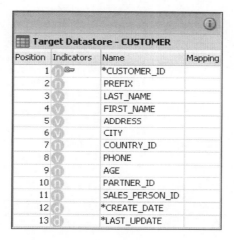

13. Now we drag-and-drop the CUSTOMER_MASTER datastore from the Oracle Customer System model into the top-left pane of the editor (the sources area). When we drop the datastore, an **Automap** dialog appears. We click on **Yes** to invoke automatic mapping.

14. ODI will perform mappings based on exact column name match and will add indicators in the target area to show where any transformation code in the mapping is to be executed.

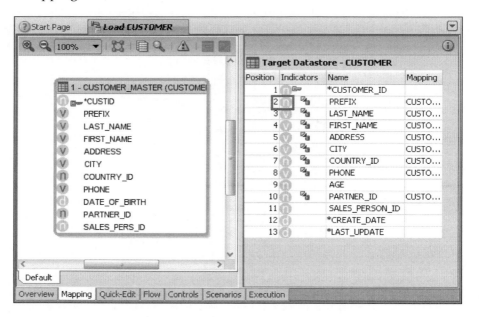

15. We need to add and amend some mappings. So we first drag-and-drop the CUSTID column from the CUSTOMER_MASTER source datastore into the CUSTOMER_ID column in the target datastore. This will perform a "straight-through" mapping (the data will be unchanged) of the source data into the target.

16. Next, we can see that the target datastore has the PREFIX column as a numeric datatype (the **n** indicator, highlighted in the previous screenshot), whereas the source datastore has it stored as a varying character value. If we click on the PREFIX column in the target datastore pane, we see the mapping implementation in the **Property Inspector** below the target and sources panes:

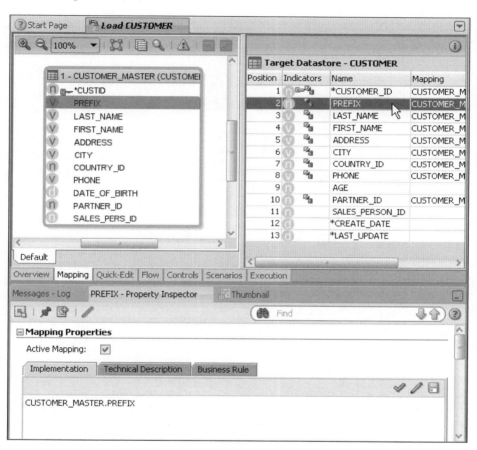

17. We change the text in the **Implementation** text box in the **Property Inspector** to read:

```
case (CUSTOMER_MASTER.PREFIX)
   when 'Mr'    then 1
   when 'Mrs'   then 2
   when 'Miss'  then 3
   when 'Dr'    then 4
else 1
end
```

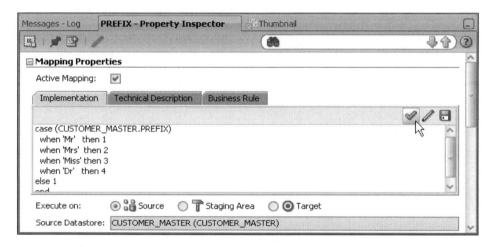

We click on the green tick icon above the textbox to force ODI to perform a syntax check of the implementation code we have entered. If you see any errors, you want to correct them before proceeding.

18. The next mapping that we will alter is the one that converts the source's DATE_OF_BIRTH column into AGE for the target. We drag the DATE_OF_BIRTH column from the sources area and drop it in the target's AGE column, then we click on that column in the target area and change the code in the implementation box to:

```
trunc(months_between(sysdate,CUSTOMER_MASTER.DATE_OF_BIRTH)/12,0)
```

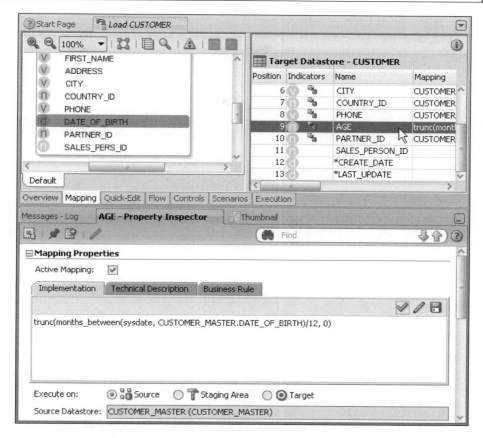

Once again, we use the syntax checker against our implementation code.

19. We drag the SALES_PERS_ID from the source into the SALES_PERSON_ID column into the target to set a straight-through mapping on that column.

20. There is no source data for the CREATE_DATE and LAST_UPDATE target columns. Instead these will be used to record modification information on the target information. We click on the CREATE_DATE target column and in the **Property Inspector**, we set the following mapping properties and behaviors:

    ○ **Active Mapping**: Checked
    ○ **Implementation**: sysdate
    ○ **Execute on**: Staging Area
    ○ **Insert**: Checked
    ○ **Update**: Not checked

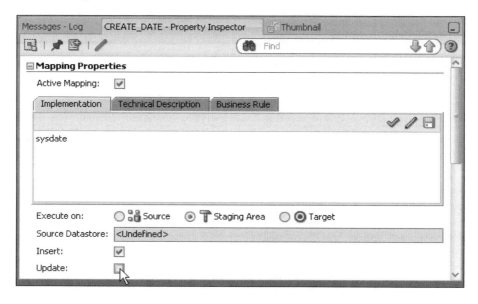

This means that the Oracle sysdate value will be evaluated on the staging system (here, our target database) and entered into the CREATE_DATE target column only when a new row is created. Here we are leveraging the SQL engine capabilities and horsepower of the target Oracle database to perform the date field transformation, while ensuring data audit quality by not allowing updates to this field in this interface.

21. We do the same for the LAST_UPDATE column, but have this value set on both insert and update operations.

22. Now that all the mappings are complete, we click on the **Flow** tab beneath the target and sources area to show the interface flow that ODI has constructed. You can see below that LKM SQL to Oracle has automatically been selected as the mechanism to load the data from the source into the staging area. This is because it is the only suitable KM for this action that has been imported into the current project.

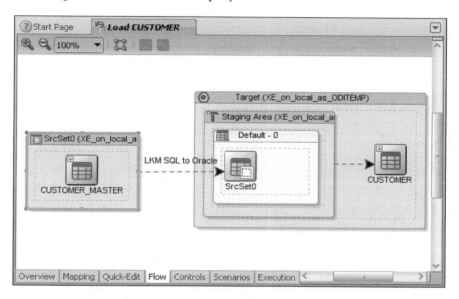

23. We click on the header bar of the Target (XE_on_local_as_ODITEMP) box in the flow diagram and we see in the **Property Inspector**, which is at the bottom of the screen, that IKM Oracle Incremental Update has been automatically selected as the integration KM for the same reason. We change the **FLOW_CONTROL** option value for this KM from <default> true to false.

The **FLOW_CONTROL** option governs whether basic data integrity controls (for example, value constraints, relationships, and key violations) are applied by ODI to the flow of data just before it is integrated into the final target datastore. This would be performed by a CKM rather than having the target database table reject the records itself. We didn't import a CKM into our project as we'll be covering Error Management in a later chapter, so that's why we're disabling flow control here.

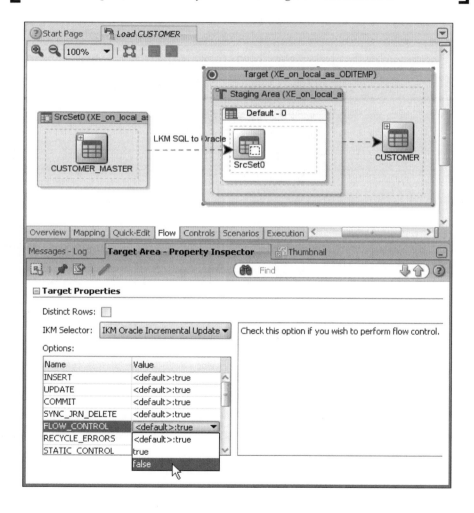

24. We have finished building and configuring the Load CUSTOMER interface, so we save all our work using the Save All icon in the ODI Studio main toolbar. A dialog may appear asking if you want to lock the object (this interface). This is to support multiple concurrent users working against the same work repository, but since we're acting as the only developer in our environment we can select **Don't show me this window next time** and click on **No** to avoid locking the object.

25. We're now ready to test our interface! We click on the Run icon in the main ODI Studio toolbar:

26. An **Execution** dialog box appears in which we can set our execution context, execution agent, log level, or we can simply simulate the execution which would generate the code for the interface but not run it (simulation is a new feature of ODI 11*g*). Since we want to actually execute the interface using all of the default values, we click on **OK**.

27. After a slight pause (while the interface code is generated), an **Information** dialog box appears telling us that the execution session has started. We dismiss this dialog box by clicking on **OK**, and we close the editor window for the Load CUSTOMER interface.

 If an error message screen pops up indicating that the **session is unable to start**, then one or more fatal errors were detected within the interface design and must be rectified before attempting to execute.

We have now built and run an interface. Let's review the steps taken:

- We created a project, then located and imported the necessary Knowledge Modules into that project to support the desired source and target technologies.

- We created an interface, specified the target and source for that interface, and had ODI automatically create the majority of the mappings for the interface.

- We then added to and modified the existing mappings, using simple, straight-through mappings, database functions, and some fairly complex SQL (the case...when mapping and the date of birth to age conversion).

- We then checked the interface flow and the KMs being used, and set the IKM so that data integrity would not be selected (since we didn't import a CKM into the project, we couldn't allow the IKM to invoke the CKM activities).

- We then saved and executed our work.

- It is important to note that we satisfied the requirements of moving and transforming the data into the data mart solely by interacting with the ODI Studio user interface. Very little SQL was required: the pre-built Knowledge Modules, enhanced with the interface field mappings, did all the "heavy lifting" of the SQL generation.

The next step is to see whether what we have built worked in the way that was expected!

Checking the execution with the Operator Navigator

This section will be our first introduction to ODI Studio's capability to show and examine execution tree details, so that we can check our development as we go along in an iterative and incremental manner. We will now do the following:

- Introduce you to the different views in execution data available in the Operator Navigator

- Examine the execution session log for the interface we've just run so that we can see the overall metrics

- Examine the detail of the steps executed and the code generated for us by ODI

To look into the details of the execution of a job, we need to follow these steps:

1. We click on the **Operator** tab in the main ODI Studio Navigator pane. The **Operator** word may not be visible, depending on the width of your Navigator pane, but the Operator icon should always be shown.

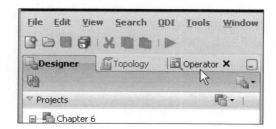

Alternatively, you can select the **ODI Operator Navigator** option under the **View** main menu item.

2. We see in the **Session List** view at the top of the Navigator that sessions can be viewed by execution date, physical agent, session name, execution status, any keywords associated with the session, the user who executed the session, or a cover-all list of all executions in session number order.

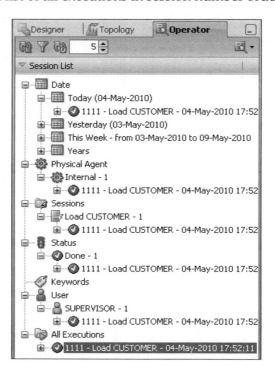

All of these views (with the exception of the **Keywords** view) will show the same session, identifiable by the session number — 1111 in this case. The green symbol with a tick icon shows that the session executed successfully.

 A brief explanation of session numbers: If you run a process, your session number will most likely be different from the one (1111) shown in the previous screenshot. That number represents session number 1 in a Work repository with an ID of 111. If instead, it were the second execution session in a repository with the ID of 100, the session number would be 2100.

3. If we close all the category nodes (for example, **Date**) except **All Executions**, and double-click on (or right-click and select **Open**) the Load CUSTOMER node that's still visible, an overview of the session will be displayed in the right-hand side of ODI Studio. This shows the overall metrics for the session, including duration, number of inserts, updates and deletes, and the execution status of the session.

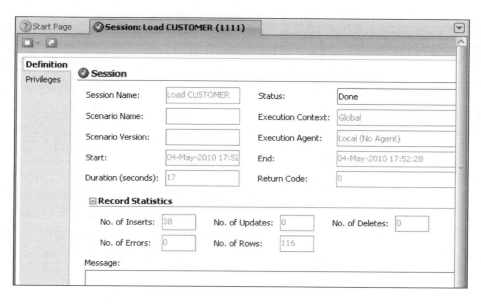

In this view we can see that 38 records were inserted, with no updates or deletes.

4. Back in the **Session List** view, we expand the Load CUSTOMER session node and we see that our session has one major step—also called Load CUSTOMER (the name of our interface). When we expand the 1 - Load CUSTOMER node, we can see all the steps that ODI created and executed to run the interface (we can scroll up and down to see them all).

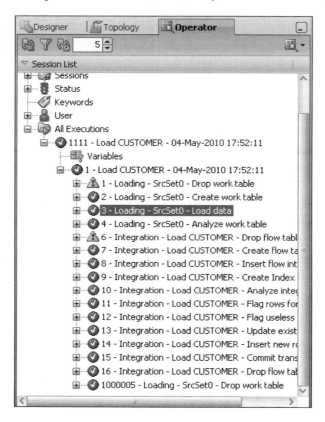

The steps labelled **Loading** are generated by the LKM; those labelled **Integration** are generated by the IKM. The steps marked by a yellow warning triangle report a warning—in this case because they are both steps to delete ODI temporary tables that may not exist at the start of execution.

5. The **3 – Loading – SrcSet0 – Load data** step is where the LKM loads the source data into the loading temporary table in the staging area. We can open this step by double-clicking to view the execution statistics.

We can see that 38 rows were processed. In this case the values in the fields for the number of inserts, updates, and deletes refer to the temporary loading work table (C$) here. We now close the session task tab.

6. We return to the session task list and select the **6 – Integration – Load CUSTOMER – Insert flow into I$ table** step.

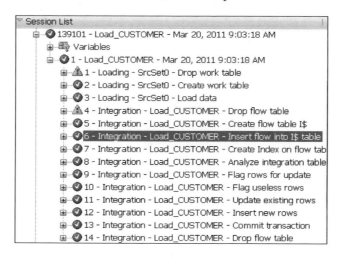

7. We double-click on the **6 – Integration – Load CUSTOMER – Insert flow into I$ table** step. This step will show the activity performed against the temporary integration work table (I$), most of whose data will eventually be integrated into the target table.

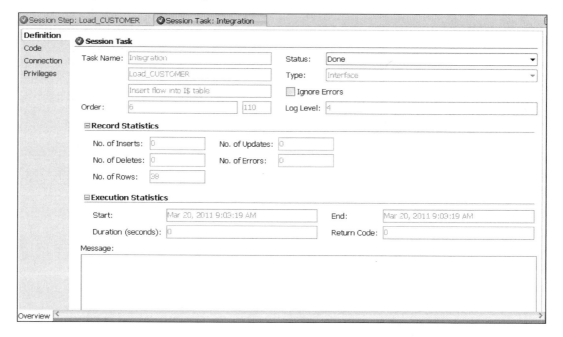

8. When we click on the **Code** tab, the **Code** view shows the SQL generated on the source for this step (the CUSTSYSTEM database) and the corresponding code for the step's target (the loading work table in the staging area). By scrolling down we see in the code for the source that the mappings we created in the interface to be executed on the source are included here, including the PREFIX and AGE transformations.

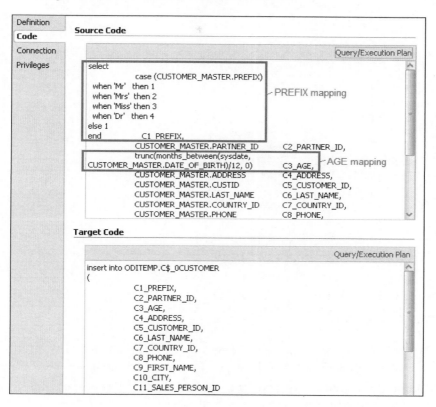

9. We now close the window for the step and open the step **8 – Integration – Load CUSTOMER – Insert flow into I\$ table**. This is the step in which the mappings configured to be executed in the staging area will be executed. The code shows the two references to `sysdate` that we set for the `CREATE_DATE` and `LAST_UPDATE` audit columns.

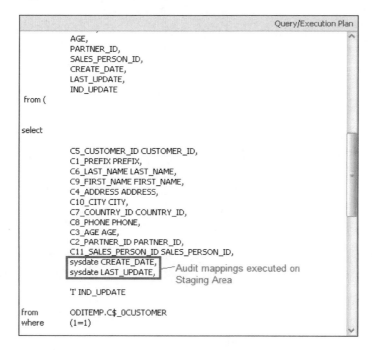

10. We can now close the **Session Task : Integration** tab window and the **Session : Load CUSTOMER** tab window and return to the **Designer** tab.

11. In the Models view, we open the `CUSTOMER` datastore in the `Oracle DataMart` model in an editor and on the **Definition** tab, we click on the Refresh icon next to the **Total:** field in the **Number of Rows** section. We can now see the field updated to a value of **38**.

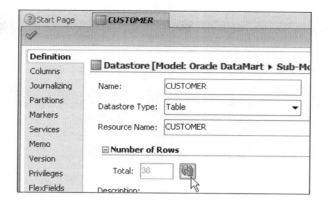

12. Another way to view the record count (and data) is by opening the
    Load CUSTOMER interface in an editor, going to the **Mappings** page,
    right-clicking on the target datastore title bar and selecting **Data...**.
    You would immediately see that there are 38 records.

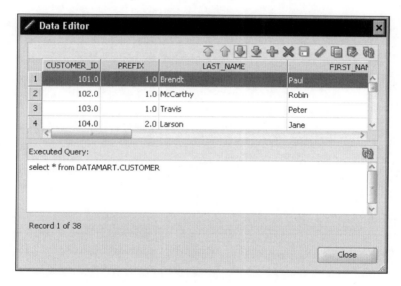

Also take note of the various columns on which our transformations have occurred; scrolling to the right we will now see that the PREFIX column has a numerical value, the **AGE** field has been calculated, and the **DATE** fields have been populated.

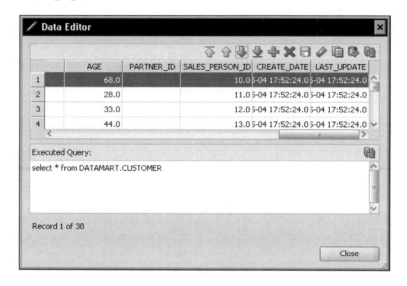

The number of records shown in either of the views previously mentioned do not necessarily reflect the correctness of the integration process; perhaps there were unintended record deletions or updates where inserts were expected. It's always best to verify the integration steps summaries as they give much more details on specific counts and what events really happened.

13. Close the Data Editor dialog and the Interface editor.

In these past few steps we've:

- Used the Operator Navigator and seen the multiple category views through which you can examine execution sessions
- Viewed overall execution session metrics
- Drilled down through the levels of session information to the individual executed steps
- Seen how those steps are linked to KMs used by the interface

- Examined the actual SQL code executed at a couple of stages in the interface flow, specifically the steps where the source and staging area mappings are implemented

- Checked that the target table has been loaded with the correct number of records and seen that key data transformations have been implemented.

Summary

In this chapter we covered most of the basics that will help you become very productive with ODI and took our first step towards implementing our PO processing solution—we populated our data mart with the enriched and transformed source data from our Customer System that met the data mart business requirements.

We began by configuring ODI's view of the physical data architecture for the source and target systems using two data servers, the Physical Schemas that they hold (one with a separate work schema), and linking these Physical Schemas to Logical Schema names via the Global context.

Next we reverse-engineered metadata from those schemas into ODI models and in one case, used selective reverse-engineering. This task resulted in two datastore definitions, namely, CUSTOMER_MASTER in the Oracle Customer System model and CUSTOMER in the Oracle DataMart model.

We then created a new project and imported the Loading and Integration Knowledge Modules that would be needed to build our interface.

Next we created a Load CUSTOMER interface that used CUSTOMER_MASTER as a source and CUSTOMER as a target. During this process, we used the Automatic Mapping feature and then supplemented this activity with a few manual mappings and transformations and enriched the data with some timestamps that could be later used for audit purposes. We also checked the Knowledge Modules being used by the interface and changed an IKM option to amend the flow to avoid any data integrity checks. We then executed the interface.

In the last few steps, we used the Operator Navigator to drill down and examine the execution tree for our interface, taking a look at the SQL code it executed. We made sure that the correct number of records had been uploaded and that the key mappings and transformations had been successfully implemented.

In the next chapter we'll add some additional complexity by introducing joins and lookups, heterogeneous data sources, data aggregation, and adding a JDBC driver to ODI 11*g* (something we didn't have to do for our Oracle databases because the Oracle driver came pre-installed with ODI).

6
Working with MySQL

ODI's normal operating environment is being surrounded by a number of different database systems. We saw in the previous chapter that ODI comes ready for use with Oracle databases, having the required JDBC driver installed automatically out of the box. However, ODI's heritage means that there doesn't have to be an Oracle database anywhere within ODI's reach. So let's take a look at how ODI interoperates with another popular database, MySQL, that historically had nothing to do with the Oracle Corporation.

The reason for choosing MySQL is simply to illustrate some additional steps that must be performed when using many third-party databases. These steps are required to make the required JDBC drivers for those databases available for ODI to use.

In the previous chapter we integrated data from one database table into another as a simple foundation example. In this chapter we're going to extend the skills we gained as follows, by incorporating a number of new elements in our work while we continue to integrate data into the data mart for our examples:

- Before we start developing anything new we will add an additional JDBC driver to ODI Studio to allow it to access and process the MySQL data and metadata
- We are going to use two methods to configure some joins between source datastores to enrich our target data
- We will introduce some aggregation in our transformation mappings to produce summary data in our data mart
- We will use "simulation" in ODI to examine the automatically generated runtime code before it is executed

In addition to these new tasks, we'll be repeating a number of operations—with some slight variations—that we performed in the last chapter, so you should begin to feel at ease with some of the most common tasks in ODI 11*g*.

What you can and can't do with MySQL

We'll be using MySQL for hosting our source data in this chapter, but MySQL is equally suitable as a target or for use as a staging area.

MySQL is one of the platforms listed in the Topology Navigator's Technologies view, so ODI knows about its database functions, datatype capabilities, SQL syntax variations and other characteristics. So the additional work to use a database such as MySQL with ODI is in fact minimal.

However, you cannot use MySQL (at least versions up to and including v5.1) as a host for ODI's Master or Work repositories. Because MySQL has a limitation in its SQL capability. This limitation is not present in all non-Oracle relational databases by any means and should you wish to use a different database for hosting ODI repositories you should consult the following ODI Certification Matrix on the Oracle support website at `http://oracle.com/technetwork/middleware/data-integrator/odi-11gr1certmatrix-163773.xls`.

ODI 11.1
Repository Database Certification Matrix
Oracle 10.2.0.4+
Oracle 11.1.0.7+
Oracle 11.2.0.1+
Microsoft SQL Server 2005
Microsoft SQL Server 2008
IBM DB2/UDB 9.7 and later FixPaks
IBM DB2/400 (V5R4+)
Hypersonic SQL 1.7.3+
Sybase AS Enterprise 15.0.x

Working with MySQL

In these step-by-step examples, we'll be adding product and inventory to our PO Processing data mart from a product system database which is hosted in MySQL. We're going to perform a mix of product data consolidation (combining base product and product category information from separate source tables into a single target table) and inventory data enrichment (converting a product number into a name).

To do this we will use two different methods in ODI 11*g* for joining information from two or more sources.

Since an ODI interface normally populates only one target datastore (though one of the newer 11*g* Knowledge Modules allows you to work around this limitation), we'll create two interfaces during this task—one for product information and the other for inventory data. As it happens, our original requirements list stated that product data was updated daily, whereas inventory information could be updated with a different frequency, so separating out these two activities would have been necessary anyway.

Obtaining and installing the software

If you want to download and install MySQL to follow-up on the examples provided here, the Community Edition of MySQL is free to download and use from `http://www.mysql.com/downloads/` or you can go to `http://download.oracle.com/` and follow the download link for MySQL from there.

The documentation for MySQL, including installation notes is available at `http://dev.mysql.com/doc/`.

The free version of the MySQL Connector/J, the JDBC driver to use (v5.0.8), is available for download at `http://dev.mysql.com/downloads/connector/j/5.0.html#downloads`.

> *Do not use the latest version of the MySQL JDBC driver.* On the main download site for the MySQL components you will see that there are driver versions later than v5.0.8 available for download. However when writing this book, the authors encountered operational errors when driver version 5.1.x was used with ODI 11*g*. These driver issues are not present in the v5.0.8 release.

Overview of the task

First we'll have to perform some infrastructure work, such as configuring ODI 11*g* to use the MySQL Connector/J, the JDBC driver, creating the topology and model for the MySQL source data, and extending the ODI model of the target PO Processing data mart to include the remaining target table definitions.

After that we'll create two interfaces, one to integrate the product data, and the other to integrate the inventory data.

Integrating the product data

This activity requires the combining of source data for products and product categories into a single target table.

Product data target, sources, and mappings

The target PRODUCT table in the PO Processing DATAMART schema has the following structure:

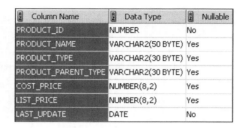

Column Name	Data Type	Nullable
PRODUCT_ID	NUMBER	No
PRODUCT_NAME	VARCHAR2(50 BYTE)	Yes
PRODUCT_TYPE	VARCHAR2(30 BYTE)	Yes
PRODUCT_PARENT_TYPE	VARCHAR2(30 BYTE)	Yes
COST_PRICE	NUMBER(8,2)	Yes
LIST_PRICE	NUMBER(8,2)	Yes
LAST_UPDATE	DATE	No

There are two source tables in the prodsystem MySQL schema, the first of which contains the base product data and is called product_base:

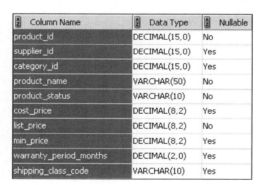

Column Name	Data Type	Nullable
product_id	DECIMAL(15,0)	No
supplier_id	DECIMAL(15,0)	Yes
category_id	DECIMAL(15,0)	Yes
product_name	VARCHAR(50)	No
product_status	VARCHAR(10)	No
cost_price	DECIMAL(8,2)	Yes
list_price	DECIMAL(8,2)	No
min_price	DECIMAL(8,2)	Yes
warranty_period_months	DECIMAL(2,0)	Yes
shipping_class_code	VARCHAR(10)	Yes

The second source table contains information used to categorize the products and is called product_category:

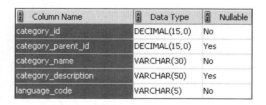

Column Name	Data Type	Nullable
category_id	DECIMAL(15,0)	No
category_parent_id	DECIMAL(15,0)	Yes
category_name	VARCHAR(30)	No
category_description	VARCHAR(50)	Yes
language_code	VARCHAR(5)	No

The column mappings for this interface are mostly straightforward and are as follows:

- The target PRODUCT_ID, PRODUCT_NAME, COST_PRICE, and LIST_PRICE columns are all populated from similarly named columns in the product_base table

- The target PRODUCT_TYPE column can be populated by the source category_name column in the product_category table, linked by category_id

- The target PRODUCT_PARENT_TYPE column can be populated from the same category_name source column, but it has to be coordinated via a self-join link from the category_parent_id column back into the same table's category_id column

- We have already populated a LAST_UPDATE column in the previous chapter, so we know how we'll achieve that mapping

Product interface flow logistics

Our source is a MySQL database and our staging area and target will be in the Oracle data mart. That means we can use the same Loading and Integration Knowledge Modules as we used in the previous chapter.

The complete interface process flow is displayed in the following figure:

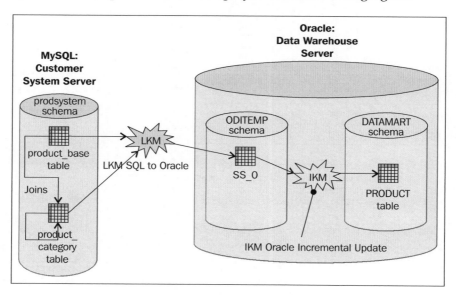

Once again, we won't be performing any data quality checking, so we won't be using any CKMs.

Integrating inventory data

The inventory data that we have in the `prodsystem` MySQL schema is provided by the product for each warehouse in our estate. The target data mart only needs sum totals, so we need to perform aggregation of the source data and we also need to perform a look-up on some of the product data that we will have just integrated in the previous interface.

Inventory target, sources, and mappings

The target for this interface is the `INVENTORY` table, which has the following structure:

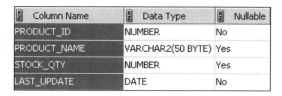

Column Name	Data Type	Nullable
PRODUCT_ID	NUMBER	No
PRODUCT_NAME	VARCHAR2(50 BYTE)	Yes
STOCK_QTY	NUMBER	Yes
LAST_UPDATE	DATE	No

The main source for this information will be the MySQL `warehouse_stock_level` table as follows:

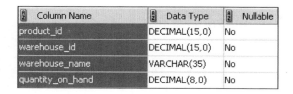

Column Name	Data Type	Nullable
product_id	DECIMAL(15,0)	No
warehouse_id	DECIMAL(15,0)	No
warehouse_name	VARCHAR(35)	No
quantity_on_hand	DECIMAL(8,0)	No

However, we'll also be reusing the `DATAMART` schema's `PRODUCT` table to provide some information in this interface, for reasons that will become clear shortly.

The column mappings are as follows:

- The `PRODUCT_ID` target column is populated from the similarly named column in the `warehouse_stock_level` source table.

- The `PRODUCT_NAME` column could have been populated by joining with the `product_category` source table again, but instead we will use the same information from the `PRODUCT` table in the `DATAMART` schema that we will have previously loaded. This is because it is already in the target system, so it won't need to be transported across any network and performance is likely to be improved. When dealing with huge data volumes, considerations such as these can make a considerable difference. The figure of the flow will make this clearer.

- We have another LAST_UPDATE target column that will be populated using the same mapping as before.

Inventory interface flow logistics

Again we can use the same LKM and IKM. The IKM is the component that will link the data mart PRODUCT table's information with the source data from MySQL to populate the INVENTORY table's columns as shown in the following figure:

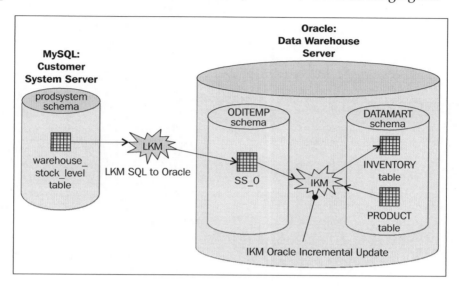

Instead of performing a database join to combine the data (as we will use for the product data interface) we will use an ODI 11*g* Lookup. In fact we will choose a lookup implementation that is resolved down to a join, but which will allow us to explore another capability of ODI 11*g*.

Using MySql with ODI

Building on the Data Topology steps we performed in the previous chapter, we'll be completing this exercise in a number of steps as follows:

- **Adding the MySQL JDBC driver**: To enable ODI Studio to access the MySQL schema and data

- **Expanding the Topology**: To add the MySQL server and schema to ODI's metadata

- **Reverse-engineering revisited**: To create a model based on the MySQL schema that we can use for our source data and also to complete the model of our PO Processing System data mart target

- **Preparing to move the product data**: By creating an interface that enriches the base product data from the source by joining some source datastores

- **Using simulation and execution**: To examine the generated code before it is executed, and then actually executing the code and checking some key metrics

- **Moving the inventory data**: Including some aggregation and enrichment achieved through the use of a an ODI lookup, followed by checking some of the execution metrics

Adding the MySQL JDBC driver

This is a very short section, since adding JDBC drivers to ODI 11*g* Studio is very simple. Follow the given steps:

1. Save all your work in ODI Studio and exit out of the program.

2. If you haven't already done so, extract the MySQL Connector/J driver JAR file called `mysql-connector-java-5.0.8-bin.jar` from the ZIP file or "tarball" you downloaded from the MySQL Connector/J download site and copy it to the location for your particular operating system given in the ODI 11*g* Installation Guide. For example, for Windows users, this is `%APPDATA%\odi\oracledi\userlib`, where `%APPDATA%` is the Windows Application Data directory for the user, which is usually located at `C:\Documents and Settings\<user>\Application Data`.

3. That's it! When we restart ODI Studio, it will scan that directory for any JAR files and will add them to its classpath automatically.

Adding drivers and classes in other locations

The directory to which you copied the JDBC driver (and this doesn't just work for MySQL, it's for all additional JDBC drivers) includes a file called `additional_path.txt`. If you want to add classes into ODI Studio's classpath (for example, JMS libraries) that you don't want to copy into this directory, you can amend the contents of the `additional_path.txt` file (following the examples it includes), to add those other class and JAR files that are located elsewhere into ODI Studio's classpath.

If you installed the Standalone Agent for ODI, and/or the Java EE agent (and created a WebLogic domain for the ODI Java EE components), then you must also make the JDBC driver available to these agents. The process for each type of agent is as follows:

1. To make the driver available to the Standalone Agent, copy the driver JAR file (`mysql-connector-java-5.0.8-bin.jar`) into the `<ODI_HOME>\oracledi\agent\drivers` directory and restart the Agent (if it is running). Similarly to ODI Studio, the Standalone Agent automatically scans this directory for driver and class files each time it starts.

2. To add the driver to a Java EE Agent, follow the vendor's instructions for adding a third-party JDBC driver for the specific flavor of application server you are using to host the Java EE components. If this is a WebLogic Server, you should add the driver JAR location to the `WEBLOGIC_CLASSPATH` entry in the `<WL_HOME>\common\bin\commEnv.cmd` file, where `<WL_HOME>` is the `wlserver_10.3` directory where WebLogic server is installed (for example, `C:\Oracle\Middleware\wlserver_10.3`). The WebLogic server instance that hosts the Java EE Agent will then need to be restarted.

 You may find a v5.0.3 version of the MySQL Connector/J JDBC driver in your WebLogic server installation below `<WL_HOME>\server\ext\jdbc`, but this isn't added into the server's classpath by default. The v5.0.8 driver can be copied to the same location and then explicitly added by altering the `commEnv.cmd` file as explained previously.

So for ODI Studio and the Standalone Agent, adding a new JDBC driver is simply a matter of copying the driver archive into a specific folder location. For the Java EE Agent, it depends on the flavor of the application server, but usually it's just a case of adding the driver archive to the server's `classpath` definition.

Expanding the topology

In this section we will perform the following:

- Add a reference to the MySQL data server to the physical architecture, specifying the appropriate credentials, driver class, and connection URL

- Create a physical schema reference to the `prodsystem` MySQL database holding the source product and inventory data

To define the Physical Architecture for MySQL, we have to do the following:

1. We start ODI Studio, connect to your Work repository and then select the **Topology** tab to start using the Topology Navigator.

2. We expand the Technologies node in the Physical Architecture node. Since we previously selected **Hide Unused Technologies** and at this point MySQL is one of those "unused" technologies, we need to toggle that option in the tab header menu (the factory icon) to reveal the complete technology list.

3. We add a new MySQL data server the way we added the Oracle ones in the previous chapter (right-click on the **MySQL** technology node), and we set the following values on the **Definition** tab:

   ○ **Name**: Local_as_prodsystem

   ○ **User**: prodsystem

   ○ **Password**: welcome1

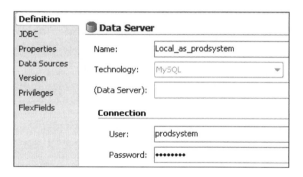

If you are following along with your own installation of MySQL, make sure to create the prodsystem user (and its password) for the prodsystem schema.

4. On the **JDBC** tab, we must manually enter the driver and URL details, as the search icons to the right of these fields do not yield any MySQL Connector/J information. The values to enter are as follows:

   ○ **JDBC Driver**: com.mysql.jdbc.Driver

   ○ **JDBC Url**: jdbc:mysql://localhost:3306/

The URL value given previously assumes that MySQL is running on the local computer and that it is listening on the default port of 3306. If either of these is not true for you, then you must change the URL accordingly.

5. We test the connection (acknowledging the dialog boxes along the way) using the **Local (No Agent)** option. Once we see the **Successful Connection** dialog, we dismiss it and close the Data Server editor.

6. We create a new Physical Schema on our new MySQL Data Server reference (right-click on the Local_as_prodsystem node). On the **Definition** tab set both the **Database (Catalog)** and **Database (Work Catalog)** values to the prodsystem schema.

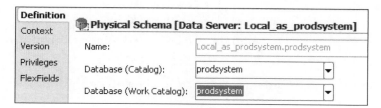

 Note that on this page the term for the data area in MySQL is **Database (Catalog)**, whereas when defining our ODI Physical Schemas for Oracle systems it was **Schema (Schema)**. It's these differences between vendor/system terminologies that ODI hides from the data integration designer by the use of Logical Schemas and models.

7. On the **Context** tab, we add a new Context mapping to a Logical Schema, entering MySQL_PRODSYSTEM as theLogical Schema name.

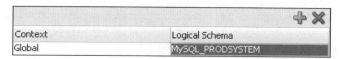

We save our work and close the Physical Schema editor.

We've now expanded our Physical Architecture to allow us to access the MySQL metadata by performing actions that were almost identical to adding references to Oracle systems. The slight differences were as follows:

- We had to enter the driver class and URL manually, because MySQL Connector/J is not included in the search lists in the **JDBC** tab of the Data Server editor

- The field labels where we set the schema names were different, but we still performed the same actions to select the data and work areas

Now that our Topology is configured, we will be able to import metadata from MySQL, and we can get ready to build interfaces.

Reverse-engineering revisited

Next we're again going to help build familiarity with ODI by creating a new model based on the MySQL schema metadata. We also need to reverse-engineer the remainder of the metadata in the data mart target system.

To reverse-engineer the metadata from MySQL, we will do the following:

1. Models are managed in the Designer Navigator, so we click on the **Designer** tab in the left-hand pane.

2. We expand the **Models** view, then click on the menu icon in the **Models** view's title bar, and choose the **New Model** option.

3. On the **Definition** tab, we name the model MySQL Product System, then we choose MySQL as the technology, and check that MySQL_PRODSYSTEM is selected as the Logical Schema.

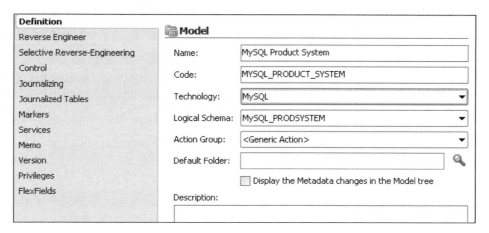

4. Next, we click on the **Reverse Engineer** tab to check that the `Global` context will be used. Then we click on the **Reverse Engineer** button in the left-hand side of the Model Editor title bar, and **Yes** in the confirmation dialog to save the model and proceed, and then we close the Model editor.

5. We expand the new **MySQL Product System** node in the **Models** view and we can see that three MySQL tables have been reverse-engineered as ODI datastores.

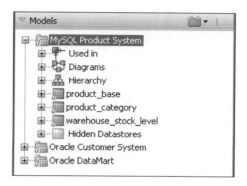

6. We can either double-click on the **Oracle DataMart** model node or right-click on **Open** to open the Model editor.

7. We click straight through to the **Selective Reverse-Engineering** tab—as the **Selective Reverse-Engineering** and **New Datastores** checkboxes should already be ticked, we click on the **Objects to Reverse Engineer** box to reveal the tables we haven't already reverse-engineered.

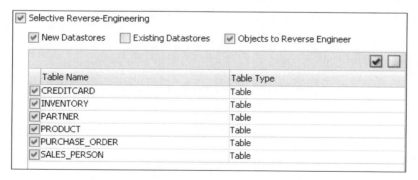

8. The remaining tables are all pre-selected as seen in the previous screenshot, so we click on the reverse engineer button in the Model editor's title bar. We then click on the save all icon in the ODI Studio main toolbar and we close the Model editor pane.

9. We expand the Oracle DataMart model node and we can see all the tables are now represented as datastores in the ODI model.

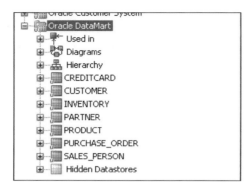

We now have the MySQL source tables and the Oracle target tables represented as datastores in ODI, ready for us to create our interfaces to populate the product-related data mart tables.

Preparing to move the product data

Next we're going to build an interface to build and enrich the product data. The task requirement means that we'll need to perform some joins between the source tables as follows:

- A join between the `product_base` and `product_category` sources to expand the product type code into a textual name
- A self-join from `product_category` back into itself to retrieve the parent category name for each product

To perform these operations, we will create an interface as follows:

1. We create a new project via the menu button in the **Projects** view title bar and we call the new project `Chapter 6`.

2. We right-click on the **Knowledge Modules** node in the **Projects** view in the Designer Navigator, and select and import `IKM Oracle Incremental Update` and `LKM SQL to Oracle` as before.

3. We expand the **First Folder** node, then right-click on the **Interfaces** node and select **New Interface**.

4. We name the interface Load PRODUCT and we select the **Mapping** tab at the bottom of the Interface editor.

5. We drag-and-drop the PRODUCT datastore from the Oracle DataMart model into the target datastore area of the **Mapping** editor.

6. We drag-and-drop the product_base datastore from the MySQL Product System model into the sources area of the editor and we accept **Automatic Mapping**. However, no mappings are performed — the column names are in different cases for the source and target, so no mapping is done for us. Instead, we map product_id to PRODUCT_ID by drag-and drop, and we map the product_name, cost_price, and list_price source columns to their respective target counterparts in the same way.

7. We drag the product_category datastore from the MySQL Product System model and we drop it just to the right of the product_base datastore in the sources area of the **Mapping** editor, this time rejecting **Automatic Mapping**, as it won't help anyway.

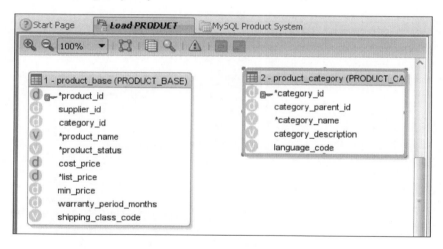

8. We drag-and-drop the `category_id` column from the `1 - product_base` (`PRODUCT_BASE`) source datastore onto the `category_id` column in the `2 - product_category` (`PRODUCT_CATEGORY`) source datastore.

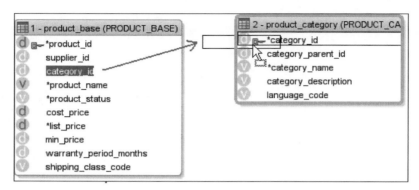

9. On releasing the mouse button to "drop" the column, a join marker appears with links from either side to the two columns. We click and drag the join marker so it sits between the two source datastores.

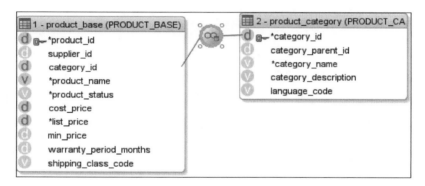

10. We drag a second copy of the `product_category` datastore from the `MySQL Product System` model and drop it just beneath the first one in the sources pane of the Mapping editor. It doesn't matter whether we click on **Yes** or **No** in the **Automatic Mapping** dialog as you may have noticed that we have no matching column names.

In the **Property Inspector**, below the sources pane, we can see that the second copy of the datastore has been given an **Alias** of PRODUCT_CATEGORY1. We change this to PRODUCT_PARENT (highlighted by the red box in the following screenshot) to more easily distinguish it from the first copy (we can change the alias name for each of the source datastores if we want to). Don't forget to hit **Return** after changing the name when you perform this operation.

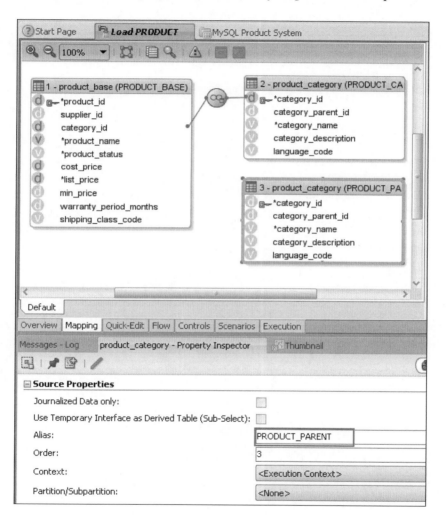

11. This time we drag the category_parent_id column from the 2 - product_category (PRODUCT_CATEGORY) source datastore onto the category_id column in the 3 - product_category (PRODUCT_PARENT) datastore to create a join between these two sources.

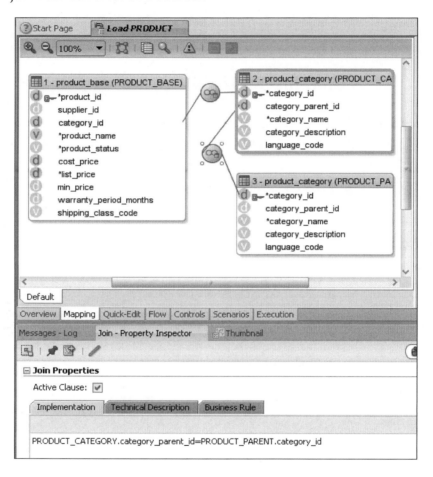

We then reposition the resulting join marker as before. In the **Property Inspector** we can see that the join clause uses the datastore aliases in its implementation text (it is also here that you can designate the type of join required—left, right, full, and so on).

12. We can see that the target's `PRODUCT_TYPE` and `PRODUCT_PARENT_TYPE` columns are both of varying character type — the same as the `category_name` column from the `product_category` sources. Therefore we can populate these target columns by dragging the `category_name` columns from each of the `product_category` source datastores to the appropriate target columns, as shown in the following screenshot:

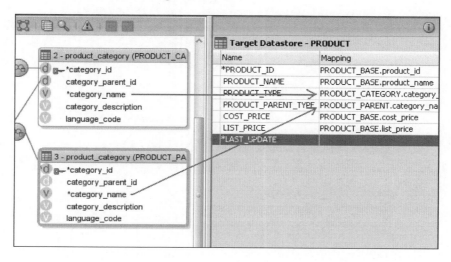

13. The `LAST_UPDATE` target column has the same mapping as was used in our previous task, namely an **Active Mapping** and an **Implementation** of `sysdate`, executed in the **Staging Area** for both **Insert** and **Update**. That completes our mappings, so now we need to configure the flow.

> We have to make sure that the `LAST_UPDATE` mapping will be executed in the **Staging Area**, and not the **Target Area**, or we would see some warning messages when we save the interface. These are related to ODI's ability to ensure that the database's `NOT NULL` condition on the `LAST_UPDATE` column is enforced.

14. We click on the **Flow** tab and we see that our two joins are going to be performed on the source system, which will reduce the "traffic" of data between the source and the target systems.

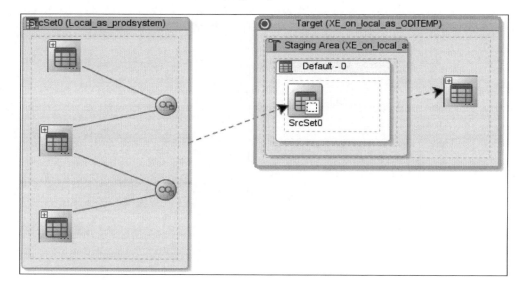

15. We click on the title bar of the source system in the **Flow** editor and in the **Property Inspector** below the diagram. In the **Property Inspector,** we can now select the LKM we just imported to define which loading mechanism will be used for our interface. We do the same for the target system, selecting the newly imported IKM and set the **FLOW_CONTROL** option to `false`. We save our work at this point.

We've finished building this interface, which contains two joins as follows:

- One between the `product_base` and `product_category` datastores to allow us to populate the `PRODUCT_TYPE` target column with the product category name

- Another that links the `product_category` back to itself (using an alias, which we changed) to enable us to retrieve the parent category name for the `product_parent_type` field in the target `PRODUCT` datastore

Before we run the interface, we'll examine the code that ODI will generate based on our design work on this interface.

Using simulation and execution

In this short section we will do the following:

- Use the new ODI 11*g* simulation capability to view the generated code before execution
- Execute the interface and check some key metrics

The steps to simulate an execution and to run the code are as follows:

1. We click on the **Execution** link in ODI Studio's main toolbar, but when the **Execution** dialog appears, we select the **Simulation** box before clicking on **OK**.

2. A **Simulation** report dialog appears which allows us to scroll through all of the steps and tasks within each step, viewing the executable code and operational parameters for each task. We have one step here, that is the execution of the Load PRODUCT interface, but there are a number of tasks that comprise this step, each task being generated from the appropriate Knowledge Module. As we scroll down through the simulation report we can see that the first task was to drop a temporary loading table (with a C$_ prefix) from our staging area (the ODITEMP schema in our oracle instance).

3. The following screenshot shows a small portion of the simulation report:

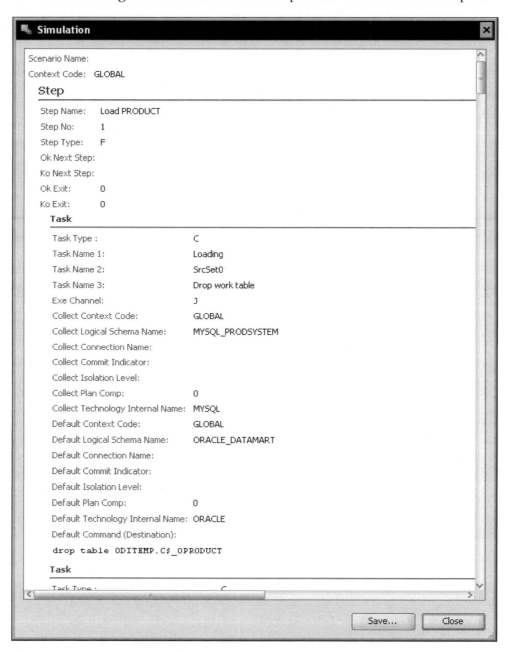

4. If we scroll down further to the third task we see the SQL generated for execution on the source system to extract the information from MySQL.

```
Loading Command (Source):
select
        PRODUCT_BASE.PRODUCT_ID    as    C1_PRODUCT_ID,
        PRODUCT_CATEGORY.category_name    as    C2_PRODUCT_TYPE,
        PRODUCT_BASE.PRODUCT_NAME        as    C3_PRODUCT_NAME,
        PRODUCT_BASE.LIST_PRICE    as    C4_LIST_PRICE,
        PRODUCT_PARENT.category_name        as    C5_PRODUCT_PARENT_TYPE,
        PRODUCT_BASE.COST_PRICE    as    C6_COST_PRICE
from    prodsystem.product_base as PRODUCT_BASE, prodsystem.product_categor
where   (1=1)

 And (PRODUCT_CATEGORY.category_parent_id=PRODUCT_PARENT.category_id)
 AND (PRODUCT_BASE.category_id=PRODUCT_CATEGORY.category_id)
```

This shows the use of the datastore aliases in the generated code, together with the join clauses we constructed graphically.

5. Just below the command for the source is its counterpart for the target system. This uses the output from the source query to insert into the loading table by the use of bind variables—all this being done behind the scenes for us automatically. You will notice that since this task loads data into the staging area, the column that is populated by a staging area mapping (the LAST_UPDATE column) is not included in the loading table.

```
Default Command (Destination):
insert into ODITEMP.C$_OPRODUCT
(
        C1_PRODUCT_ID,
        C2_PRODUCT_TYPE,
        C3_PRODUCT_NAME,
        C4_LIST_PRICE,
        C5_PRODUCT_PARENT_TYPE,
        C6_COST_PRICE
)
values
(
        :C1_PRODUCT_ID,
        :C2_PRODUCT_TYPE,
        :C3_PRODUCT_NAME,
        :C4_LIST_PRICE,
        :C5_PRODUCT_PARENT_TYPE,
        :C6_COST_PRICE
)
Task
```

6. Having had a quick look at the generated SQL, it's time to actually execute the interface to move the data. We close the **Simulation** dialog and click on the **Execute** toolbar link again, this time executing the interface without simulation.

7. This time we see an information message that a session has started, which we can dismiss.

8. Opening the **Operator** Navigator (leaving the Interface editor open), we expand the **All Executions** node and then we open the Load PRODUCT session (double-click or right-click on **Open**). We see that 67 records were inserted with no updates, deletes, or errors.

Record Statistics					
No. of Inserts:	67	No. of Updates:	0	No. of Deletes:	0
No. of Errors:	0	No. of Rows:	203		

9. We close the **Session: Load PRODUCT** tab and back in the Interface editor we click on the **Mapping** tab, we right-click on the **Target Datastore – PRODUCT** title bar and we choose **Data...** to see the newly inserted records.

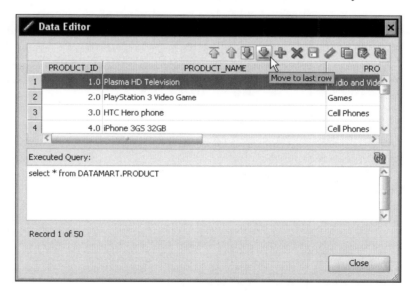

The **Data Editor** window initially shows **Record 1 of 50**, but if we click on the **Move to last row** button then we see that in fact 67 records exist (the Data Editor window retrieves the datastore records in batches — 50 records at a time).

10. If we scroll through the records we see that there are three parent category names – Media, Electronics and Office, which have been retrieved and populated by the join from product_base into product_category and that datastore's self-join (driven by the alias we renamed to PRODUCT_PARENT).

11. We close the **Data Editor** dialog and the Load PRODUCT interface editor.

We have seen, rather than executing the interface and then looking at the code that was executed, we used ODI simulation to view the code before (and without) execution.

In this interface we used a couple of joins on the source side—even if one of the joins was from a table back onto itself. In the next interface, we'll use a join in a different way and we'll add some data aggregation for good measure.

Moving the inventory data

In this section, we will perform the following:

- Create another interface, this time to move inventory data from our MySQL Product System into our PO Processing data mart

- We'll use an ODI Lookup as an alternative join mechanism, this time retrieving data from the PRODUCT table on the target (that we've just loaded) to enrich the inventory information

- The data from the source system will be aggregated across all warehouse holdings to have a single total for each product

- We'll then execute the interface and have a look at the resulting information and compare it with the source inventory data set

The steps required to implement this new interface are:

1. With ODI Studio still open, we click on the **Designer** tab to return to the Designer Navigator.

2. We create another new interface in **First Folder** in the Chapter 6 project and we call it Load INVENTORY.

3. In the Mapping editor, we use the INVENTORY datastore from the Oracle DataMart model as the target and the warehouse_stock_level datastore in the MySQL Product System as the source (once more there are no **Automatic Mappings**, as the case of the column names between the datastores is different).

4. We map warehouse_stock_level.product_id to INVENTORY.PRODUCT_ID via drag-and-drop.

5. We do the same for the source `quantity_on_hand` column, mapping it to the target STOCK_QTY column. However, this not complete, as we will see. We know we have just populated the target PRODUCT table with 67 records, but how many inventory records do we have? We right-click on the `warehouse_stock_level` datastore in the Interface editor's sources pane and select **Number of Rows....** The **Data Editor** dialog shows that there are in fact 601 source inventory records. This is because the source table holds inventory records from a number of different warehouse locations, so we need to aggregate them.

6. We close the **Data Editor** dialog, we click on the target STOCK_QTY column, and in the **Implementation** field in the **Property Inspector** we change the implementation to SUM(WAREHOUSE_STOCK_LEVEL."quantity_on_hand") and also change the mapping location to be executed on the **Staging Area**.

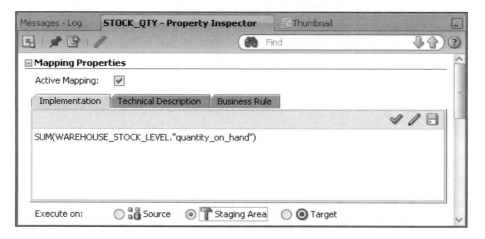

7. We add the (by now familiar) mapping for the target's LAST_UPDATE column, that being an **Active Mapping** of `sysdate` executed on the **Staging Area** for **Insert** and **Update**.

8. We still need to populate the target's PRODUCT_NAME column and for this we're going to use a **Lookup** rather than a join, simply to use a different approach. We click on the **Add a new Lookup** icon in the source area's toolbar.

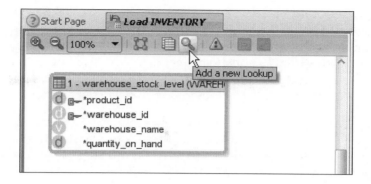

9. The Lookup Wizard starts and displays screen 1 of 2.

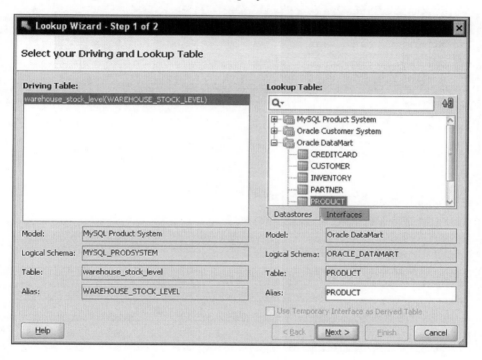

The **Driving Table** is pre-selected as `warehouse_stock_level`, as we only have one source table in our **Mapping** diagram. If we had more in our diagram they would all be listed in the left-hand field and we would have to select the appropriate one to drive the lookup. However, in the **Lookup Table** field we need to expand the `Oracle DataMart` model and select the `PRODUCT` datastore (as in the previous screenshot), then click on **Next**.

10. In **Step 2 of 2** we choose the column in each of the **Source** and **Lookup** that hold the product ID values and we click on the **Join** button. We select the option for the lookup to be executed on the **Staging** Area and we also set the **Lookup type** to be an **SQL left-outer join in the from clause**. We click **Finish**.

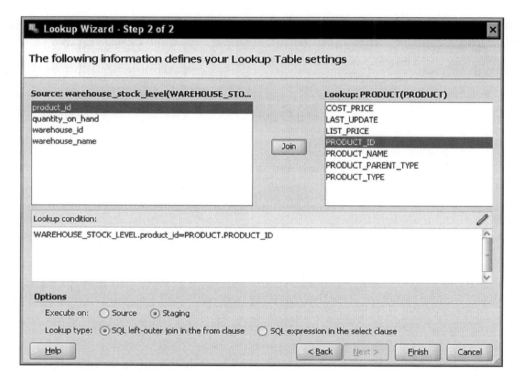

11. Back in the Mapping editor, the `PRODUCT` lookup is now linked to the `warehouse_stock_level` source datastore.

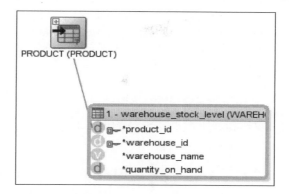

12. We expand the PRODUCT lookup either by clicking on the little cross in the top-left of the marker, or right-click and select **View As | Symbolic**. It is now represented similarly to any other datastore in the sources area, but it has a green title bar and a slightly different title icon. We right-click on the lookup and select **Optimize Shape Size | Height and Width** to reveal all the column details (we can always rearrange the size afterwards).

13. We drag-and-drop the PRODUCT_NAME column in the PRODUCT lookup into the target PRODUCT_NAME column to create the final mapping.

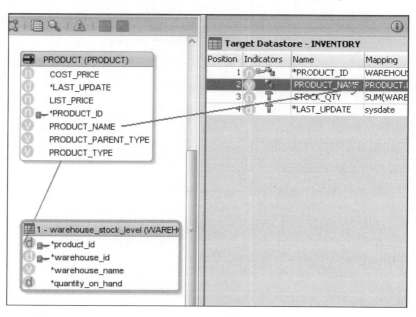

14. We click on the **Flow** tab. Since we imported a suitable LKM and IKM into our project for the last interface, they've been pre-selected here. However, we must still set the **FLOW_CONTROL** on the IKM (click on the title bar of the target server) to be `false`. The flow diagram shows (in the following screenshot) that data from the `warehouse_stock_level` table is transferred to a work table in the staging area (**dotted arrow**) where it is joined by information from the PRODUCT lookup—driven by the `warehouse_stock_level` table (**solid arrow**) and those two combine to populate the target INVENTORY table (**dotted arrow**).

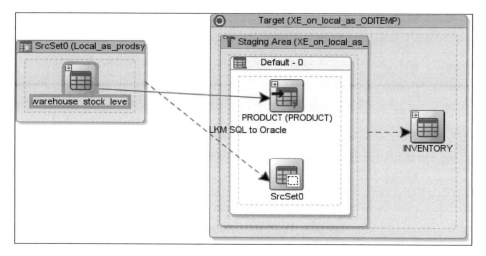

15. We click on the main toolbar's **Execute** button to run the interface, agreeing to have the interface saved when prompted and not using simulation. We dismiss the **Session Started** informational message.

16. We switch to the Operator Navigator and refresh its view (this can be done by clicking on the left-most button in its header bar—seen with a red box around it in the following screenshot).

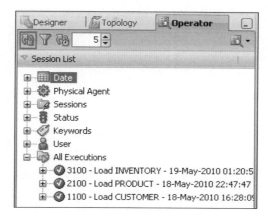

17. We double-click on the Load INVENTORY session that reveals (in the **Record Statistics** section) that 67 inserts took place.

18. We expand this session node and the Load INVENTORY step node to reveal the task nodes. We double-click on the task called 8 - Integration Load INVENTORY – Insert flow into I$ table and we click on the **Code** tab. We saw in the example in the previous chapter that inserting rows into the I$ (integration) table takes place in the staging area and this is where our staging area mappings and lookups are executed.

By scrolling down the code window we can see that our lookup has been included in a subquery within the main SQL statement and that a GROUP BY clause has been added to make sure our SUM aggregation calculates correctly.

```
insert into     ODITEMP.I$_INVENTORY
(
                PRODUCT_ID,
                PRODUCT_NAME,
                STOCK_QTY,
                LAST_UPDATE,
                IND_UPDATE
)
select
PRODUCT_ID,
                PRODUCT_NAME,
                STOCK_QTY,
                LAST_UPDATE,
                IND_UPDATE
 from (

───────  Subquery Including Lookup
select

                C1_PRODUCT_ID PRODUCT_ID,
                PRODUCT.PRODUCT_NAME PRODUCT_NAME,
                SUM(C2_QUANTITY_ON_HAND) STOCK_QTY,
                sysdate LAST_UPDATE,

                'I' IND_UPDATE

from            ODITEMP.C$_0INVENTORY   LEFT OUTER JOIN DATAMART.PRODUCT    PRODUCT ON
C1_PRODUCT_ID=PRODUCT.PRODUCT_ID
where           (1=1)


Group By C1_PRODUCT_ID,  ⎤   Aggregation Group By
         PRODUCT.PRODUCT_NAME ⎦   Clause


) S
where NOT EXISTS
        ( select 1 from DATAMART INVENTORY T
```

19. We close the **Session Task** and **Session** panes, returning to the **Load INVENTORY** editor. We click on the **Mapping** tab and we view the data now held in the target table. If we jump to the last row, we see that there are 67 records (aggregated from the 601 source records), one for each product. We close the **Data Editor** window and the **Load INVENTORY** editor pane.

In this final section we've created an interface to load the inventory data, performed an aggregation (the SUM SQL function), and used an ODI Lookup instead of the previous join mechanism to translate the source inventory data's product ID into a product name.

We then ran the interface, had a quick look at the generated staging area code including the added lookup elements, and then briefly checked integrated INVENTORY data.

Summary

You should now be starting to feel comfortable with some of the common activities in ODI. After first installing a third-party JDBC driver (MySQL), you were presented with two examples which led us through a series of activities representing many of the most frequently performed tasks within ODI.

Following those examples, we built several topology entries for data servers and physical schemas and linked them to logical schema names via contexts. We then used those logical schemas to reverse-engineer physical, vendor-specific metadata into a logical, platform-independent data model.

We then created a new project folder and imported the specific Knowledge Modules that would be needed based upon the interface requirements. We then built two separate interfaces in order to populate a target from one or more sources linked together either by joins or lookup relationships. We added simple column mappings using both the Automatic Mapping or standard drag-and-drop methods. We also augmented those mappings with more complex (yet still SQL) mapping code and implemented an aggregation function.

In the last few steps, we executed the interfaces and viewed the execution tree information using the Operator Navigator. We were also given an opportunity to examine the results of an ODI simulation.

In the next chapter we are going to cover another popular SQL database, namely Microsoft SQL Server, and introduce more features of ODI, including using the Expression Editor to avoid having to remember and manually enter SQL function names.

7

Working with Microsoft SQL Server

So far, we have seen how ODI can simplify and expedite data integration challenges when using Oracle and MySQL databases. But what if your company has a site license for Microsoft SQL Server? Or what if the majority of your database administrators and data architects are from a SQL Server database background? Not to worry! ODI supports Microsoft SQL Server as a first class database technology.

As we have seen in the previous chapters, ODI is effective at abstracting away the nuances of a given database technology and virtually eliminating the hand coding of SQL as compared to a traditional ETL project approach. Using our Purchase Order example, we'll be covering the following topics in this chapter:

- Provide a third (Oracle, MySQL, and now SQL Server) exposure of going through the process of working with ODI to create and test integration interfaces

- Define a SQL Server Data Server using Topology Navigator

- Introduce the Expression Editor and learn how to generate SQL-based transformation syntax without having to know the variants of SQL syntax for each database technology

- Define and configure the use of temporary indexes within ODI Designer to achieve faster interface execution

Example: Working with SQL Server

This chapter builds upon the incremental example scenario created in *Chapter 5, Working with Databases*, and *Chapter 6, Working with MySQL*. It is best to read through those chapters first.

Overview of the task

We will be accomplishing the following tasks in this chapter:

- Expand the ODI Topology to enable access to a SQL Server database
- Revisit the reverse-engineering process to create a model based on the SQL Server source database and also to complete the model of our PO processing system target data mart
- Prepare to move the Sales data by creating interfaces that enrich and transform the source Sales Division data
- Check ODI interface execution using Operator Navigator, viewing the execution status along with sampling portions of the SQL code generated and run by ODI

Integrating the Sales data

In this example, we will be populating the Sales Person data to the data mart. This new data mart supporting our PO processing example needs the Sales Person data to accurately and appropriately calculate bonuses for a Sales Division.

Our PO processing example solution requires a subset of today's Sales Person data to be appropriately moved to the corporate Data Warehouse at regular intervals to reflect changes in the Sales Division personnel.

Source

The source data resides on a single instance SQL Server and is owned and administered by the Sales Division business team. There are two tables of interest in this SQL Server SALESSYSTEM database, the first of which contains information on employees who hold the title of Sales Person and is called SALES_PERSON_MASTER:

Column Name	Data Type	Allow Nulls
SALES_PERSON_MASTER_ID	numeric(18, 0)	☐
FIRST_NAME	varchar(30)	☑
LAST_NAME	varchar(30)	☑
SALARY	numeric(18, 0)	☑
COMMISSION_PERCENT	numeric(18, 0)	☑
REGION_ID	numeric(18, 0)	☑
DATE_HIRED	date	☑
LAST_UPDATE	date	☐

The second table was created to satisfy the needs of the business team to summarize and analyze the sales team performance by geography and is called REGIONS:

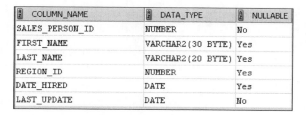

Target

The target SALES_PERSON table in the data mart schema has the following structure:

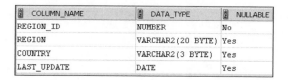

COLUMN_NAME	DATA_TYPE	NULLABLE
SALES_PERSON_ID	NUMBER	No
FIRST_NAME	VARCHAR2(30 BYTE)	Yes
LAST_NAME	VARCHAR2(20 BYTE)	Yes
REGION_ID	NUMBER	Yes
DATE_HIRED	DATE	Yes
LAST_UPDATE	DATE	No

The target REGIONS table in the data mart schema has the following structure:

COLUMN_NAME	DATA_TYPE	NULLABLE
REGION_ID	NUMBER	No
REGION	VARCHAR2(20 BYTE)	Yes
COUNTRY	VARCHAR2(3 BYTE)	Yes
LAST_UPDATE	DATE	Yes

Prior to the initial load from the SALESSYSTEM database, both SALES_PERSON and REGIONS tables in the DATAMART schema have zero rows.

Integrations

The SALES_PERSON_MASTER and REGIONS tables have been identified as the two tables having relevant and required data for populating the data mart. Initially, a full load will be performed to populate the data mart with a near current version of the operational sales data subset.

Two ODI interfaces are created for this example as follows:

- **Load Sales Person**: This interface loads SALES_PERSON_MASTER data from SQL Server to Oracle as represented by the following figure:

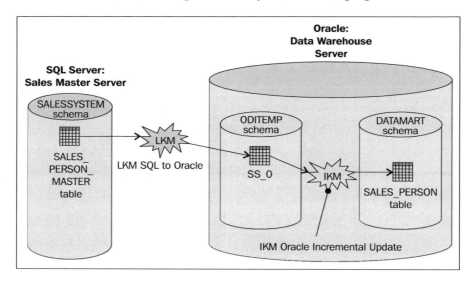

- **Load Regions**: This interface loads REGIONS data from SQL Server to Oracle as represented by the following figure:

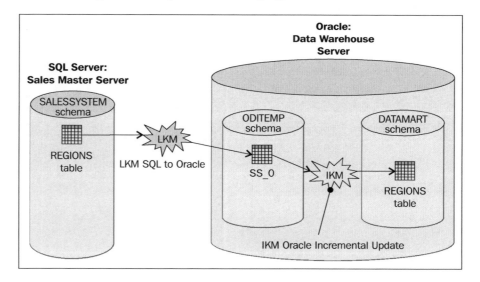

Sample scenario

Now that we understand the requirements, goals, scope, and structure of the source and target sales data definitions, let's start building another increment of the PO processing example solution.

Expanding the ODI topology

In this section we will:

- Create the Topology references to our source and target servers and schemas
- Create a Logical Schema name for the newly created Sales schema in order to be able to create our new Sales model in Designer Navigator
- Associate our Logical and Physical Schemas using the default Global context

Setting up the topology

We will go through the following steps in order to configure the topology:

1. If you are following along with your own installation of ODI, first make sure your Oracle instance that hosts your ODI repositories is up and running. Start ODI Studio Navigator (**Oracle | Oracle Data Integrator | Oracle Data Integrator Studio** on the Windows **Start** menu) and connect to your default repository.

2. We click on the **Topology** tab to switch to the Topology Navigator. Then we expand the **Technologies** node in the Physical Architecture node.

3. We right-click on **Microsoft SQL Server** and select **New Data Server.** We enter Local_as_SALESSYSTEM for the name of our source SALESSYSTEM data server. We add sa and welcome1 for the **User** and **Password** information on the **Definition** tab:

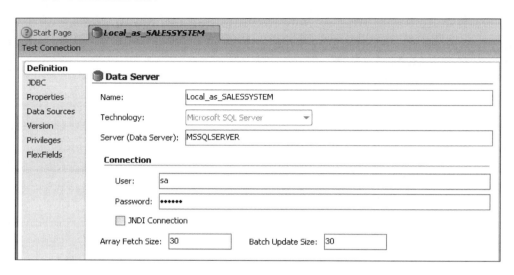

4. We select the **JDBC** tab to configure the **JDBC Driver** and **JDBC Url** for the SALESSYSTEM data server. Then we click on the magnifying class to configure the **JDBC Driver:**

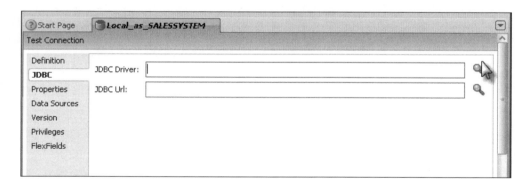

5. After the **JDBC Driver** magnifying class has been clicked, the **Drivers** dialogue appears showing available drivers. We select **Microsoft SQL Server Datadirect Driver**, and then press **OK**.

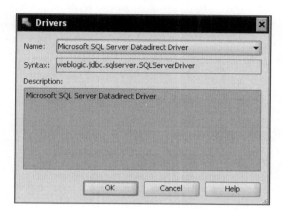

6. Now it is time to set the **JDBC Url**. We click on the magnifying glass to the right of the textbox associated with the **JDBC Url**. A template entry for the **JDBC Url** is generated based on the selected driver — `jdbc:weblogic:sqlserver://hostname:port[property=val ue[:...]]`. We replace the template text with `jdbc:weblogic:sqlserver:// localhost:1433`

7. The **JDBC** tab entries now look similar to the following screenshot:

The **JDBC Url** used in this example assumes that SQL Server is running on your local computer and installed using the default port number `1433`. Changes to the **JDBC Url** value will need to be made if one or more of those assumptions are not true.

8. We click on the **Test Connection** button (it becomes a button when the mouse moves over it) in the header bar for the editor. When asked if we want to save our data to continue, we click on **Yes** in the **Confirmation** dialog. We press **OK** if an information dialog appears asking to **register at least one physical schema**. Then we click on the **Test** button for the **Test Connection for:** dialog. We leave the **Physical Agent:** selection as **Local(No Agent).** Finally we see the **Successful Connection** dialog and we close the Data Server editor. We have now created the ODI Data Server corresponding to the SQL Server database.

Now that we have created our Data Server, we need to create the Physical Schema(s) that contains data that we would like to integrate. Having seen this Data Server to Physical Schema to Logical Schema process with Oracle, MySQL, and now SQL Server, you may have noticed a similar process being used within ODI, independent of the vendor of the relational database. That is not by accident. Data servers and Physical Schemas are defined in Topology Manager and mapped to a Logical Schema. The number of ODI users interacting with Topology Navigator is typically much smaller than those using ODI Designer.

In Designer, the only construct users need to be concerned with is the last construct of the process mentioned earlier—the Logical Schema.

9. We create a new Physical Schema on our new SQL Server Data Server node. We right-click on the **Local_as_SALESSYSTEM** data server node located under Microsoft SQL Server technology and select New Physical Schema. On the **Definition** tab we set both the **Database (Catalog)** and **Database (Work Catalog)** values to the SALESSYSTEM schema. We also set both the **Owner (Schema)** and **Owner (Work Schema)** to dbo.

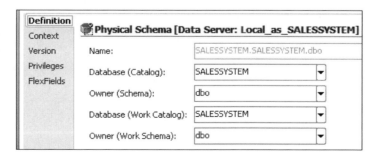

The name of the Physical Schema is automatically generated and is read only.

10. As ODI Designer operations work using Logical Schemas within the Designer user interface, and to support the functionality of contexts where Logical Schema to Physical Schema mapping is performed, we add a Logical Schema definition for our new Physical Schema. The Logical to Physical Schema mapping is created on the **Context** tab of the Physical Schema creation dialog. We add a new context mapping to a Logical Schema, entering SQLSERVER_SALESSYSTEM as the Logical Schema name.

11. Finally we save our work and close the Physical Schema editor.

We've now expanded our Physical Architecture to allow us to access the SQL Server metadata by performing actions that were similar to adding Oracle (*Chapter 5, Working with Databases*) and MySQL (*Chapter 6, Working with MySQL*) systems. The differences were as follows:

- We used the SQL Server JDBC driver provided with ODI 11*g* (**weblogic.jdbc. sqlserver.SQLServerDriver**) on the **JDBC** tab of the Data Server editor

- The Physical Schema definition field labels where we set the schema names were different, but we still performed the same actions to select the data and work areas

We have now completed the additional physical resource definition and configuration (think Topology Navigator when physical resources are involved) to add the SQL Server connectivity and metadata enablement (Data Server, Physical Schema, and Logical Schema creation). We can now move to the next step that is, reverse-engineering SQL Server hosted Sales data. The remainder of the SQL Server example scenario will focus on ODI Designer Navigator to create Model and datastores and design interfaces for data movement and transformation.

Reverse-engineering the Model metadata

In this section we will create a SQL Server Sales model for our SALESSYSTEM database. Without a model and the datastores contained within, we would not be able to create our interfaces.

We will now create a Model:

1. We click on the **Designer** tab and expand the **Models** accordion and subsequent tree view list.

2. Then we click on the menu icon in the **Models** view's title bar and choose the **New Model** option

3. On the **Definition** tab, we enter SQLServer2008_ SALESSYSTEM, choose Microsoft SQL Server as the technology and check that SQLSERVER_SALESSYSTEM is selected as the Logical Schema.

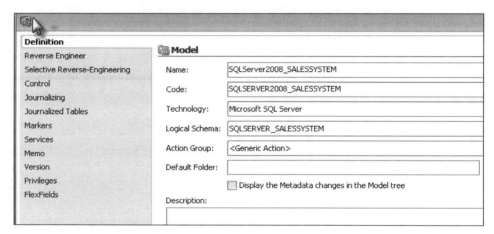

4. We click on the **Reverse Engineer** tab to check that the Global context will be used and on the **Reverse Engineer** button to the left-hand of the Model editor title bar. We click on **Yes** in the confirmation dialog to save the model and proceed, and then we close the Model editor.

5. Finally we expand the new **SQLServer2008 SALESSYSTEM** node in the **Models** view and we see that two SQL Server tables have been reverse-engineered as ODI datastores, namely, REGIONS and SALES_PERSON_MASTER.

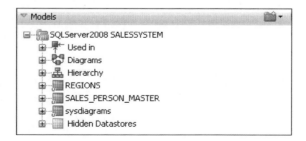

Creating interfaces and mappings

We now have the required SQL Server sales system source tables and the Oracle data mart target tables represented as datastores in ODI. We are ready to build our Sales data interfaces to populate and update the data mart for our PO processing example. In this section, we will:

1. Create a project.

2. Create the Load Sales Person interface and mappings to satisfy the target data mart requirements using enrichment, aggregation, and transformation of the source data.

3. Take a quick peek at the new ODI 11*g* Property Inspector toolbar and Property Inspector Auto Extend feature.

4. Examine and use the Expression Editor for improved productivity.

5. Create a temporary index for enhanced interface execution performance.

6. Create the Load Sales Region interface and mappings.

We start by creating a new project via the menu button in the **Projects** accordion view title bar and enter Chapter 7 SQL Server as the project **name**, then we press the **save** icon. Our ODI interfaces will be created in this project.

Load Sales Person interface

Now it is time to create our first interface for loading the source Sales Person data residing on Microsoft SQL Server to the Sales Person table in the Oracle data mart. To do so, we follow these steps:

1. We expand our **Chapter 7 SQL Server** project node and the **First Folder** node it contains, then we right-click on the **Interfaces** node and select **New Interface**. We then enter Load Sales Person as the interface **Name** and keep Global as the **Optimization Context**. Finally we click on the **Mapping** tab at the bottom of the Interface panel.

2. We drag-and-drop the `SALES_PERSON_MASTER` datastore from the `SQL Server 2008 SALESSYSTEM` model into the source datastore area of the **Mapping** editor.

3. Then we drag-and-drop the `SALES_PERSON` datastore from the `Oracle DataMart` model created in *Chapter 5, Working with Databases*, into the target datastore area of the **Mapping** editor and accept **Automatic Mapping**.

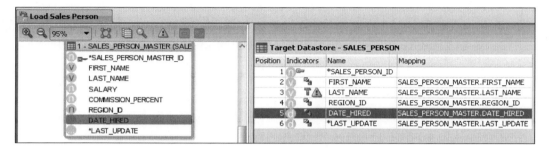

Property Inspector toolbar

The **Property Inspector** toolbar is new in ODI 11*g*. In addition to the recommendations made in *Chapter 5, Working with Databases*, regarding overlaying the three panes (**Messages – Log**, **Property Inspector**, and **Thumbnail**) into one tabbed collection, the **Property Inspector** toolbar can add additional usability to the day-to-day mapping user experience. While its presence may not be obvious when first using ODI Studio, the toolbar offers additional user control of the size and visual behavior of the frequently used **Property Inspector** dialog. The first image in the toolbar is **Enable/Disable Auto-Extend**. The default behavior is off. Press the **Auto-Extend** image on the toolbar to turn on/off **Auto-Extend** and see if you like the dynamic behavior of the Property Inspector dialog.

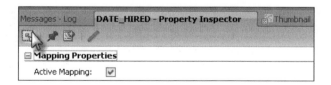

Load Sales Person mapping

Now that we have defined the source and target of our Load Sales Person interface we will start working on the mappings definition:

1. In our example, the primary key SALES_PERSON_ID was not mapped during **Automatic Mapping**. We select the source SALES_PERSON_MASTER_ID column and drag it to the target SALES_PERSON_ID column to populate the mapping column.

2. The business requirement for DATE_HIRED is that the data is set once and only once reflecting the original hire date of the Sales Person. By default, both Insert and Update are turned on within the Mapping interface. We uncheck the **Update** field to ensure no updates to this column will be made.

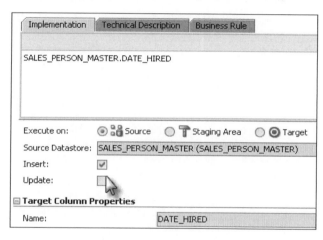

3. We find out that the warning indicator stays enabled, indicating potential issues in our interface.

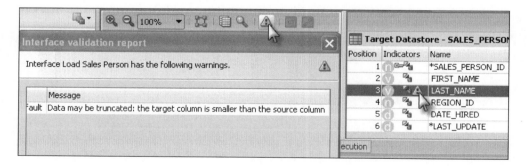

4. The warning message says the LAST_NAME data mart column is defined as smaller than the LAST_NAME source column. While there are better solutions for this particular issue than the SUBSTRING solution demonstrated next, the mismatch in column size was intentionally designed into this example to illustrate the use of the ODI Expression Editor. One solution is to transfer only the first 20 characters of the 30 character format LAST_NAME source column. But what SQL syntax for the substring operation should be used—SQL Server? Oracle? The ODI Expression Editor provides a graphical editor for those developing Mapping interfaces but who may not be familiar with all of the SQL syntax nuances between Oracle, SQL Server, DB2, Sybase, and so on.

> **Expression Editor**: Use the Expression Editor for generating the database SQL that is appropriate for execution on the source, staging, or target database selected in the **Execute on** radio button group in the Property Inspector dialog for a given field being mapped. The Expression Editor is always available to the **Mapping Properties** dialog user by pressing the pencil symbol. When launched, the Expression Editor will always specify the database platform being targeted for SQL syntax generation appropriate for execution on that platform. Standard editing functions (cut/copy/paste/undo/redo) are also available using the toolbar buttons. In the expression entry panel below the toolbar, you can directly type code for execution, or drag-and-drop elements from the other panels.

5. We select the column LAST_NAME on the Target Datastore – SALES_PERSON. We ensure that the **Source** radio button is selected on the **Execute on:** radio button group of the **LAST_NAME - Property Inspector** dialog. Then we launch the Expression Editor by selecting the pencil icon in the implementation tab menu bar for the **Property Inspector** dialog.

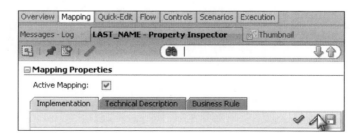

6. With the Expression Editor launched, we note that **SQL(Microsoft SQL Server)** is present on the toolbar because **Source** (SQL Server) was selected on the **Execute on:** radio button group.

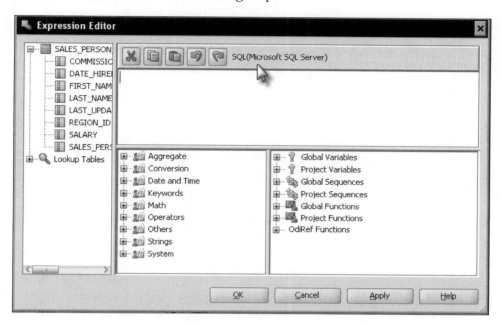

7. As we've seen previously, there is a schema mismatch between the SALESSYSTEM source and DATAMART target datastores for the LAST_NAME column. While both are character data, the lengths of the columns are different. By reducing the length of the source data to that of the target length, the interface execution can proceed without issue. As we are looking to operate on string data, one of the functions listed under **Strings** in the technology function panel is a good starting place to look for our needed solution. We expand the **Strings** function tree display. Then we select the SUBSTRING function and drag it into the expression panel to build the expression. The substring template SUBSTRING(<string>, <start>, <length>) appears. The <string> parameter should be populated by the LAST_NAME column of the SALES_PERSON_MASTER datastore residing on SQL Server. We select LAST_NAME and drag it over the centre of the <string> template parameter to obtain SUBSTRING(SALES_PERSON_MASTER.LAST_NAME, <start>, <length>). We know the desired length (20), and the desired starting character position (1), so by editing the <start> and <length> template parameters, we obtain a complete operation of SUBSTRING(SALES_PERSON_MASTER.LAST_NAME, 1, 20).

This can be seen in the following screenshot:

8. We press **OK** to apply and close the **Expression Editor** dialog. The text within the expression panel of the Expression Editor now appears in the `Target Datastore - SALES_PERSON` mapping for `LAST_NAME`.

Since one of the benefits of using the Expression Editor is hiding the syntax details and differences of operations across various database technologies, let us examine the syntax generated for the substring operation for the Oracle technology. Since syntax elements are defined by the technology that will run the operation, we select **Staging Area** (the Oracle data warehouse) on the **Execute on:** radio button group when the `LAST_NAME` target mapping column is selected.

9. We open up the **Expression Editor** again and notice that SUBSTR is provided rather than SUBSTRING in the expression panel of the **Expression Editor** dialog. This is because SUBSTRING is the appropriate operation when SQL Server is the execution platform, and SUBSTR is the appropriate syntax when executing on Oracle.

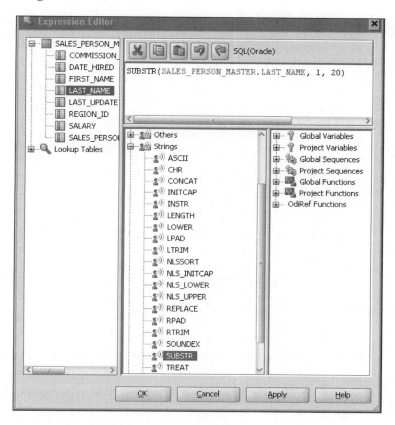

10. We again select **Source** on the **Execute on:** radio button group to restore SQL Server as the execution platform for the LAST_NAME target mapping.

Automatic Temporary Index Management

The ability to create temporary indexes during interface execution is new in ODI 11*g*. When performing *filter* or *join* operations, ODI can create a temporary index to provide enhanced interface execution performance.

To illustrate Temporary Index Management, we will follow these steps:

1. To illustrate Temporary Index Management, we will add two
   filters on the source datastore—one to **SALARY** and the other to
   COMMISSION_PERCENT:

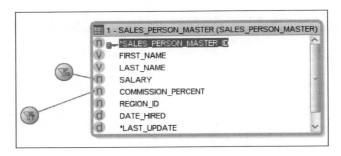

2. We select each filter, and in the **Filter Properties** dialog, we specify the
   following for **SALARY**:

   ○ **Active Filter:** checked

   ○ **Implementation:** SALES_PERSON_MASTER.SALARY<1000000

   ○ **Execute on:** Source

   ○ **Create Temporary Indexes:** None

   and the following for **COMMISSION_PERCENT**:

   ○ **Active Filter:** checked

   ○ **Implementation:** SALES_PERSON_MASTER.COMMISSION_PERCENT>0

   ○ **Execute on:** Target

   ○ **Create Temporary Indexes:** Non-Unique

   This will create a temporary index for **COMMISSION_PERCENT** each
   time the interface is executed as the generated SQL for the **COMMISSION_
   PERCENT** filter is executed on the Oracle target. Because sales commission
   are not guaranteed unique, **Non-Unique** is specified for the temporary index
   drop-down. A runtime error would occur and be visible within the ODI
   operator if **Unique** was selected in the drop-down.

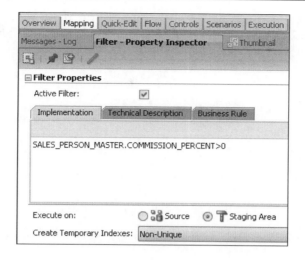

3. We have now completed the mappings. There are still a few additional tasks to perform before we are ready to execute and test the **Load Sales Person** interface. We switch from the **Mappings** tab to the **Flow** tab and we verify that the proper Integration Knowledge Module has been set. We click on the header bar of the **Target (XE_on_local_as_ODITEMP)** box in the flow diagram and we can see in the Property Inspector below that the **IKM Oracle Incremental Update** has automatically been selected. We decide not to check the data being integrated, so we set the **FLOW_CONTROL** option to `false`.

We will execute the **Load Sales Person** interface shortly. Our next task is creating the interface for loading the Sales region data. The steps are similar to creating the **Load Sales Person** interface.

Load Sales Region interface

Region data allows business owners to analyze historical sales data by region. We will now create the **Load Sales Region** interface which moves and transforms data from the operational sales database to the data mart:

1. In Designer, we expand the Projects accordion view, the **Chapter 7 SQL Server** project node, and the **First Folder** node it contains. We right-click on the **Interfaces** node and select **New Interface** to create a new interface. We enter `Load Sales Region` as the interface **Name** and keep `Global` as the **optimization context**.

2. We click on the **Mapping** tab and drag-and-drop the REGIONS datastore from the SQL Server 2008 SALESSYSTEM model into the source datastore area of the Mapping editor. We also drag-and-drop the SALES_REGIONS datastore from the Oracle DataMart model into the target datastore area of the Mapping editor and accept **Automatic Mapping.**

3. The source key REGIONS_ID needs to be mapped. We select the source REGIONS_ID row and drag it to the REGION_ID column on the Target Datastore - SALES_REGION

4. The COUNTRY column needs to be mapped to a shorter length (50 to 3). ODI automatically maps the source COUNTRY field to the target COUNTRY column. Next to the COUNTRY target column we can see a warning icon which provides a visual notification warning about the field length mismatch:

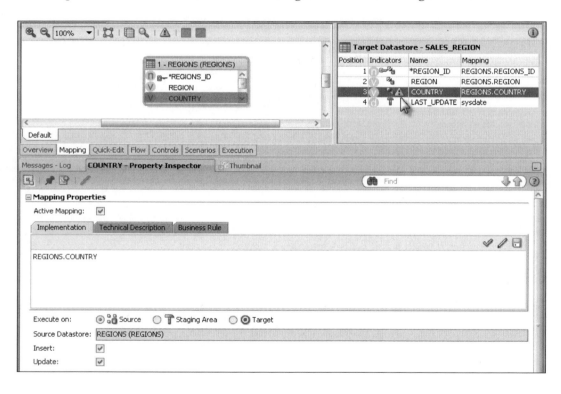

5. To solve the COUNTRY column mapping issue, we will use a CASE statement to convert UNITED STATES to USA and INTERNATIONAL to INT. Should it not be either one, the value will be set to ERR.

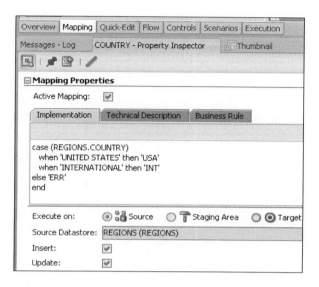

6. For the final mapping column, LAST_UPDATE, the sysdate operation executed on the Oracle staging environment will meet the requirements, creating or updating the field whenever a given REGION entry is added or changed within the data mart. We select the LAST_UPDATE mapping column. We click on the LAST_UPDATE target column and within the Property Inspector panel, we set the following mapping properties and behaviors:

    ○ **Active Mapping**: Checked
    ○ **Implementation**: sysdate
    ○ **Execute on**: Staging Area
    ○ **Insert**: Checked
    ○ **Update**: Checked

7. We then click on the **Flow** tab, and then click on the title bar for **Target (XE_on_local_as_ODITEMP)** to view **Target Properties**. We set the property **FLOW_CONTROL** to `false`.

 When executing interfaces, if you get a message, **Cannot start execution** with the first line of the Details stack trace being `com.sunopsis.tools.core.exception.` `SnpsSimpleMessageException : CKM not selected`, it is likely that the `FLOW_CONTROL` property has the default value set to `True` and no CKM has been selected. If a Check Knowledge Module is not being needed, set **FLOW_CONTROL** to `false` to resolve the problem.

So far, we have looked at and completed the following interface and mapping creation topics:

- Created a project and two interfaces — Load Sales Person and Load Sales Region
- Examined the Expression Editor feature
- Created a temporary index for a filter execution

Checking the execution with the Operator Navigator

Now that we have built the Load Sales Person and Load Sales Region interfaces, we will execute them to verify the execution in ODI Operator and examine the executed SQL to identify where and how the mappings, filters, and temporary index appear in the SQL generated by ODI. In this section we will:

- Execute the Load Sales Person interface
- Verify and examine the generated SQL and results, in particular, where and how the generated SQL appears for the filters and temporary index
- Execute the Load Sales Regions interface and verify and identify where and how the generated SQL for the interface mappings appear

Execute the Load Sales Person interface

We will execute the interface and monitor its execution using Operator Navigator. To do so we follow these steps:

1. We open the **Load Sales Person** interface in Designer Navigator, and press the green execute button in the ODI icon toolbar.

2. We then press the **OK** button on the **Execution** pop-up dialog, and **OK** on the **Information** pop-up dialog.

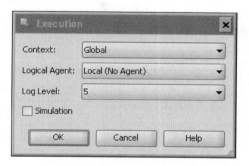

Verify and examine the Load Sales Person results

Using ODI Operator Navigator, we will examine key details of the generated SQL and resulting values in the SALES_PERSON table in the data warehouse.

1. We click on the **Operator** tab to switch to Operator Navigator. We open the tree view for **All Executions** within the **Session List** accordion dialog. The first entry is our just executed Load Sales Person results and details. The parent green checkbox tells us that the interface executed to completion successfully:

Each number under the parent **1 – Load Sales Person** represents an executed portion of the Knowledge Module(s) used during the interface execution. The **Loading – SrcSet0** steps come from the LKM SQL to Oracle. The **Integration – Load Sales Person** steps come from the IKM Oracle Incremental Update.

2. We double-click on step 3 **Load Data,** and then select the **Code** tab to examine the SQL code generated and executed for this step. The SQL generated as a result of the salary filter we created earlier in the Interface with the **Source** radio button chosen on the **Execute on:** option is shown next to the arrow:

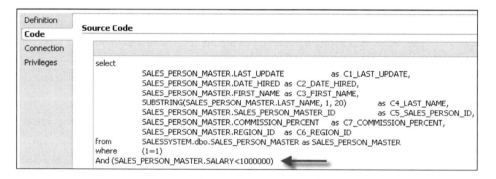

3. Now we double click on step **9 – Integration – Load Sales Person – Insert flow into I$ table** and select the **Code** tab. Here we can see the filter that is executed on the Oracle data warehouse as a result of setting the **Execute on:** option in the filter property inspector to **Target**.

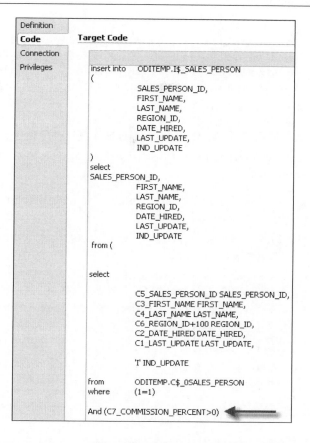

4. We click on step **4 – Loading – SrcSet0 – Create Temp. Indexes On Work**, then select the **Code** tab. This step is generated only if a temporary index is specified on the Oracle target (staging) area. While used here for illustrative purposes only, temporary indexes enable increased performance for filter and join operations operating on large tables.

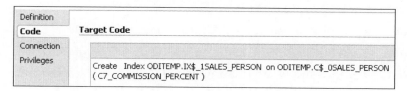

> The creation of temporary indexes may be a time-consuming operation in the overall flow. It is advised to review the execution statistics and to compare the execution time saved with the indexes to the time spent creating them.

Verify and examine Load Sales Region results

We will now execute the **Load Sales Region** interface and follow its execution within Operator Navigator:

1. We execute the **Load Sales Region** interface in a similar manner to the earlier steps for **Load Sales Person**.

2. We select the **Operator** tab, and view **All Executions.** We then open the tree view for **Load Sales Region**.

3. We double click on step **3 – Loading – SrcSet0 – Load Data**, then select the **Code** tab to view the generated SQL for this step. Here we can find the COUNTRY column mapping we added in Designer.

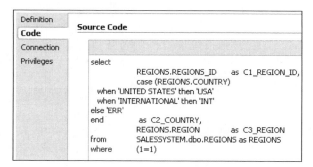

We have looked at the following execution and validation topics:

*   A refresher on how to execute an interface
*   Examining how and where the SQL for filters is generated
*   Examining where and how temporary indexes are created
*   Examining how and where mappings made in ODI Designer can be found in the SQL code provided by Operator Navigator

Summary

We have now completed the third incremental solution to the Order Processing example scenario. You should now be more comfortable with creating interfaces while simultaneously being exposed to selected new features of ODI 11*g*.

In this chapter, we started by using Topology Navigator to create a physical Data Server pointing to our SQL Server database server. We then created the required Physical and Logical schemas.

In Designer Navigator, we used the newly created Logical Schema to create a new Model and initiate a reverse-engineering process to retrieve the SQL Server datastores we were interested in, namely, SALES_PERSON_MASTER and REGIONS. Using those datastores we designed two interfaces to load the Sales data from SQL Server to our Oracle data mart. While setting up the interfaces, we saw several ways to create mappings in ODI—using the Automatic Mapping feature, by dragging-and-dropping source columns into the target columns and using the Expression Editor. We then had a look at the Loading and Integration Knowledge Modules as well as their options like FLOW_CONTROL.

Finally we executed our two interfaces and used Operator Navigator to review the steps created by ODI as well as the SQL code it generated.

8
Integrating File Data

While databases are obviously extremely significant in the realm of data integration, a large amount of data is held in flat files.

In this chapter, we'll be taking a look at how ODI plays a significant part in simplifying the integration of flat-file data using concepts and approaches that are identical to those used with database-hosted data, thereby dramatically reducing the learning curve. It also helps simplify the developer skills needed to use some of the specialized bulk data import/export functionality that databases provide, since that specialized functionality is encapsulated in Knowledge Modules.

Specifically what we'll cover in this chapter is:

- Extend the ODI Topology definition to refer to some input files and then reverse-engineer the input file metadata from both fixed format and delimited files
- Integrate data from a file using Oracle External Tables as the mechanism for the data import

This will give us the skills to get started with using files and also expand our knowledge of ODI capabilities in general.

ODI also has a lot of capabilities for detecting, moving, and transferring files, but these fall outside the scope of this "Getting Started..." book. There are a number of examples covering this specific area at http://blogs.oracle.com/dataintegration/. A lot of the content is also available in the archives of this blog, which can be accessed directly from that same link.

One type of file that we won't specifically be covering in this chapter is the XML file. We'll be covering it in the next chapter.

Working with flat files

In this example we'll be adding partner information into our data mart from flat files.

Scope

Briefly put, this example will perform the initial data loads of the Partner data. ODI also has built-in capabilities for using FTP and SFTP as well as sophisticated file and folder management functionality—files can be gathered securely from remote hosts, marshaled and processed by ODI, then archived locally or once more transferred to a remote storage location. ODI can even wait for "trigger files" to be detected at any stage before proceeding with the next phase of data integration processing. However, to keep things simple and to comply with our "Getting Started..." flavor, we're only going to be dealing with locally hosted files in a fixed folder location.

Prerequisites for flat files

There are no additional system elements that need to be installed to enable ODI to work with file data; it comes with its own JDBC driver for flat files.

ODI can also leverage database utilities for flat file processing. One important point to keep in mind is that both files and utilities have to be accessible to the ODI Agent that will process the files (either they are on the same server, or the files and utilities are on a shared directory that is visible to the agent).

Integrate the file data into an Oracle table

Integrating the file data into an Oracle table will be done by using an external table, adding files schema entries to the ODI Topology.

ODI Topology comes out of the box with a generic data server entry for the Files technology. However, we will still need to add an ODI Physical Schema entry to refer to the operating system folder in which our input files are held. For our example this will be `C:\po\input`.

As we know well by now, we must also associate this Physical Schema to a Logical Schema name via the context name that we're using.

Partner data target, source, and mappings

The target PARTNER table in the PO Processing DATAMART schema has the following structure:

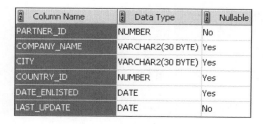

Column Name	Data Type	Nullable
PARTNER_ID	NUMBER	No
COMPANY_NAME	VARCHAR2(30 BYTE)	Yes
CITY	VARCHAR2(30 BYTE)	Yes
COUNTRY_ID	NUMBER	Yes
DATE_ENLISTED	DATE	Yes
LAST_UPDATE	DATE	No

This will be populated from a fixed format file called `partners.txt` which is in the `C:\po\input` folder. It has five columns with the following structure:

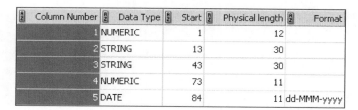

Column Number	Data Type	Start	Physical length	Format
1	NUMERIC	1	12	
2	STRING	13	30	
3	STRING	43	30	
4	NUMERIC	73	11	
5	DATE	84	11	dd-MMM-yyyy

There are no header rows containing column names in this file, but the data is held in the file in the same column order as the target table.

 The format for the date is significant. ODI needs to be told how to interpret a date column in a file as a date value, rather than as a character string. ODI being written in Java uses the Java date formatting rules. In this example dd represents the day of the month with a leading 0 for days numbering less than 10; MMM represents a 3-character abbreviation of the month name; and yyyy represents the 4-number year value. The punctuation characters are read literally, but do not influence the date value; the - used here could be replaced with / if this is what is used in the file.

Once the file is properly defined, including formats where needed, we can use it in our mappings

 A full list of Java date formatting rules and examples can easily found via your favorite internet search engine using Java SimpleDateFormat as keywords.

The mapping of the file data to the target table is straightforward: the first source column maps to the first target column (PARTNER_ID), with each subsequent source column mapping to the next sequential target column in order. As before, the target LAST_UPDATE column will be filled with the date that the record was last changed.

During the reverse-engineering process, we will be able to overwrite the name of the file columns, so that we can leverage ODI's automatic mapping facility.

Partner interface flow logistics

Our source is a flat file, our target is the Oracle data mart and our staging area will also be in the Oracle server hosting the data mart (remember that a staging area *must* be in a relational database).

For our Loading Knowledge Module we're going to use `LKM File to Oracle (EXTERNAL TABLE)`. Even if you've never used Oracle External Tables before, don't worry; we will have used one by the time we are finished with this example, and you'll see how easy ODI makes it!

For integrating the data from the staging area into the target table, we're going to use the same IKM as before (`IKM Oracle Incremental Update`).

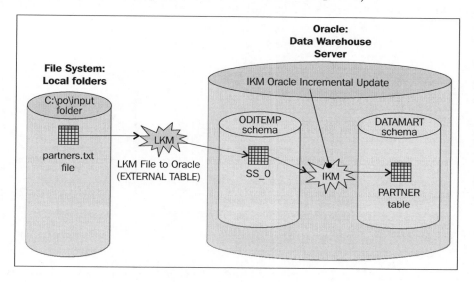

Once we've executed the interface we'll look at the results of our data load.

Step-by-step example

We now know what we'll be doing, so let's get started!

Expanding the topology for file handling

As we saw in the overview of the task, the first step is to expand the topology to add a reference to the file folder that holds the input files.

1. We first click on the **Topology** tab to switch to the Topology Navigator.

2. As we expand the **Files** technology node, we see the default **FILE_GENERIC** data server under the file technology.

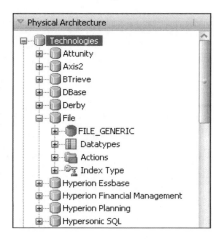

3. If we double-click (or right-click and select **Edit**) on the **FILE_GENERIC** data server node, the window that opens shows that the username and password fields are blank.

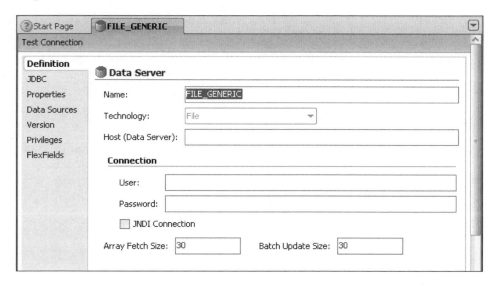

File access permissions

ODI will use the file access permissions of the operating system's user while executing the runtime code to process the files. So when using ODI Studio (as we are for this example), it will be the user who started Studio; when using a Standalone Agent, it will be the user that started the agent process; when using a Java EE agent running in WebLogic Server, it will be the user associated with the WebLogic Server instance's process.

4. When we click on the **JDBC** tab, we see that a JDBC driver is used to access file data (so SQL will still be used to access and manipulate the data), but the JDBC URL doesn't include any references to network information, such as a hostname or address. That's because the ODI file JDBC driver only allows access to files that are "visible" from the local machines; they can be on local drives, mapped network drives, NFS mounted disks, and so on.

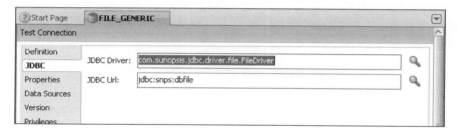

There are some optional properties that can be added to the file driver's **JDBC Url** field—these are documented in the ODI 11*g* documentation in the Connectivity and Knowledge Modules Guide for Oracle Data Integrator. We'll just be using the default settings here.

Since the FILE_GENERIC data server definition can be used to access any locally visible flat file, there is normally no requirement to add another data server definition to access file data. However, if you need to access files that use a specific character set (the default is ISO8859_1), then you should add a new file data server definition with the appropriate character set encoding option and value set in the **JDBC Url** field and use a data server name that reflects these changes from the settings of the generic file data server.

5. We only looked at the **FILE_GENERIC** definition to understand how it is defined, but we do not need to change anything, so we close it.

6. Under the server definition, we create a new Physical Schema (right-click on the FILE_GENERIC node). In the new window, we can click on what looks like a drop-down list next to the **Directory (Schema)** and we replace the **<Undefined>** text with C:/po/input (you can actually type the name directly in that field). We do the same for the **Directory (Work Schema)** field.

 Note that ODI uses the Java convention for file system paths. You can use the forward slash character / as the folder separator for all operating systems—Windows and Unix alike.

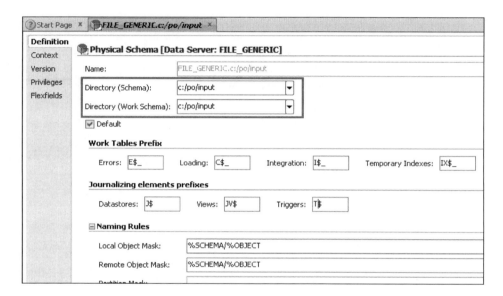

7. We then click on the **Context** tab and add a mapping in the **Global** context to a new Logical Schema named FILE_PO_INPUT (and hit *Enter*).

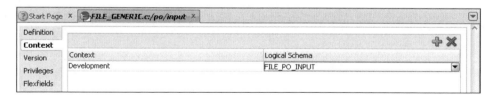

That's it in terms of expanding the topology. If we wanted to access more folders than just c:\po\input, then we'd add a new Physical Schema (and associated Logical Schema name) for each folder. We can now move to integrating the Partner data into the data mart.

Integrating the Partner data

In this section we have a number of subtasks:

1. First we need to create an ODI model for our input file and then we need to create a datastore entry for the Partners file. This isn't quite the same as reverse-engineering from a database table, as you'll see.

2. Then we'll create a new project for this example and import the Knowledge Modules for the interface to integrate the Partner data. Then we'll actually build the interface to integrate the data from the Partners input file.

3. Then we'll execute the interface and check on the integrated data, creating the Model and PartnersFile datastore definition.

Let's get started with these tasks:

1. We click on the **Designer** navigator tab and expand the **Models** accordion panel. We use the menu icon in the **Models** panel title bar to create a **New Model** and call the model **File PO Input Folder**. We select **File** as the **Technology** and the FILE_PO_INPUT entry is automatically selected for us in the **Logical Schema** field since we only have a single file Logical Schema so far.

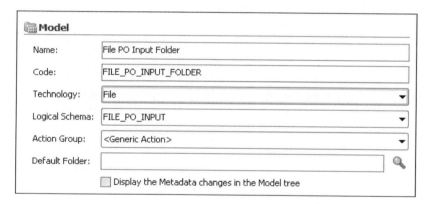

Previously we had used the Model editor (the window currently open) to perform reverse-engineering. However, as we touched on earlier, this is not possible when dealing with flat files as we first need to describe the file structure. So we just save our work and close the editor window.

2. In the **Models** accordion panel, we right-click on the **File PO Input Folder** node and select **New Datastore**.

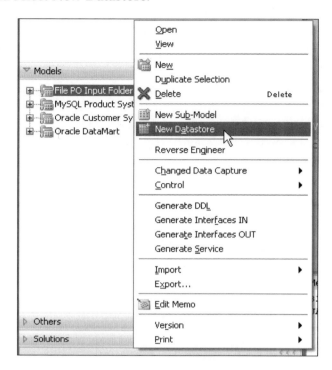

3. In the Datastore editor, we click on the search icon (the magnifying glass) to the right of the **Resource Name** field so that we can browse for the C:\po\input folder\partners.txt file and then click on the **Open** button.

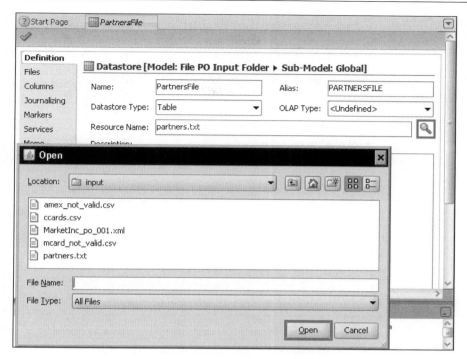

4. Back in the Datastore editor we set the **Name** to `PartnersFile`. The **Alias** field automatically picks up the first three characters of this name. However, since this is the name that will be used in the SQL for the interface mappings, we can make this alias a bit more explicit and unique, so we change the **Alias** field to `PARTNERSFILE`. We can ignore the **OLAP Type**, as it is not relevant for flat files.

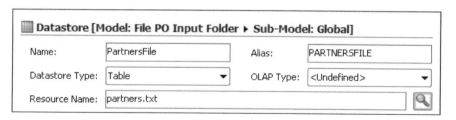

5. If you were to open the `partners.txt` file in something such as a Notepad, you'd see that the file has a fixed length column format, with the values being padded with spaces, and doesn't have any column heading information.

```
Partners.txt - Notepad
File  Edit  Format  View  Help
100          Oracle Direct          Redwood Shores          1
101          Vision Plus            Lyon                    33
102          Eurodisc               Munich                  49
103          Play Online            Cambridge               44
104          Cell Culture           Austin                  1
105          Macs Headroom          Atlanta                 1
106          Fujiama Supplies       Tokyo                   81
107          Still Stationary       Kobe                    81
108          The Way To Read        San Francisco           1
109          Pact Publishing        Birmingham              44
110          Hanstall Handhelds     Bristol                 44
111          Bordeaux Biblio        Bordeaux                33
```

When dealing with flat files, always make sure that the owner of the file gives you a precise description of the structure of the file. There is nothing worse than assuming that the file has a fixed structure when, in fact, it has a separator. If we were to only look at the `partners.txt` file, there is no way to know for sure whether it is a fixed format or a tab delimited file!

6. Back in the Datastore editor in ODI Studio, we click on the **Files** tab. We set the **File Format** to `Fixed`, we make sure that the **Heading (Number of Lines)** value is `0`, we leave the **Record Separator** as **MS-DOS**, and as we have a fixed format we do not need a **Field Separator**. We save our work at this point, but we do not close the editor.

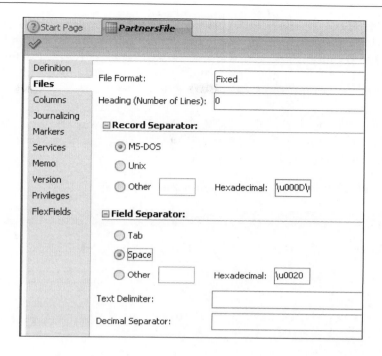

There are a few options that we have ignored here:

Field Separator: This entry can be ignored. But for a delimited file, this is where we would specify the separator characters. You can use one or several characters.

Text Delimiters: Some files will enclose text fields with double quotes for instance, to make sure that characters in text strings are not confused with separators. Use this field if your files are using text delimiters.

Decimal Separator : Some countries use a comma, whereas some use a point or period. When dealing with files from different countries, you can ensure that decimal separators are properly handled for each file.

We then click on the **Columns** tab.

7. The left-most icon in the title bar above the column area starts the reverse-engineering wizard. Be careful to not click on the words **Reverse Engineer**, as they refer to reverse-engineering a COBOL copybook file, which we're not doing here. The icon that we click on has been surrounded by a red box in the following screenshot:

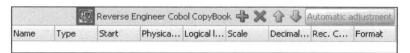

8. The **Column Setup Wizard** appears as follows:

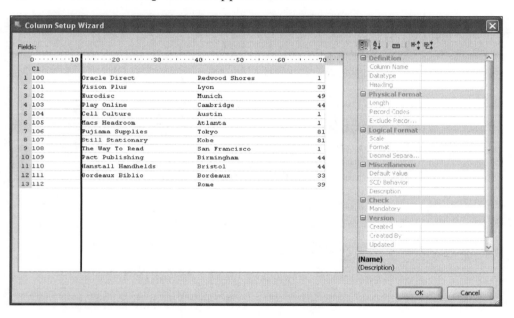

By default, all the data will be collected into a single column called **C1** and you'll see that the actual file data is being used in this wizard. However, if you move your mouse over (or just below) the column ruler at the top of the wizard dialog you'll see a vertical black line stretching down through the data (like in the previous screenshot). If you move your mouse along the rule to the start of each column of data below and then click, the black line changes into a little red spot on the column ruler and you'll see that additional column names are added (**C2**, then **C3**, and so on). This is the way that you specify the column boundaries in the file.

If you make a mistake, simply click again when the black line covers the offending red spot and it'll be removed. This file has five columns of data, so you should end up with columns **C1** to **C5** being defined, with no leading spaces for any of the columns (apart from the second column of the last row of course!). We can either enter the column names and types here, or close the wizard and finish the work in the File editor. Here we click on **OK** to close the **Column Setup Wizard**.

9. Back in the Datastore editor we now see the output from the wizard in a tabular form:

Name	Type	Start	Physica...	Logical I...	Scale	Decimal...	Rec. C...	Format
C1		1	12	12				
C2		13	30	30				
C3		43	30	30				
C4		73	11	11				
C5		84	11	11				

To make the most of auto-mapping later, we're going to name our columns exactly the same as those in the PARTNER target table in the data mart.

10. We are setting names and attributes for these columns per the following table, leaving the Start, Physical Length and Logical Length values as they are:

Name	Type	Format
PARTNER_ID	Numeric	
COMPANY_NAME	String	
CITY	String	
COUNTRY_ID	Numeric	
DATE_ENLISTED	Date	dd-MMM-yyyy

As we saw in the introductory section, the date format string given here is the correct type required for Java (ODI 11*g*) to read and interpret the file text as a date value. As with most things in Java, case *is* important in the date format string.

11. Once we have the correct column names and types set along with the date format, we can save our work and close the File editor. Now if we expand the **PartnersFile** node in the **Models** pane in the Designer Navigator, the **PartnersFile** datastore node will be shown. If we right-click on this node and select **View Data...** we see a data browser window open with the file data displayed. Any misalignment or missing data would indicate an issue with the definition of the structure of our file.

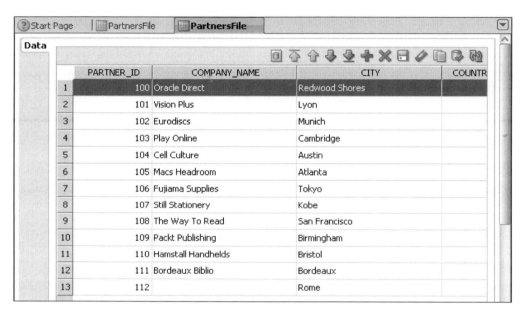

12. Before we close any editor windows we're going to perform one more check. Open up a Windows Explorer window and navigate to the `C:\po\input` folder. If you see any files called `partners.bad` or `partners.error`, then something has been entered incorrectly. Open these files in a text editor to see what the errors are and the affected rows. Correct the errors in the datastore definition for **PartnersFile**, delete the `partners.bad` and `partners.error` files and open another **View Data...** window for the datastore again. Hopefully this time there won't be any `.bad` or `.error` files created, but if there are, you now know what to do!

13. Once you can successfully see all the data in the data view window and no error files are created when you do so, save all your work, close the **PartnersFile** data view and datastore editor windows in ODI Studio.

We have now successfully modeled the metadata for the Partners datafile in ODI.

> Note that a lot of what we did here comes from the lack of information in the file. In a delimited file, you only have to specify the separator, you do not have to manually define where columns start and stop. Similarly, if the file has a header row that describes the column names, then we would not have to manually enter the column names and that would be true for both fixed and delimited files.

Creating and preparing the project

First we're going to create the project and import the Knowledge Modules we're going to use for the first interface.

1. With the **Projects** accordion panel in the Designer Navigator expanded, we create a new project that we call **Chapter 8**.

2. We expand the **Chapter 8** project node, right-click on the **Knowledge Modules** node and select **Import Knowledge Modules**.

3. Using the **Import Knowledge Modules** dialog, we import IKM Oracle Incremental Update and LKM File to Oracle (EXTERNAL TABLE) into the project.

> As with any database operation, you need to make sure that ODI has enough privileges to perform the required operations. With the External Tables LKM, ODI can create the necessary directory in the database to define the external tables, or reuse an existing one. The choice of letting ODI creating the directory (and having the necessary privileges) is usually in the hands of the DBAs.

Creating the interface to integrate the Partner data

To create an interface, follow the given steps:

1. We can now expand the **First Folder** node in the **Chapter 8** project and right-click on the **Interfaces** node to create a **New Interface**.

2. We call the interface Load PARTNER and we click on the **Mapping** tab.

3. In the **Models** panel we select the PARTNER datastore from the **Oracle DataMart** model and drag-and-drop it into the **Target Datastore** area (top right) of the Mapping editor.

4. From the **File PO Input Folder** model, we drag-and-drop the PartnersFile datastore into the sources area of the Mapping Editor, clicking on **Yes** in the auto-mapping dialog.

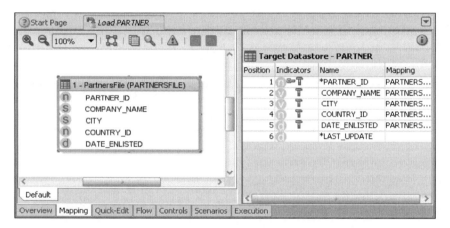

The work we put in making sure that the file datastore column names matched those for the target in the data mart has just paid off. All the source columns are correctly mapped, leaving us with only the LAST_UPDATE column to map. We click on the column name, and in the property panel set the execution location to the **Target** and **Type** to SYSDATE for the mapping.

5. Now we can click on the flow tab and view the integration flow generated by ODI.

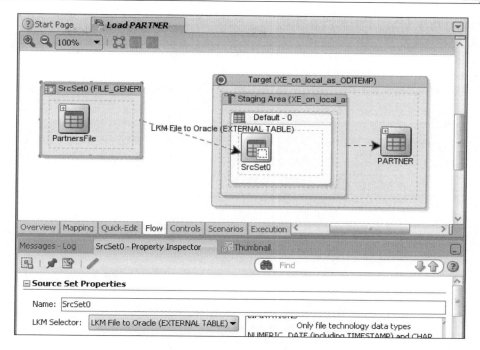

This shows that **LKM file to Oracle (EXTERNAL TABLE)** has been selected by default to load the file data into the staging area.

> If you scroll down the list of options for this particular KM, you'll see that the **EXT_PARALLEL** option has been set by default to have the Oracle database use parallelization, which will result in faster loads—especially of large data files. This kind of optimization that takes advantage of platform-specific capabilities would not be available in a generic Knowledge Module, a compelling reason to use a platform-specific KM.

The IKM we imported will have been selected to perform the integration. We are setting the **FLOW_CONTROL** option to **false** as we will not control the data.

We're now ready to run the interface and use an Oracle External table.

Running the interface

To run the interface and check the result, we do the same as we have done in the previous chapters:

1. We click on the run button in the main ODI toolbar (the green triangle), we accept the defaults in the **Execution** dialog, and we dismiss the **Session Started** dialog when it appears.

2. We click on the Operator Navigator tab to view the execution status. Click on the refresh button if necessary to see the latest execution highlighted by a red box as shown in the following screenshot:

We can examine the code generated and executed to use the External Table.

3. In the **Operator** Navigator **All Executions** list, we expand the **Load PARTNER** session node and the **Load PARTNER** step node below that to show all the **Loading**, **Integration**, and **Control** commands that were executed by the interface.

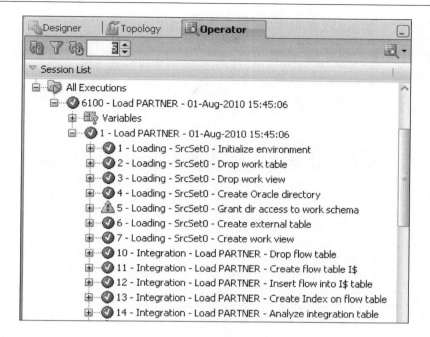

Here we can see that the LKM creates the Oracle directory, grants access to that directory, creates the external table reference, and then creates a view on that external table. It doesn't actually move any data—it just makes it available directly from the file as an Oracle table.

You can always open up any of these execution steps and take a look at the code needed to use an Oracle external table. But if you just want to bask in the glory of having used an Oracle External Table without having to know the specifics of commands and syntax, that would be OK too.

4. We click on the **Designer** Navigator tab and locate the **PARTNER** datastore in the **Oracle DataMart** model. We right-click on this node and select **View Data**. A data view window opens displaying the newly integrated contents of the PARTNER table in the data mart and shows the 12 rows that were loaded.

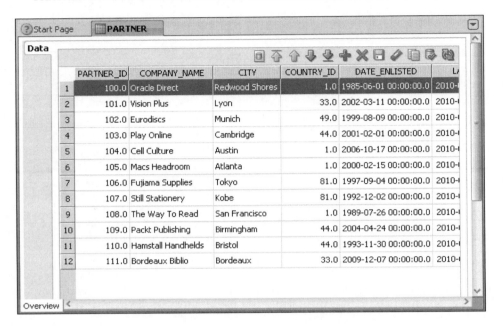

That's it for our file example. We have:

- Successfully added a Physical Schema to allow access to file data
- Defined a Model for the flat file
- Loaded data using an Oracle External Table and seen how effectively ODI Knowledge Modules can encapsulate the expertise to use proprietary database extensions and utilities

Summary

Here's what we've covered in this chapter:

- We've learned about the FILE_GENERIC data server and what we'd need to look out for when using different character sets in files

- We've seen how to reverse-engineer metadata from both fixed format and delimited files and how the two methods differ

- We've used an Oracle External Table without having to learn the detailed database syntax to achieve this, because the Knowledge Module we used encapsulated all that expertise and made it easily reusable

- We also saw that there are still circumstances (such as setting the necessary database permissions) when some additional preparatory work is needed before we can use platform-specific Knowledge Modules

We've integrated data from a flat file into a database. Next we're going to deal with a form of file that has massively growing significance in the business IT world, namely XML files.

9
Working with XML Files

Extensible Markup Language (XML) has grown rapidly in importance over the last few years. It has a strong association with web services and **service-oriented architecture (SOA)** initiatives, but it is working its way into all kinds of areas in IT. As a result, XML is often a significant factor in enterprise data integration projects.

ODI 11*g* is in a very strong position when it comes to XML as it has an extremely powerful and rather elegant JDBC driver that works directly with XML structures, as we shall discover in this chapter. What we will cover is:

- A very brief introduction to XML, just to cover the basics, and to make sure that we use a common vocabulary when exploring XML and ODI's capabilities

- An overview of the ODI JDBC driver for XML and the essentials of how it works: this is important to understand certain aspects of how to use ODI with XML and will include explanations of the most commonly used JDBC driver flags

- A brief look at some of the more advanced capabilities of the XML driver

- A sample tutorial in which we'll be reading a simple XML file and integrating its data into our data mart

Introduction to XML

XML files employ a format in which data is contained in a nested, hierarchical structure of tags which give context and meaning to the data contained between and within the tags. It has been described as similar to HTML because both in XML and in HTML the tags used can each have attributes, can surround data value elements (in HTML these are mostly text strings to be displayed), and can support deeper nesting of tag structures.

Where tags surround data or a deeper structure, they have opening tags balanced with closing tags, those nested inner tags always being closed before outer tags as in this snippet of HTML:

```
<b>This text will be displayed as bold <i>and this as bold italics
  </i></b>.
```

Where a tag has attributes, but doesn't surround any data or other elements, the opening and closing tags can be combined into one, with a closing "slash-bracket":

```
<meta content="text/html; charset=utf-8" http-equiv="Content-Type" />
```

However, a big distinction is that HTML was designed to *display* data, whereas XML was designed to *carry* data—albeit that XML was always intended to be suitable for the web.

The limited range of tags and the known structural rules in HTML mean that quite a lot can be inferred in a sequence of HTML. So you frequently see "unbalanced" tags in HTML pages. This is never true of XML: it isn't designed for a limited set of clients or interrogators, so it doesn't have a pre-defined set of tags or structures (after all, it's extensible!), so each tag must explicitly be closed in XML, as the opening of any particular tag type cannot imply the closing of any previous tags.

Since XML is so extensible, the definitions of the tags being used in a document or file together with the structural and datatype metadata for those tags are held in a separate, but associated definition document or file, typically either as a:

- A Document Type Definition (DTD), which is an early, rather terse method of defining tags, their attributes, and their hierarchies, or

- An XML Schema Definition (XSD), which is itself an XML-based method of defining an XML structure including:

    ◦ Tag names, attributes, and value types (using standard datatypes such as string, integer, and decimal.

    ◦ Complex types, which are user defined substructures of tags and attributes.

    ◦ Namespaces, which are conceptual "containers" in which complex type definitions can be organized to help clarity and avoid naming conflicts. Once a user-defined complex type has been defined to reside in a specific namespace, an XML document need only refer to the namespace in order to use and leverage that complex type.

In fact, since an XSD is an XML document, it needs to conform to a schema definition itself. Fortunately there are standard organizations that have agreed to a common format and content for these foundation definitions of elementary types, tag names to use to define new types, how to specify namespaces, and so on.

If you are a total newcomer to XML, there are many websites (your favorite search engine will oblige) and books that cover the subject, but the authoritative source of information is the World Wide Web Consortium (W3C) and they have a section of their website dedicated to XML at `http://www.w3.org/standards/xml/`—their *XML Essentials* section is a very good introduction to the basic concepts of XML.

XSD and DTD files are the most prevalent vendor-neutral forms of schema definition for XML, and even though XSD has to a large extent eclipsed DTD by being more easily understood, more flexible, and more powerful, both are still in use—and both can be used with ODI 11*g*.

Introducing the ODI JDBC driver for XML

As we've mentioned before, ODI uses JDBC in order to access data, so it needs a JDBC driver to access XML data. Fortunately it comes with an extremely sophisticated driver right out of the box. It will be essential for us to understand some of the characteristics and working methods of the driver for us to use it correctly and effectively, so we'll cover the basics here.

ODI and its XML driver—basic concepts

We now know that XML documents contain a hierarchical, nested structure of elements (each of which may have attributes), all of which are contained within a single root element.

We also know that ODI is a very SQL and relational-oriented tool that models things in a very table-like way.

The ODI JDBC driver for XML marries these two paradigms by representing a single XML file as a hierarchy of table-like datastores that are related to each other through primary, foreign key relationships:

- Each XML element (tag) that contains subelements (nested tags) becomes a table
- Each attribute becomes a column of the associated element's table

- Lowest level elements that only contain data values and no nested tags also become columns of the containing element's table

- To preserve the order of elements in the correct sequence within an enclosing tag pair, an ORDER column will be added for each enclosed element—whether that element is mapped to a table or a column within a table

- To maintain the correct hierarchical nesting of elements, the driver will also add numeric primary and foreign key columns to the tables

As an example, let's take a look at a simple XML file that has a root element that only contains one level of subelement:

```
<?xml version="1.0" encoding="UTF-8"?>
<Building>
   <StreetAddr>32 Lincoln Road</StreetAddr>
   <Locality>Olton</Locality>
   <City>Birmingham</City>
   <StateOrProv>West Midlands</StateOrProv>
   <PostCode>B27 6PA</PostCode>
   <CountryCode>44</CountryCode>
</Building>
```

If reverse-engineered into ODI, this would resolve to a table called Building that has columns called StreetAddr, Locality, City, and so on. There would also be columns created in the table in the model called StreetAddrORDER, LocalityORDER, CityORDER, and so on that would hold numbers that represent the order in which those elements appear in the XML file.

The use of the term "table" here is significant: what the XML driver does is it creates these tables and columns in a relational schema and uses that schema for the management and manipulation of the data in the XML file. By default this relational schema is created in memory, but the driver can be configured to use an Oracle or non-Oracle database, which enables ODI to work with huge (tens or hundreds of megabytes and even more) XML files.

Although ODI 11g does allow the use of an external database such as Oracle to be used as a data manipulation area purely for the XML JDBC driver (as distinct from a staging area used in an ODI interface), this chapter will only cover the default out of the box behavior which has this "in-driver" XML data manipulation occurring in memory.

If the XML file holds a nested structure of elements, such as a building that has floors and rooms on each floor, the XML driver will create a hierarchy of related tables in its relational schema, as shown in the following figure:

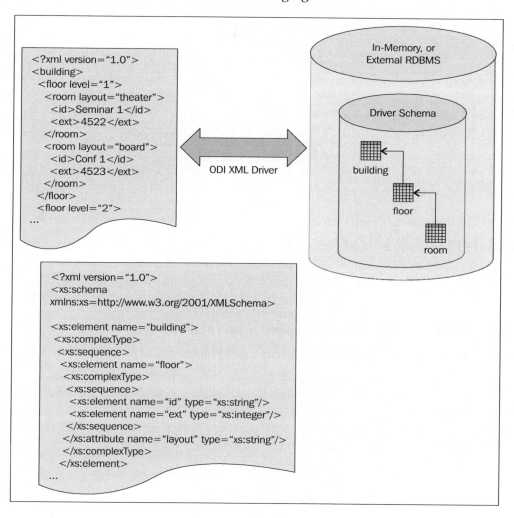

Each XML data file is represented in the ODI topology by its own Physical Data Server. Within that Data Server a single Physical Schema will represent the hierarchical schema and the contents of the XML file. This differs from comparable objects for database technologies (where each Data Server will have access to all of the individual schemas available via a single database server connection string) or for flat files (where a single Physical Data Server covers the whole accessible filesystem structure for the hosting machine and each Physical Schema represents a filesystem folder).

> There is an in-depth description of the ODI XML JDBC driver in the ODI 11*g* documentation, specifically in *Appendix B* of the *Connectivity and Knowledge Modules Guide*, available (at the time of writing) at the Oracle Technology Network at `http://www.oracle.com/technetwork/middleware/data-integrator/documentation/index.html`.

Example: Working with XML files

In this example we're going to be reading simple XML files with ODI. Along the way we're also going to introduce ODI Procedures and build a couple of examples.

Requirements and background

The examples in this chapter build on the expertise gained in previous chapters.

Our overall sample scenario covers a Purchase Order (PO) processing environment and here we're going to be dealing with handling Purchase Order data. So what we'll focus on in this section is how ODI can integrate incoming Purchase Order data into the data mart from which those other PO processing elements could retrieve the purchase orders for further sequential processing.

The PO data we must handle is provided in the following format:

- We have an online order capture system that outputs each order as an XML message as they are placed. These messages are stored as individual XML files. The files that we receive from the online system are always for orders placed today.

Scope

As we've noted earlier, we're going to be reading XML files and examining the behavioral characteristics of the XML driver when used in its default configuration. We will not be using an external SQL database for the XML driver to store the schema and data, nor will we be using special character sets in the XML.

As we progress through this example we will also need to run a number of procedures and interfaces that we create in a piecemeal, manually-driven way. How this can be orchestrated and performed by ODI itself will be covered in the next chapter.

Overview of the task

We're going to break down the task of integrating a single Purchase Order from our sample file into smaller parts. This will include:

- Setting up the topology entries for the file
- Reverse-engineering the metadata from the XML schema
- Building an interface to map and enrich the data into the target table
- Executing the interface and checking the results of our execution

We'll also take a first look at ODI Procedures and use two interactively in relation to our XML file integration.

Integrating a Purchase Order from an XML file

By now it will come as no surprise that we will be creating topology entries for a Data Server, a Physical Schema and a Logical Schema. What we will see is both the similarity to and difference from the way that we specified corresponding entries for flat files.

Creating models from XML files

Once again we'll be reverse-engineering metadata on a file-by-file basis, but we'll also see that using the ODI XML driver adds significance to the concept of schemas in the topology when it comes to the reading, writing, and manipulating of XML data and the relationships.

We'll also see after the reverse-engineering process that the new columns that are added in the model allow ODI to preserve element order and hierarchical association information between nested structures of elements.

Integrating the data from a single Purchase Order

We'll be integrating data into the PURCHASE_ORDER table in the data mart. This table has the following format:

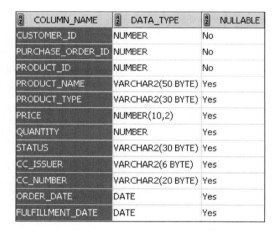

COLUMN_NAME	DATA_TYPE	NULLABLE
CUSTOMER_ID	NUMBER	No
PURCHASE_ORDER_ID	NUMBER	No
PRODUCT_ID	NUMBER	No
PRODUCT_NAME	VARCHAR2(50 BYTE)	Yes
PRODUCT_TYPE	VARCHAR2(30 BYTE)	Yes
PRICE	NUMBER(10,2)	Yes
QUANTITY	NUMBER	Yes
STATUS	VARCHAR2(30 BYTE)	Yes
CC_ISSUER	VARCHAR2(6 BYTE)	Yes
CC_NUMBER	VARCHAR2(20 BYTE)	Yes
ORDER_DATE	DATE	Yes
FULFILLMENT_DATE	DATE	Yes

The table will be populated from an XML file called order_20001.xml which is in the C:\po\input folder. It has a single record of data that conforms to the following XML schema definition shown in the following figure. This XML schema is composed of those main elements:

- The root element is called PurchaseOrder and is of type PurchaseOrderType (the po: prefix refers to the http://xmlns. oracle.com/ns/order namespace)

- PurchaseOrderType has a sequence (the oval with three red dots) of nine subelements, some of which are optional (the dotted outline boxes)

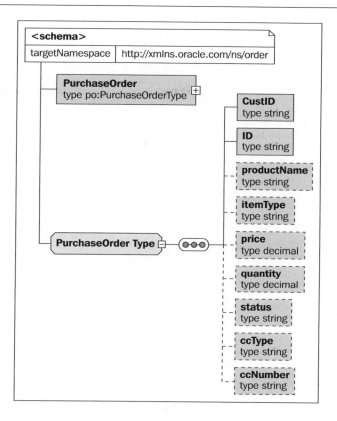

The mappings are all straight-through (no data modification) from the source XML file apart from four columns in the target:

- ORDER_DATE is taken to be the date on which the order data is integrated (these XML files are processed on the day the order is received)

- FULFILLMENT_DATE will be left blank (null) for now as we don't have that information yet

- The PRODUCT_ID will be obtained by a lookup into the data mart's PRODUCT table based on the product name held in the XML file

- The STATUS of the order can be changed to Approved if either the value is less than $1000 or if there is a valid credit card number for orders of $1000 or above

- Orders of $1000 or above with an invalid credit card will need their status set to InvalidCreditCard

We also have a requirement that each order must be associated with either a sales person or a partner so that we can calculate commission correctly. Rather than performing a join with the CUSTOMER table in the data mart, we have created two ODI constraints on the data mart's PURCHASE_ORDER table so that non-compliant purchase orders are diverted into an error table from where they can later be corrected and fed back into the next interface execution. The first constraint checks that the CUSTOMER_ID in the Purchase Order links to a valid customer and the second checks that the linked customer either has a SALES_PERSON_ID or PARTNER_ID entry. The advantage of this is that the constraints will be reused by all interfaces that feed into the PURCHASE_ORDER table — we don't need to check that all the interfaces include the correct join.

We'll be using CKM Oracle to divert these non-compliant records by using flow control in the interface.

Single order interface flow logistics

Our main source is an XML file and our target is our Oracle data mart. We're also going to perform a join into the PRODUCT table which is in the data mart, so it makes sense to have the staging area in the data mart server and the join can be performed there without having to move the PRODUCT table data out of its hosting server. This is one benefit of ODI's **Extract, Load,** and **Transform (ELT)** architecture.

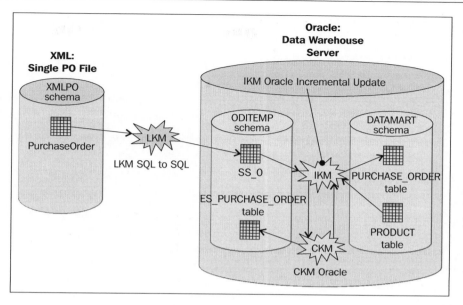

We decided to use LKM SQL to SQL to show that you don't have to use a platform-optimized Knowledge Module if you don't want to. The LKM SQL to Oracle can also be used for this example scenario.

After we've run the interface to integrate the data we're going to investigate some of the nuances of dealing with individual XML files and employ some techniques that are commonly used when dealing with files of this type.

The schema name **XMLPO** shown for the source in the previous figure for the XML file region is simply a value that we'll pass as a parameter to the driver so that it can name the region of memory it sets up to hold the relational representations of the underlying XML file data. Being able to name schema regions in this way means that the driver can segment and keep separate the work it performs for multiple different interfaces if that is needed.

Sample scenario: Integrating a simple Purchase Order file

In this section we will:

- Create the necessary topology entries to be able to interrogate the XML file and its schema to access both the data and metadata

- Reverse-engineer the XML file into an ODI model and take a quick look at the structure that gets created

- Use the ODI model to build an interface to read the data from the XML file and move it into the target table

- Improve the approach we've taken so that it can better cope with multiple similar XML files—bearing in mind that we'll get one incoming file per Purchase Order captured by the online system

- Highlight one of the key things to remember when dealing with the ODI XML driver…

So with that last thought hanging, let's get started!

Expanding the Topology

As you'd expect, the first thing to do is to expand the Topology definitions to include the XML file we want to integrate.

1. With ODI Studio open and connected to a Work repository, we click on the **Topology** navigator tab.

2. We scroll down the list of technologies right to the bottom, then right-click on XML to add a new XML data server and we call it `XML Single PO File`. We can leave the fields labeled **(Data Server)**, **User**, and **Password** all blank and go straight to the **JDBC** tab.

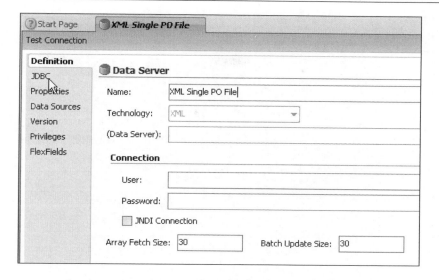

3. We click on the browse icon (magnifying glass) to the right of the **JDBC Driver** field and when the driver selection dialog appears we click on **OK** to accept the default choice of the **ODI JDBC Driver for XML**.

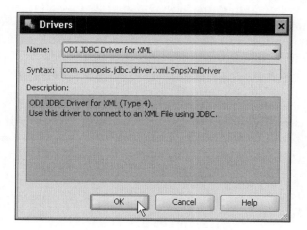

4. Next we click on the browse icon to the right of the **JDBC Url** field to open the **URL examples** dialog.

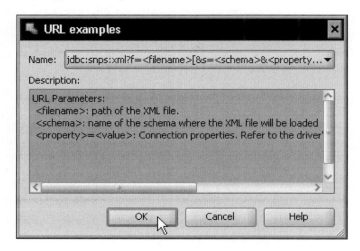

The URL parameters description mentions the **f=** parameter for the filename and the **s=** parameter for the name of the relational schema that the ODI XML driver will create in memory and it also hints that there are a number of other parameters that could also be specified. This is very true, but we're going to use only one of those additional parameters, that being the **d=** parameter, which specifies the location of the DTD or XSD document that specifies the definition of the XML schema being used by the data file.

We click on **OK** to accept the default example URL template.

5. We modify the **JDBC Url** field to reflect the location of the XML and XSD files. We also choose to call the schema XMLPO (s= parameter):
   jdbc:snps:xml?f=C:/po/input/order_20001.xml&d=c:/po/
   xmlschemas/po.xsd&s=XMLPO.

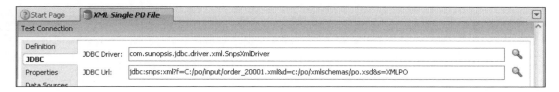

This means that we'll be accessing `C:\po\input\order_20001.xml` file (remember the Java preference for forward slashes for folder separators), using a definition of an XML schema held in `C:\po\xmlschemas\po.xsd` and the driver will create an in-memory area at the ODI Agent level that it will refer to as the **XMLPO** schema and create our relational representations of the XML data in there.

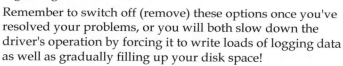

Obtaining log information from the ODI XML JDBC driver

If the Test Connection operation were to fail by raising an error, we can add another couple of JDBC URL parameters to switch on driver logging and specify a log file to which it will write. For example, adding the text, `&ll=255&lf=c:/po/input/xml.log`, to the end of the URL we've been using will set the log level to 255 (the most detailed level) and will write all entries to the `C:\po\input\xml.log` log file. This should help with diagnosing and resolving any problems we might have, or at the last resort will help any conversations with Oracle Technical Support about issues regarding our XML files.

Remember to switch off (remove) these options once you've resolved your problems, or you will both slow down the driver's operation by forcing it to write loads of logging data as well as gradually filling up your disk space!

6. We click on **Save All** and dismiss the informational dialog about creating a Physical Schema—we'll do that soon. For now we click on the **Test Connection** button in the Data Server editor's toolbar. After a slight pause we see a **Successful Connection** informational dialog appear.

It's useful here to reflect on what happened in that *slight pause*. The XML driver opened up the XSD file we referenced in the connection URL and used the structure defined within it to create a table (just one in this case) in an in-memory area that it created and called **XMLPO**; it then loaded the data from the XML file into that table. From here on the XML driver will be using the in-memory data until and unless we instruct it to do otherwise. This means that the **Test Connection** check is extremely thorough—it checks that the XSD (or DTD) schema is valid and also checks that the data held in the XML file conforms to that schema.

7. Now that we have a successful connection we close the Data Server editor tab.

8. We expand the **XML** technology node and right-click on the new data server to create a **New Physical Schema**.

9. In the Physical Schema editor that appears we use the drop-down lists to select the newly created in-memory schema **XMLPO** for both the **Schema (Schema)** and **Schema (Work Schema)** values.

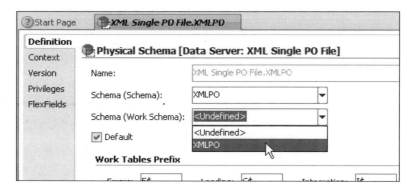

10. Finally we click on the **Context** tab and add a new Logical Schema reference for the **Global** context, typing in the name XML PO (and hit the *Enter* key). We click on **Save All** and close the Schema Editor tab.

Reverse-engineering the metadata

Next we'll reverse-engineer the XML file to create a new model for the data that we're going to integrate. The process to create a model is as follows:

1. We switch to the **Designer** navigator tab and add a **New Model**, calling it XML Single PO and we select the **XML** technology: the XML PO Logical Schema will automatically be selected for us as it's the only compatible one defined so far. We click on the **Selective Reverse-Engineering** tab and then click on the checkboxes to select **Selective Reverse-Engineering** (the **New Datastores** box should automatically get checked) and to view the **Objects to Reverse Engineer**. A table called PURCHASEORDER can be reversed, so we select it, click on the **Reverse Engineer** button in the Model editor's toolbar and close the Model editor tab.

2. In the Models accordion pane, we expand the **XML Single PO** model, double-click on the **PURCHASEORDER** datastore node to open up the Datastore editor, and then click on the **Columns** tab.

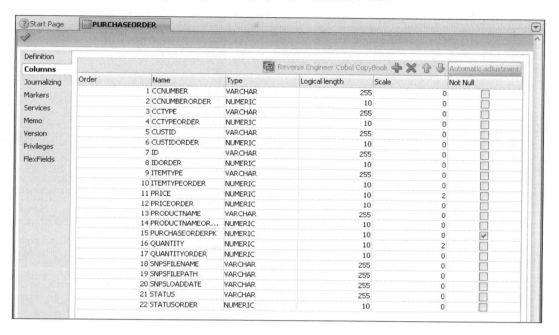

We can see that all the columns appear in alphabetical order, with each of the data columns having a corresponding numbered **ORDER** column which will indicate the actual order in which the elements appear in the XML file. There's also a **PURCHASEORDERPK** column been added to ensure that ODI can distinguish between XML records that may have identical information (there is nothing to stop this in XML data) — this column being marked as **Not Null**. Three additional columns have been added, all with a prefix of SNPS (a hangover from "Sunopsis" days): these columns hold information about the filename, path, and time when the file was accessed to retrieve this data (which was when we tested the connection).

We can also see that all the XML "string" type columns are reverse-engineered as VARCHAR(255) in our model and all the "decimal" type columns are translated to NUMERIC(10,2). We can anticipate that when mapping from some of these source columns to corresponding columns in our target that have types such as VARCHAR2(30) or NUMBER with no decimal places that we're likely to receive warnings.

We could change these column definitions here and save our changes to avoid those warnings, but for now we just close the Model editor without altering any details.

 There is a case sensitivity parameter that we could have set in the connection URL for the driver. Since we didn't set this parameter, we're seeing the default behavior of all datastore and column names being in uppercase.

Creating the Interface

We're done with the metadata, so we need to start to create an interface to move the data.

1. We create a **New Project**, called **Chapter 9**, save it, and close the Project editor.

2. Within **First Folder** in the **Chapter 9** project, we create a **New Interface**, call it **Load Single PURCHASE_ORDER**, and move to the **Mapping** tab.

3. We drag-and-drop the PURCHASE_ORDER datastore from the Oracle DataMart model as the target and the PURCHASEORDER datastore from the XML Single PO model as the source, accepting automatic mapping.

4. We notice that a couple of yellow warning triangles have appeared next to two out of the three mappings that ODI automatically created. We click on the matching warning symbol above the sources area to see what these mean.

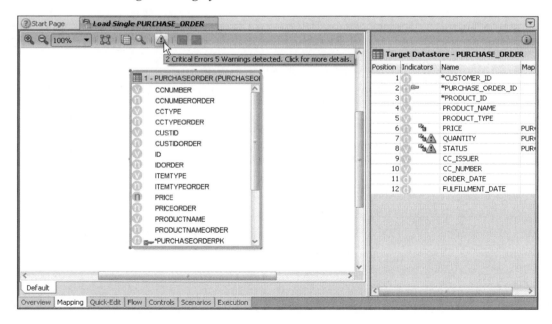

5. The top two messages in the dialog that appears (if we scroll across) inform us that the warnings for the two fields that we have mapped relate to the possibility of data being truncated. In the case of the STATUS column, it's because the default field length given from reverse-engineering an XML "string" type is 255 characters as we saw earlier, whereas our target column is considerably smaller. As we map the other "string" columns we'll see more warnings of this type. The QUANTITY column is specified as a "decimal" XML type and this is translated to be a number with up to two decimal places when reverse-engineered into ODI. The column we're mapping into is specified to have no decimal parts, so it's these that would be at risk of truncation in the interface. We'll simply ignore these warnings for this interface as none of our data will in fact be truncated.

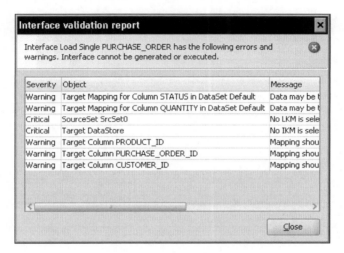

The next two messages—those with a **Critical** status—relate to Knowledge Modules not being selected for the interface and this is because we haven't imported any into this project yet. We'll address this soon.

The final three warning messages tell us that we're missing some mandatory mappings, which we will address next, so we can close the **Interface validation report** dialog.

6. Before we get carried away and start creating mappings too quickly, we need to take note of a couple of things:

    ○ The source CUST_ID and target CUSTOMER_ID columns are of different types, the former being a character string and the latter a number

    ○ The same distinction is true of the source ID and target PURCHASE_ORDER_ID columns

    ° We don't (yet) have any means to populate the PRODUCT_ID column, so we'll have to rectify that soon with a join or lookup

    ° There are a number of name mismatches (which is why automatic mapping didn't pick them up), such as ITEMTYPE mapping to PRODUCT_TYPE, CCTYPE mapping to CC_ISSUER

    ° The FULFILLMENT_DATE mapping needs to be left empty as we don't have that data yet

Bearing these points in mind, we create mappings for the CUSTOMER_ID and PURCHASE_ORDER_ID columns that use a TO_NUMBER() conversion function executed on the staging area. We then map the ORDER_DATE target column to SYSDATE, again on the staging area. The rest of the mappings (except obviously PRODUCT_ID and FULFILLMENT_DATE) can be created simply by drag-and-drop from the source column to the appropriate target column.

Target Datastore - PURCHASE_ORDER

Position	Indicators	Name	Mapping
1		*CUSTOMER_ID	TO_NUMBER(PURCHASEORDER.CUSTID)
2		*PURCHASE_ORDER_ID	TO_NUMBER(PURCHASEORDER.ID)
3		*PRODUCT_ID	
4		PRODUCT_NAME	PURCHASEORDER.PRODUCTNAME
5		PRODUCT_TYPE	PURCHASEORDER.ITEMTYPE
6		PRICE	PURCHASEORDER.PRICE
7		QUANTITY	PURCHASEORDER.QUANTITY
8		STATUS	PURCHASEORDER.STATUS
9		CC_ISSUER	PURCHASEORDER.CCTYPE
10		CC_NUMBER	PURCHASEORDER.CCNUMBER
11		ORDER_DATE	SYSDATE
12		FULFILLMENT_DATE	

> If we wished we could either use appropriate database functions in the mappings, or set the XML table's column width and scale settings at the datastore level to actually reflect our data to remove these warning symbols.

7. Next we need to add the PRODUCT_ID data, so we'll create a join with the PRODUCT table in the Oracle DataMart model to provide that data. We drag this datastore from the **Models** accordion panel into the sources area, accept automatic mapping to create the PRODUCT_ID mapping, and then create a join between the PURCHASEORDER and PRODUCT sources based on PURCHASEORDER.PRODUCTNAME=PRODUCT.PRODUCT_NAME.

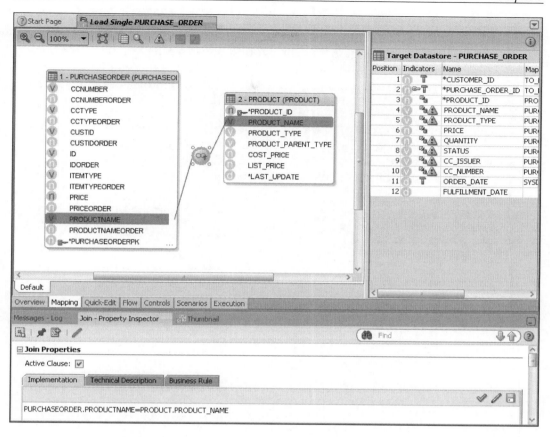

Before we go leaping ahead thinking that we've finished our mappings, we haven't addressed the requirements for the STATUS column in the target. If you remember, these require automatic approval for orders below $1000 and validation of the supplied credit card number if the order value is above this threshold. We have the quantity and price for each Purchase Order, so we can easily calculate the value, but within this interface we don't (yet) have access to the credit card's validation status—and we need to cope with the situation where a fictitious (or incorrect) card number is supplied.

If we simply create a default (inner) join between the PURCHASEORDER source and the data mart's CREDITCARD table, it will result in ODI ignoring any purchase orders where the given card number does not match one in our table of credit card data—which is most definitely not what we want to achieve. Instead we'll use an outer join, which will result in all the purchase orders being handled, but any credit card details that are missing due to unmatched numbers will be presented as null values.

1. We drag-and-drop the CREDITCARD datastore from the Oracle DataMart model into the sources area and create a join by dragging the CCNUMBER column of the PURCHASEORDER datastore and dropping it into the CCARD_NUMBER column of the CREDITCARD datastore.

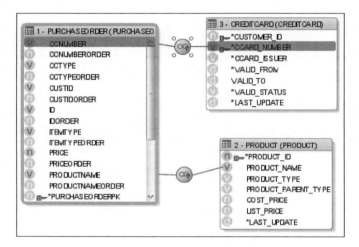

2. We click on the join symbol (it will highlight the joined columns as in the previous screenshot) and scroll down in the Property Inspector so that you can change the join type to a **Left Outer Join**. The description text will explain that all of the PURCHASEORDER rows will be included in the join, even if there is no matching CREDITCARD row.

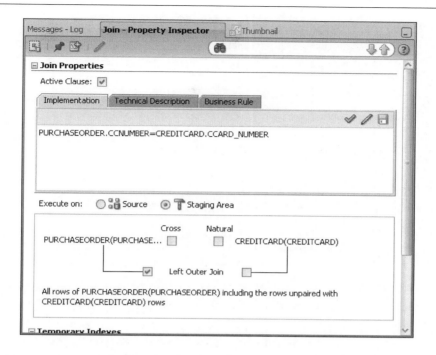

3. Now that we have all the data we need, we can correct the mapping for the STATUS column in the target table. We click on this column and set the mapping text to be:

```
case
  when PURCHASEORDER.QUANTITY * PURCHASEORDER.PRICE < 1000 then
    'Approved'
else
  case
    when CREDITCARD.VALID_STATUS = 'VALID' then 'Approved'
  else 'InvalidCreditCard'
  end
end
```

We mark the mapping to be performed on the staging area.

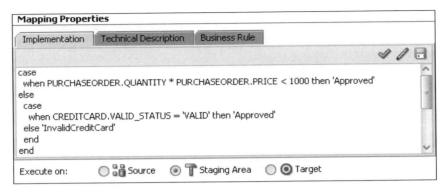

If we were going to use this mapping again later, it would be a candidate for a reusable user function, but we'll leave it as it is for this example.

4. We click on the Flow tab and click on each of the **Source** and **Target** box headers in turn, noting that for each of them the selected Knowledge Module is <Undefined>.

5. We right-click on the **Knowledge Modules** node in the **Projects** accordion panel within the **Chapter 9** project and choose **Import Knowledge Modules...**. We see a list of importable Knowledge Modules and choose CKM Oracle, IKM Oracle Incremental Update, and LKM SQL to SQL, then click on **OK** to import these three KMs.

6. Back in the Flow diagram, we click on the **Source** box header bar and then in the **Property Inspector** below the diagram we set the LKM to be LKM SQL to SQL.

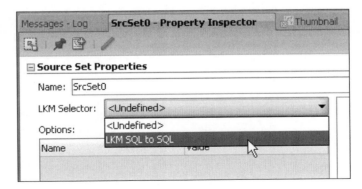

7. We perform a similar operation on the header of the **Target** box and set the IKM to be IKM Oracle Incremental Update.

8. Then we click on the **Controls** tab and set the **CKM Selector** value to CKM Oracle.

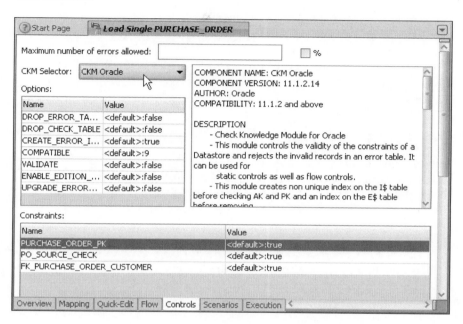

9. Finally we **Execute** the interface (accepting the execution defaults) and check that the data made it to the target table successfully using Operator.

Since the start of this chapter's sample exercise we have:

- Added Topology definitions for an XML data server to map onto our source file and the ODI Physical and Logical Schemas associated with it

- Reverse-engineered the XML file into an ODI model

- Used the datastore representing the XML file as a source in an interface to integrate the data into our source data mart

- Executed the interface and checked that the intended data was loaded into the target table

While we were doing this you may have noticed once more that once we had the model reverse-engineered into ODI, we could access XML data in exactly the same way as RDBMS or flat-file data.

However, it is also the case (similar to the flat files we were dealing with in the previous chapter) that the file name is hardcoded either in the Topology definitions (for XML files) or in the datastore definitions (for flat files). So what do we do if we have multiple XML files that all need to be integrated, like for our Order Processing situation? Having separate data server definitions in our Topology for each and every XML file is unwieldy and totally impractical.

In practice there are multiple ways this can be addressed, but we're going to look at a simple approach next that also highlights a very important factor when dealing with XML files in ODI (remember we left a thought *hanging*). The approach we're going to take exploits ODI Procedures to do some file manipulation.

Creating procedures

Imagine if you had your XML Data Server definition set up using a fixed, but dummy filename and you copied or renamed each of the desired source files in turn to have the right name to be picked up by the Data Server definition. We'll go through the following steps to create a procedure which will copy and rename our XML files:

1. In ODI Studio, we switch back to the **Topology** navigator tab and open the **XML Single PO File** data server entry for editing. On the **JDBC** tab, we change the **f=** parameter to refer to the `c:/po/input/single_po.xml` file.

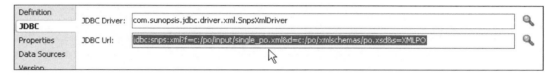

2. We switch to the **Designer** navigator tab and in **First Folder** within **Chapter 9** project we create a **New Procedure**.

3. In the Procedure editor we set the name to `CopyXMLOrderForInput` on the **Definition** tab and leave the source and target technologies as `<Undefined>`.

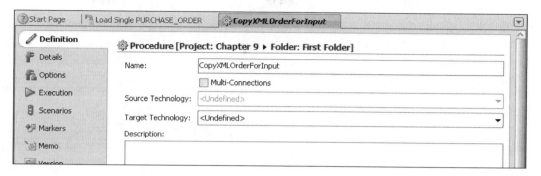

4. We then click on the **Details** tab and add a new command step by clicking on the green plus sign above the (currently empty) command list.

5. In the **Command** tab that opens, we name the command `Copy XML PO File`, in the **Command on Target** subtab we set the **Technology** to **ODI Tools** and enter the following text (all on one line) in the **Command** field leaving all the other values as they are:

```
OdiFileCopy -FILE=c:/po/input/order_20001.xml
  -TOFILE=c:/po/input/single_po.xml -CASESENS=yes
```

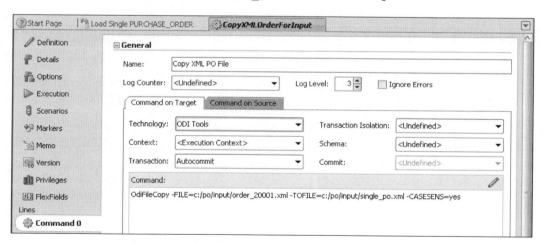

 `OdiFileCopy` is an ODI Tool, which we'll cover in the next chapter along with the packages.

6. We save our work and click on the **Execute** button in the main ODI Studio toolbar using the default settings. After execution we can see that a new `single_po.xml` file has been created in the `C:\po\input` directory.

This approach is still not going to work because we hardcoded the original file name in the text of our procedure. What we need to do is pass in the original filename as a parameter, in this case we'll use a Procedure option.

7. We expand the **Procedures** node in **Chapter 9 | First Folder**, right-click on our new procedure's node and select **New Option**.

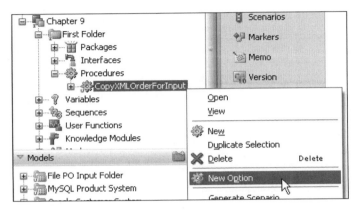

8. We call the option `POSourceFileName`, set its **Type** to **Value**, its **Position** to `0`, and its **Default Value** to `C:/po/input/order_20001.xml`.

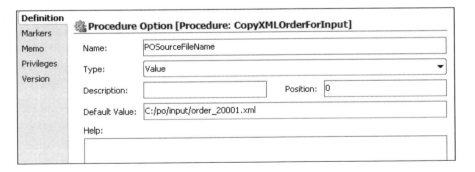

9. Next we need to alter the procedure so that it uses the value of the option rather than our hardcoded source filename, so we save all our work, close the Option editor and back in the procedure command field we change the first parameter passed to the `OdiFileCopy` command to be:

```
-FILE=<%=odiRef.getOption("POSourceFileName")%>
```

getOption() is an ODI substitution method which substitutes the value of the option at execution time into the code generated by ODI. In our example it will return the source filename that we're going to copy into our "known" location which we set in our topology definition.

There are many more substitution methods which can be used to create generic code in ODI. Their documentation is part of the *Knowledge Module's Developer Guide* which can be found (at the time of writing) at http://www.oracle.com/technetwork/middleware/data-integrator/documentation/index.html

Now what would happen if we changed the default value of our procedure to use a different XML file such as C:/po/input/order_20002.xml? If we were to re-execute our procedure with this new value and then look at the data in Designer, we would still see the data from the previous file (C:/po/input/order_20001.xml).

Recall that the XML driver loads data into an in-memory area for manipulation. Well we've done nothing to force the driver to reload its in-memory data from the file so it's still running off the old data. We need to create a new Procedure so that ODI can refresh the in-memory data.

10. We create a **New Procedure** called RefreshSingleOrderData and on the **Details** tab add a new command. We call the command Synchronize From File, set the **Technology** for the **Command on Target** to be **XML**, the **Schema** to be **XML PO**, and enter the **Command** text, SYNCHRONIZE FROM FILE, as shown in the following screenshot:

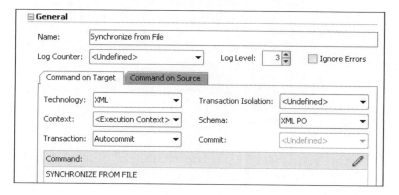

11. We save and execute this procedure and then view the data in the XML PURCHASEORDER datastore again. This time we can see the data from the new XML file.

When integrating this last file we've seen three things:

- Changing the contents of an XML file doesn't automatically change the contents of the in-memory representation of the file that the ODI XML driver holds (and the reverse is also true). This is one of those things that can occasionally "bite" if you don't watch out.

- There are times when it is necessary (not just desirable) to perform a predictable sequence of operations, even just to integrate data into a single table:
  - ° Renaming/copying a file
  - ° Synchronizing with that file
  - ° Running an interface to integrate the data it contains
  - ° Usually renaming/copying the processed file into an archival area

  We will cover this kind of orchestration in the next chapter when we examine ODI Packages and Load Plans.

- When running a procedure manually, the only way we could change the value of the Option (parameter) we created was to change its default value. What you'd expect to be able to do is use some kind of variable as the parameter and change the value of the variable based on some other processing. ODI variables can be used for that purpose, however variables in ODI *only* take on values inside a Package, a Scenario, or a Load Plan, so we won't be using them in this chapter.

 If you don't want to continuously have to copy XML files around (and if they're large, you would probably want to avoid this) you can in fact use an ODI variable in the Topology definition for the XML Data Server (in the connection URL) to represent all or part of the filename. This would mean that you could only connect to a new file, synchronize the data, and so on from within a Package, but for production running this isn't really a limitation because normally everything is run as part of a Package. Also be aware that this approach would *only* work if all the XML files have the *same structure*.

Summary

In this chapter we've successfully consumed XML files in our integration activities. Along the way we've explored a number of aspects of working with XML as well as some other extremely useful capabilities of ODI 11*g*:

- We've seen how XML Data Servers are associated with file references — both for the datafiles and their schema definitions and how, by using ODI Procedures, we can manipulate those files to enable a single data server access to multiple sets of file data.

  There are other, more sophisticated ways to achieve this, but at least we've covered enough to "get started".

- We took a look at how the XML driver breaks down a hierarchical tag structure from a file into a number of related in-memory tables and how it adds columns to maintain the ordering of entries and the relationships between them.

- We've experienced the separation between the file data and those in-memory tables and how care must be taken to ensure that these are synchronized if changes are made to one or the other.

- We also had our first glimpse at ODI Procedures and the requirement for sequencing (also known as orchestration) of data integration activities.

In the next chapter, we'll take a deeper look at the orchestration of data integration tasks and investigate some of ODI's comprehensive and flexible capabilities in this area.

10
Creating Workflows—
Packages and Load Plans

Once individual interfaces have been created, you will want to orchestrate their execution. Part of the orchestration will be the definition of the order in which the interfaces have to be executed, which elements will be executed in parallel or in a series, and which other operations you will want to add to your processes to make the overall orchestration more sophisticated. In this chapter, we will review three elements that will be needed to achieve these goals: Packages, Load Plans, and ODI Tools.

Packages

Packages are the basic element of orchestration in ODI. This is where you will sequence your interfaces, and define what operation to perform when a step (or interface) fails. One important point to keep in mind is that packages can be very sophisticated with the use of tools, but the execution of the different steps in a package is always sequential. For execution of steps in parallel, we will look into Load Plans a little further down in the chapter.

Creating a package

Since you cannot use an interface from a different project in a package, packages will be created in the same project as the interfaces.

Further, for the code to be easier to maintain, one approach is to organize interfaces and packages in a folder (and as many subfolders as needed) so that a folder only contains one package and the interfaces needed for that package. Interfaces that would be shared across packages can be grouped in a separate folder, still in the same project.

To create a package, go to the **Packages** entry under your folder, right-click on **Packages** and select **New Package**.

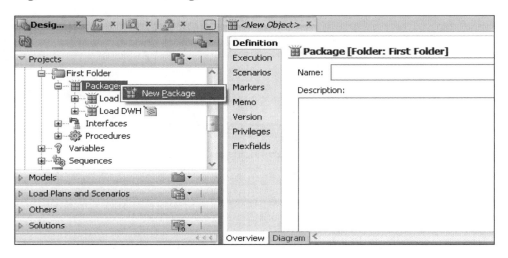

The very first task will be to name the package. You will not be able to save a package without a name. You then have to click on the **Diagram** tab at the bottom of the package definition to start designing your package.

Before we look into building a package, you need to be aware of some characteristics of packages:

- A package has only one entry point (or first step). The first step is marked with a green triangle at the bottom right of the icon of the step itself.

- Steps are sequenced in terms of successes (*Ok*, or green arrows) and errors (*Ko*, or red arrows). If a given step is successful, ODI will follow the green arrow to the next step. If the step fails, ODI will follow the red arrow to the next step (if any).

- If no arrow follows a step, the execution will stop. If that last step is successful, the entire package is successful. If that last step fails, then the entire package fails. One consequence is that if on one step you decide to have the green and red arrows point to the exact same next step, then errors in that step will basically be ignored.

Adding steps into a package

There are two ways to add steps in a package. You can either close the package and drag-and-drop the objects you want to add to the package on the package name in the tree view. If you add the objects in the order in which you want them sequenced in the package, ODI will do all the sequencing for you (the first object added will be the starting point and the green arrows are drawn for you from step to step).

The other approach is to open the package **Diagram** and to manually position the objects and draw the arrows to define the sequence of execution.

The objects that you can drag-and-drop on a package are interfaces, variables, procedures, scenarios, models, and tables.

Variables are outside of the scope of this chapter, but generally speaking different actions are possible for variables:

- **Declare variable**: Positioned at the beginning of the package, variables would receive values passed as parameters to the package

- **Refresh variable**: Run the SQL query associated with the variable to refresh its value

- **Evaluate variable**: Compare the variable value to some value (or other variable) and branch out following a *True* (Green) or *False* (Red) arrow

- **Set Variable**: Assign a value to a variable

Models and tables are used in packages to automate CDC operations (Changed Data Capture, or detection of changes on a system) — start CDC, stop CDC, and more advanced operations related to CDC.

Interfaces, procedures, and scenarios will be added to the package to define the order in which they will be executed. Tools will be added to enhance the workflow behavior. We will have more details on tools later in this chapter, but a few examples of tools would be detection of events, sending e-mails for notifications, or invoking operating system commands.

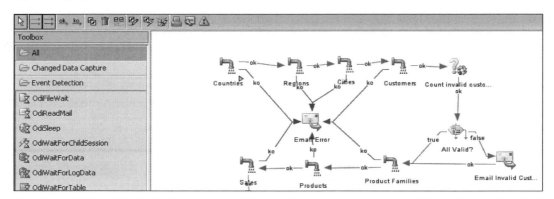

When a Package is designed manually, the ok arrows (success) and ko arrows (failure) must be drawn manually—change the cursor by clicking on the single green arrow or single red arrow in the toolbar. Then left-click on the first object (do not release the mouse button), drag the cursor to the next object in sequence and release the mouse button. The arrow will be drawn between both objects. If the arrow does not end up the way you want (releasing the mouse button would typically end up in an arrow that loops on the same object) you can simply repeat the operation—since there will be only one *Ok* (green) and one *Not Ok* (red) arrow per object, redrawing the arrow will replace the earlier definition.

You can also select the arrow and hit the *Delete* key on your keyboard to remove an invalid arrow if needed.

At run time, ODI will follow the "green" arrows as long as execution is successful. When an execution error is encountered, ODI will follow the "red" arrow. If an object has no arrow to follow, the execution will stop and the status of the entire package will be the same as the status of that last object: success or failure. In other words, if you do not process execution errors, the package ends in error.

Adding tools in a package

The most sophisticated of packages will leverage ODI tools. Outside of ODI tools, an ODI package does not do much more than what can be done with stored procedures in a database (except that thanks to the use of the graphical interface and KMs, you should be much more efficient at getting the job done). ODI tools can be organized in different categories: Changed Data Capture (CDC), Event Detection, Files, Internet, Metadata, ODI Objects, Plugins, SAP, and utilities.

Changed Data Capture

CDC tools will be used to allow the package to wait for new data in CDC tables. Other tools will force a refresh of the count of CDC tables (the journals) or investigate the journal tables.

Event Detection

Beyond CDC, other events can be detected: flat files detection, new e-mails, completion of other ODI scenarios, and so on, all very convenient for a more advanced orchestration than basic scheduling.

Files

File operations will include detection of new files on the operating system, moving, copying, deleting files, creating files (as a result of a SQL query or otherwise), zipping and unzipping files, and splitting and concatenating XML files. These operations will be very handy when file handling is a great part of the data integration process. For instance, detect that new files are available, archive them once they have been processed, and wait for more files to be available.

Internet

Often times, the data that must be processed has to be accessed remotely, or the result of the data integration process has to be pushed to a remote location. Web Services, FTP, SFTP, SCP, and e-mails can all be used to retrieve or send data.

Metadata

Metadata tools are rarely used as is in packages. They are commonly used in Reverse-engineering Knowledge Modules to import metadata from databases.

ODI Objects

These tools manipulate objects in the ODI repository (import, export, delete, and regenerate scenarios). They can be very useful to automate lifecycle management.

Plugins

The plugins are typically custom-coded tools. If you decide to create your own tools, they will appear in the Toolbox as Plugins.

SAP

One way to exchange data with SAP applications is to leverage IDocs files that are close to an XML format. Dedicated tools are provided to communicate with SAP by using actual XML files. The tools will translate XML to and from IDocs.

Utilities

A series of other tools are available to perform all sorts of operations: invoke operating system commands, beep, invoke the data quality tool, ping the ODI agent, purge the ODI logs, start a load plan or a scenario, and so on.

Adding tools to a package

When you click on the name of a tool in the toolbox, the mouse cursor will change into a crossbeam. From then on every click in the package will add a new instance of the tool. When you want to release the tool selection, click on the arrow cursor in the package toolbar. The mouse cursor will return to the default arrow. If you end up adding more instances of a tool than needed, click on the arrow cursor in the toolbar and select the extra tools. You can then either right-click on the icon and select **Delete** or hit the *Delete* key on your keyboard.

Using ODI Tools

When it is added to a package, each tool will display a grid where parameters can be entered (in the **General** tab).

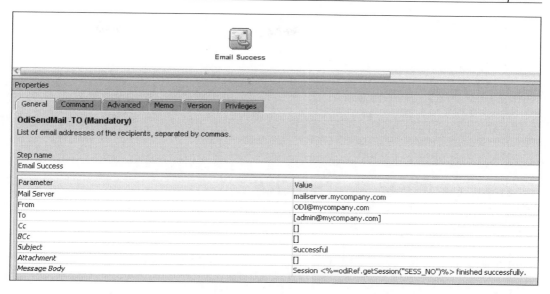

The grid will help with a contextual list of possible values for each parameter. The **Command** tab will display an API version of the same command. This API version can be used in procedures when the technology for a given step is set to **ODI Tools**. You can set and modify the parameters in either the **General** view, or the **Command** view.

Retry versus fail

Every step of a package can be defined so that in case of error the step is tried again for a certain number of times before failing (or before going down the path of a "red" arrow).

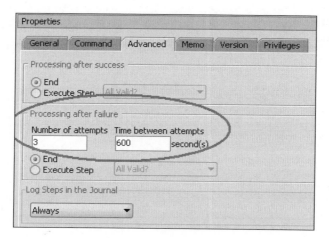

If you click on any of the steps, the properties window will have an **Advanced** tab. In the **Processing after failure** portion of the window, you can enter the **Number of attempts** and the **Time between attempts** (expressed in seconds) that you want to wait before trying again.

This feature can be extremely useful if you know that one of your connections is prone to failure when you are supposed to process the data. You can have ODI keep trying to process during the expected downtime. If the downtime exceeds the normal duration you can error out—and typically send a notification to some administrator.

Best practice: No infinite loop

You will quickly notice that it is easy—and convenient—to define loops into your packages. One point to pay attention to though is as long as the package is running, the same job generates new steps in the Operator logs and this job cannot be purged until it is completed. For the sanity of your logs—and to make it possible for human operators to understand what is happening—remember to never have an infinite loop in your packages. Packages must finish eventually. What you can do though is use the tool ODIStartScen and start the same scenario asynchronously (the scenario is a compiled version of the package—more on this will be covered in the following section). An asynchronous call means that you will fire up a new process and continue. If this is your last step, the package finishes. If you start the scenario with version "-1" you will always execute the latest version of that scenario.

Generating a scenario from a package

The scenario is the "compiled" version of the package. More accurately, it is a frozen version of the package where the code has been pre-generated. Only the topology information has not been defined, so that it can be updated based on the context selected at execution time.

To generate a scenario, right-click on the package name in the tree.

A scenario is made up of a name and a version. ODI will automatically increment the scenario version with each scenario generation from the package. You can of course modify the version number as needed: if ODI increments from 1.1 to 1.2 and you would rather increment to 2.0, you can definitely do so by overwriting the version number.

If you want to regenerate a scenario and overwrite its previous definition, you have to right-click on the scenario itself and select **Regenerate Scenario**. ODI will refuse to overwrite a scenario with the same name and version number if you are generating from the package name.

Load Plans

As we have seen so far, packages only handle serialized execution. Each step executes after the previous one and before the next. Load Plans will bring additional functionalities that will allow for more advanced orchestration of the processes.

Serial and parallel steps

When a Load Plan is defined, the first operation is to define if steps will be executed in sequence or in parallel. You can obviously mix and match serialized and parallel branches as needed.

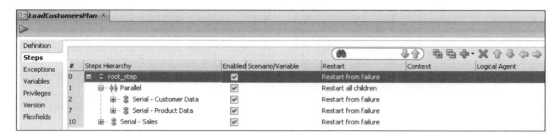

In the previous example, we will load our *Customer* data and our *Product* data in parallel, since there is no dependency between these two sets. Each set can be made of several steps that can be, in turn, executed in a serialized or parallel fashion. You can see here that steps in each set are executed in sequence. When both sets are completed, we then process our *Sales* data. This step is serialized because it is dependent on both customer and product data.

Objects that can be used in a Load Plan

The following objects can be used in a Load Plan:

- Scenarios
- Interfaces
- Variables (in particular to use as decision points with a "case…when…" syntax)

These objects can be dragged from the **Projects** tree on the left directly into the Load Plan to create a new step. However, whenever an object is added to a Load Plan, what is added is a scenario generated from this object. If you add an Interface or a Variable, ODI will automatically generate a scenario and add this scenario in the Load Plan. This means that if you perform changes to the object after it has been added to the Load Plan, you will have to either regenerate the scenario, or generate a new version of the scenario and edit the version number in the load plan. One way to limit the amount of edits is to use "-1" for the version number, so that the load plan always uses the most current version of the scenarios.

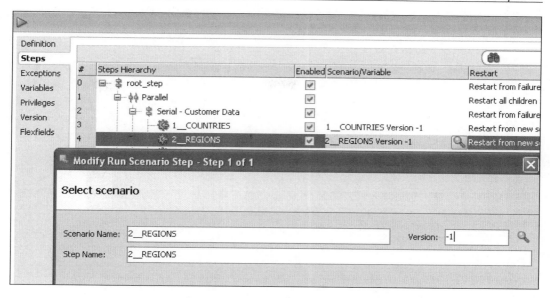

To modify the version of a scenario that will be executed in a Load Plan, click on the Load Plan step; a magnifying glass will appear. Click on the magnifying glass to edit the version number.

You can also right-click on a step to modify its references: regenerate the scenario that is currently used, or update the scenario version to the latest one that has been generated.

Exception handling

Exception handling can be quite complex and there is a need to go beyond what is offered by packages. The default behavior in a package is to restart a package from the last point of failure. This is very good in a sequential execution, but when processes start to invoke other processes and run in parallel, restarting a job gets to be trickier. Do you want to restart from the point of failure, or to restart the entire step? Or maybe the entire branch?

Load Plans allow you to specify for each step what the behavior must be in case of an exception.

In addition to choosing the restart point, you can also define ODI behavior in case of error in each step.

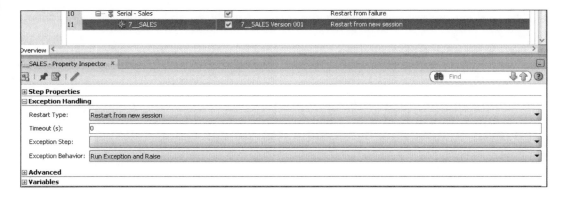

As shown in the previous screenshot, the properties panel lets you choose for each step of the Load Plan an **Exception Step** to execute in case of failure. Raising an exception (which would stop the process) can be set to **Raise** or **Ignore**. **Raise** will stop the execution and report an error in the operator window.

Exception steps are defined in the **Exceptions** tab of the Load Plan.

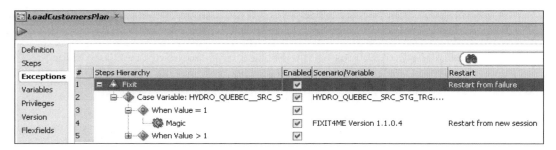

Rather than simply error out and wait for the operator to take some action, you can trigger all necessary actions immediately, whether you want to notify an operator or start some-self correcting process in the form of an ODI scenario.

Using Packages and Load Plans

Packages have a natural place in Load Plans: they can be used to define complex operations that are executed in sequence and multiple packages can be executed in parallel within a Load Plan.

Load Plans are "execution" objects. They can be created directly in the production environment if needed. However, Load Plans can be invoked by packages with a tool called OdiStartLoadPlan that is very similar to the tool used to start scenarios.

Summary

In this chapter, we have seen how to orchestrate processes in ODI, whether it is with packages or Load Plans. Both approaches offer different sets of benefits, from the sophistication of the processes in packages to the flexibility of the Load Plans. By combining both, you will be able to orchestrate the most advanced deployments for your data integration projects.

11
Error Management

If only everything we developed and used worked perfectly each and every time! Unfortunately in the real world the topic of error management — how to discover, diagnose and correct errors — is a fundamental part of "business as usual" operations. It's also one of those areas of knowledge and skill which constantly grows with experience and familiarity with a product or system.

There are three main categories of errors and error management when it comes to ODI, namely:

- **Data errors**: These occur when we encounter "bad" data during data integration tasks. This subject area covers ODI's error tables, detecting and diverting non-compliant records, and correcting and recycling error records — essentially ODI's basic data quality capabilities and mechanisms.

- **Execution errors**: These occur when one or more steps in an interface, procedure, package, or scenario fail to complete successfully. We've already spent some time looking at execution logs in Operator Navigator of ODI Studio and seen the use of error paths in package orchestration flows, so we'll only have a brief recap here.

- **Operational errors**: These arise if one or more of the underlying platform-level or infrastructure components encounter some kind of exception. This area forms part of management and monitoring, especially locating and viewing system component (for example, ODI Agent) log files and is primarily described in a later chapter, although we'll cover a high-level overview here.

So it's the first category of error management listed previously that is the main focus in this chapter. The major topics we'll cover are:

- Detecting and diverting data errors in ODI
- Correcting and recycling those data errors

Managing data errors

Data errors in the context of ODI refer to records that do not conform to a set of keys, constraints, references, and conditions that describe the values, patterns, uniqueness, and relationships we require of that data. Examples in the context of an Order Processing scenario include:

- An order where the customer ID is incorrect or missing
- An order where the customer ID exists and is correct, but the corresponding customer record has an incorrect or missing reference to a sales person or partner to whom we can pay commission as the source of the sale

What we're really dealing with here is a basic level of data quality enforcement.

Detecting and diverting data errors

The first step in managing errors of any kind is to identify when they arise and isolate their effects. When dealing with data quality we typically want data that does not comply with our quality rules to be temporarily diverted into some kind of holding area (occasionally called an "error hospital") where corrections can be applied before the amended data can be re-introduced into the main environment. But first we need to detect the violations of our quality rules.

Data quality with ODI constraints

So how can we spot the data errors listed earlier? We would need to specify the required quality characteristics of the data we integrate into a data mart by setting ODI constraints on the target tables we populate. We would then detect and divert the non-compliant records by making sure that an appropriate Check Knowledge Module is specified in the interface performing the data integration and trigger its use by setting the FLOW_CONTROL option of the Integration Knowledge Module to true.

If instead we simply add the constraints to the underlying database schema, what would happen? Well, if we don't reverse-engineer those constraints into the ODI models for the amended database tables, ODI would be unaware of the additional data integrity requirements and would try to insert or update records into the database tables which would trigger errors. Those errors raised would have been database errors, which would cause the whole insert, update, or merge database statement to fail. The only sensible steps for ODI to take when it receives a database error are to halt its processing immediately and mark the accompanying session as having failed.

Remember that ODI performs set-based SQL operations which either succeed or fail in their entirety, as opposed to the conventional approach of row-by-row processing where the same rule may be applied, but at the row level, allowing the appropriate action to be taken, but in a slower overall way.

The key point is that even one "bad" column value in one record could stop the whole set of data from being integrated into the desired target.

It's not often that you want one mistyped entry on an order to stop your complete sales Order Processing system in its tracks. So by taking the approach of adding the constraints into the ODI model for the corresponding tables, we enable ODI to detect which of all the records being integrated don't comply with the quality rules, allow all of the other records to continue to be processed normally, and only divert the non-compliant records into some kind of error hospital.

Ideally we would want to have the quality rules applied directly in the database and in ODI, so that we still see the error handling behavior of ODI; but the data is protected from corruption by other systems, applications, or direct access. This can be achieved by adding the new constraints to the underlying tables and then repeating the reverse-engineering process for ODI, making sure that the **Existing Datastores** checkbox is selected in the **Selective Reverse-Engineering** tab to enable incremental reverse-engineering.

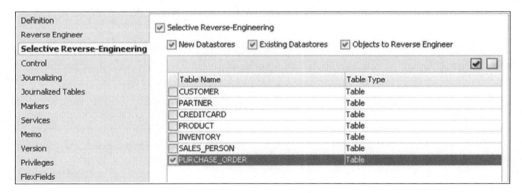

In our example, as seen in the preceding screenshot, we have selected the PURCHASE_ORDER table to be reverse-engineered into the current data model.

Incremental reverse-engineering in ODI

Reverse-engineering in ODI is purely additive: if we were to *drop* a column or constraint on the underlying table, this would *not* be reflected in the ODI model of that table, so care must be taken when taking this course of action. (The underlying reason for not dropping metadata information from a datastore is that such an action might easily break interfaces which are currently referencing the datastore in question. Therefore, deleting existing metadata becomes a manual process.)

Furthermore, if a database object (constraint, index, and column) has been renamed since the time when the datastore was first modeled, then there is a potential for a "doubling" of metadata elements.

There may be circumstances where you cannot have the constraints defined both in the database and in ODI. For example, you may not have the privileges to edit the database metadata. This is where ODI has an advantage because ODI constraints are defined at the metadata level, so in some circumstances ODI is able to impose a higher level of quality on the data than the database itself.

There are three types of ODI constraints:

- **Keys** correspond to primary keys, alternate keys, or indexes in the ODI metadata.
- **References** represent foreign keys which link two datastores together.
- **Conditions** are business rules expressed in SQL which are used to validate the data in the datastore. It is possible to set a specific error message per condition. This error message will appear in the error tables along with the invalid records.

ODI constraints are created at the datastore level in Designer Navigator as you can see in the following screenshot.

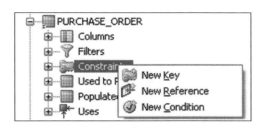

Remember that adding new constraints in the ODI metadata will not impact the underlying database. In case you would like to reflect the modifications you made in ODI at the database level, it is possible to generate a Procedure containing the DDL statements. This can be done from a model using the Generate DDL menu item.

ODI error table prefix

We saw how we could view the errors that had been diverted out of the integration flow of the interface by right-clicking on the datastore in the Models accordion pane in ODI Studio and selecting **Control | Errors**, but where are those errors actually held?

You may remember from previous chapters that when we set up the topology details of a physical schema, there are some **Work Table Prefix** fields just below where the schema names are specified.

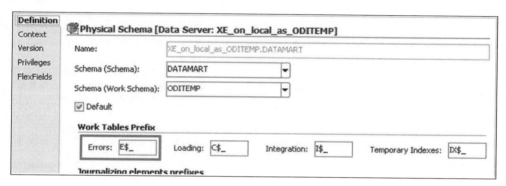

As you can see in the preceding screenshot, the prefix for the table that contains errors is **E$_** and it is the default prefix. Therefore if data errors are detected by the CKM when loading a CUSTOMER table in our DATAMART physical data schema, those errors will be diverted into a table called E$_CUSTOMER located in the ODITEMP schema since that's our chosen work schema name.

We can also see that these fields are not greyed out (unlike the automatically created ODI schema name), so if we desired we could change these prefixes. Indeed, there are some systems and programs that have problems accessing tables that include characters such as $ in their names. So if we wanted to use one of these programs or systems directly to read the error records from our error tables to correct those errors, we would have to change the prefix to something else, such as ERR_. The ODI Knowledge Modules and ODI Studio environment pick up these prefixes internally by using substitution methods, so changing a prefix should not normally damage ODI's behavior.

> Be aware when changing prefixes, some databases have a maximum length that can be used for table names. Do not use excessively long prefixes or you may introduce unexpected problems in ODI's operation.

Contents of an error table

ODI error tables have a structure that includes all the columns and definitions of the corresponding data table with additional columns to record information such as whether the error was detected during static or flow control ("S" or "F" error types), the message associated with the error, the check date, the originating ODI object (the interface or scenario that raised the error), constraint name and type (for example, "FK" for a reference, "CK" for a condition), and the ODI session number that detected the error.

This additional information is used by ODI to identify which error rows are candidates for recycling when a specific interface or scenario is re-executed.

> Note that the structure of the 11*g* error tables is different from the 10*g* error tables, so existing error tables will need to be rebuilt to avoid 11*g* runtime failures. This can be done automatically using the UPGRADE_ERROR_TABLE option of the 11*g* CKMs.

Using flow control and static control

So far we have seen how to use flow control—non-compliant records have been diverted out of the integration flow before they ever reach the target datastore. As an alternative (or supplement) to this, the IKM can be configured to have the CKM perform a *static* check on the complete target table once the complete interface flow has been integrated into the target.

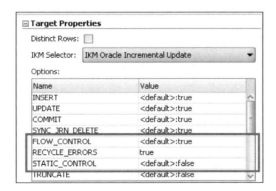

This is especially useful if the ODI constraints are more rigorous than those defined on the underlying database and where a data change may break constraints for existing data in the target table.

Say we have a table of employees with their employee IDs and a column that identifies their manager via their manager's ID. If you have an update where an employee's ID is changed (for whatever reason), their manager's ID may still be valid. However, if they also managed a number of other people, their team members' records would now have an invalid manager ID—despite the fact that those records themselves weren't changed at all.

When used in this way, static control also creates entries in the corresponding error table for the target of the interface. However, using flow control will mean that these records are diverted before they reach the target table. Static control leaves the non-compliant records in the target table and simply copies the record information into the error table. This is because ODI cannot be sure of the origin of those records and whether their removal will cause downstream errors or failures to other systems.

You can configure whether you want an individual constraint to be applied during flow control and/or static control by selecting checkboxes on the **Control** tab of the definition of the constraint on a datastore. The following is a screenshot of the **Control** tab of a constraint where you can see the two control checkboxes, namely, **Flow** and **Static**.

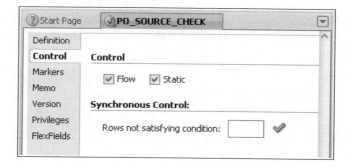

The **Synchronous Control** section shown in the previous screenshot allows ODI to simply count the number of records that violate the chosen constraint (which is expressed in the form of an SQL WHERE clause) when the tick is clicked. This kind of check does not add records to the corresponding error table. It is also valid to perform this kind of check for simple homogeneous conditions such as evaluating the uniqueness of a new key, or the number of records that fall outside a required value range.

Using error thresholds

While we probably don't want to halt an entire data integration process due to one piece of bad or missing data, we want to protect against flooding our error handling system if we receive a set of particularly poor quality or corrupted data. This is especially true if we're working with outside agencies and we have no control over the generation or extraction of the data that we are required to integrate into a data mart or data warehouse. For example, receiving a set of 90000 orders from a new partner's website might seem to be a welcome sales boost on the surface, but if every product ID in those orders is based on the partner's unique and proprietary coding system rather than the scheme that we rely on in-house, then we'd most likely end up with 90000 error records to deal with. It would probably be easiest and best in the long run to reject the whole batch and firm up our service level terms with that partner to specify which coding scheme must be used.

ODI allows us to guard against unusually poor quality source data by letting us place thresholds on the maximum number (or percentage) of non-compliant records it will divert into the error table before it places the whole interface execution into a failed state and suspends the processing of the session. The threshold value chosen for an interface is set in the **Control** tab of its definition, the same place where the CKM for the interface is specified. When selecting a threshold value, you may choose either a percentage or an absolute record count. When a percentage is indicated, this value will get checked after the whole set of conditions has been evaluated. However, when a specific number is specified, then as soon as the total number of errors after each check exceeds the threshold, execution is halted; a subtle but useful distinction when there is large volume of data or a large number of checks to be performed.

As you can see in the following screenshot, the threshold value can be set using the **Maximum number of errors allowed** field in the **Controls** panel of an interface.

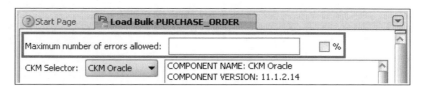

Correcting and recycling data errors

We know that we can set the difference between good and error records by adding constraints. We also know that we can apply these constraints and detect all the error records by using flow and/or static control in an interface. We also know where all the error records are stored. But what do we do about them?

The process of rectifying incorrect or missing data will depend on numerous factors, including:

- The "ownership" of the source data—if it comes from an outside agency, or direct from user or citizen input, and do you have the "right" to change it

- The nature of the data error—if it's missing or partially corrupt such as having one incorrect letter or digit), can it be found or inferred from elsewhere, and so on

- Whether the error is temporary

- Organizational policy—some organizations will have rules, some of which may be legally imposed upon them, when dealing with data corrections

These points will hopefully make it clear that the mechanisms and process for correcting errors form too wide a topic to be covered in this book. Indeed, this is one of those issues for which there is no single correct answer.

There will also be occasions where an error is only temporary and *doing nothing* to the error record is the correct policy. Say we process orders by integrating incoming data at several points during the day, but we only integrate customer data once each day at the start of operations. We're very likely to have orders arriving from new customers where the customer data doesn't exist in the data mart. However, all we have to do is wait until the next day, by which time the new customer data will have been added and then re-process the order data without change.

This latter case can be handled automatically by ODI by configuring the **RECYCLE_ ERRORS** option of an IKM to **TRUE**—as it was in the screenshot of the IKM options in the *Using flow control and static control* section. This simply signals to the IKM to extract the data from previous runs of the interface out of the error table for the interface target and re-insert it into the integration flow just before the flow control checks are performed. If the constraints are passed successfully the second (or later) time around, the data is integrated into the target without any further intervention. Note however, if any of the data integrity checks fail again during the next integration cycle, the offending data will once more be diverted into the error table.

This capability is also extremely useful when considering an overarching error correction process when dealing with ODI: if we correct the individual data errors in the error table (add missing fields, modify incorrect values, and so on) and have error recycling enabled, then the corrected records will automatically be integrated into the desired target on a subsequent run of the interface that originally detected and diverted the errors in the first place.

Generally speaking, it is not considered best practice to correct data errors solely by effecting changes to the data contained in the error tables without also attempting to get the source system(s) that provided the original data to make similar corrections. To do so will mean that the same non-compliant data could return and create the same errors sometime in the future.

The actual error modification can be performed by an external system — the important thing is that the error table is updated with those modifications.

There is an *Oracle By Example* tutorial available in the Fusion Middleware section of the Oracle Learning Library called "Creating an ODI Error Hospital that uses BPEL Human Workflow" (https://apex.oracle.com/pls/apex/f?p =44785:24:3481539500422101::NO:24:P24_CONTENT_ ID,P24_PREV_PAGE:4350,29) which shows the use of Oracle SOA Suite to orchestrate the correction and recycling of ODI errors. Although this example was built using the 10*g* versions of both Oracle SOA Suite and ODI, the principles hold true for the 11*g* versions of each product.

Recycling errors and ODI update keys

A short explanation of part of a mechanism used in ODI interfaces to uniquely identify each and every record will add clarity here.

ODI and the IKM being used in an interface must be able to identify individual records when integrating data into a target, for example to determine whether the record will result in an insert of a new record or an update of an existing row in the target table. This is achieved by making sure an update key exists for the target datastore.

By default, ODI extracts the update key information from the primary key definition of the datastore in the ODI model (originally reverse-engineered from the underlying database). If we want to add more columns to the update key we could alter the ODI metadata definition of the primary key constraint on the target datastore. We can even ignore the primary key definition altogether and choose a different update key or set of columns on the target datastore properties sheet of the mapping tab of the interface.

So when considering which records to re-insert into the integration flow, the IKM only extracts records from the error table that were caused by a previous execution of *the same interface or scenario* and also ensures that recycled error records do not clash with (that is have the same update key as) incoming records from the source datastore.

Precedence is given to the source records over the error records—it would be extremely annoying and somewhat confusing if you corrected the non-compliant data in the source table, re-executed the interface, and yet the previous error data continued to overwrite the newly corrected source data.

Managing execution errors

Execution errors can be categorized in a number of ways, but for the sake of simplicity we'll use a simple matrix to divide between design-time and run-time in one dimension, and anticipated versus unexpected in the other, to distinguish between the tools and approaches that are most likely to be used in each circumstance:

	Anticipated	Unexpected
Design-Time	Error path in ODI package or scenario	Operator Navigator in ODI Studio
Run-Time	Error path in ODI package used to build scenario	ODI Console

Handling anticipated errors

If we can anticipate that an error might occur, such as a database server being offline or unreachable, then we should be able to specify what should happen in the event of such an error. We should build our systems (ODI packages, scenarios, or load plans) to cope with this type of error.

The mechanism to use for this in ODI is the error (KO—or "not OK") path in the ODI Package editor. By using this technique we can send alerting e-mails, perform automated investigation or mitigation activities, and so on.

> An important point to remember is that if our post-error processing completes successfully (for example, the alert mail is correctly sent), then the session will be marked in the session log as having completed successfully. If we want the session to be marked as having failed, and this will depend on each organization's operational policy, then we will have to force the last step executed in a package (or its derived scenario) to fail.

Causing a deliberate benign error with OdiBeep

A "trick" frequently used to force a session to be marked as having failed is to use the OdiBeep tool step as the last activity in an error path. This tool step, found in the **Utilities** category in the Package editor, can take a sound file as a parameter value (using a `FILE=` syntax) and would normally play that sound file on the host executing the package or scenario.

However, if you deliberately specify an incorrect parameter on the **Command** tab for the step, the step will fail on execution—with no other adverse effects on system resources or data. It's probably best to rename the package step to reflect its intention.

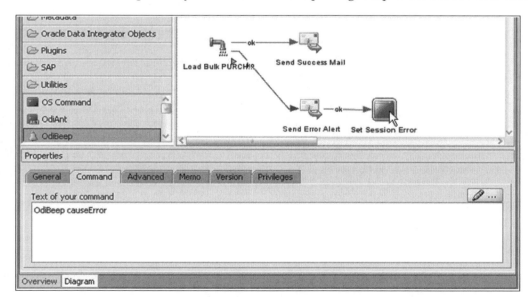

Handling unexpected design-time errors

We've already used the Operator Navigator of ODI Studio and seen that when data errors occur then the status indicator of an execution session is changed to show a warning symbol. You may already have seen what happens when a full error is encountered and the execution session fails:

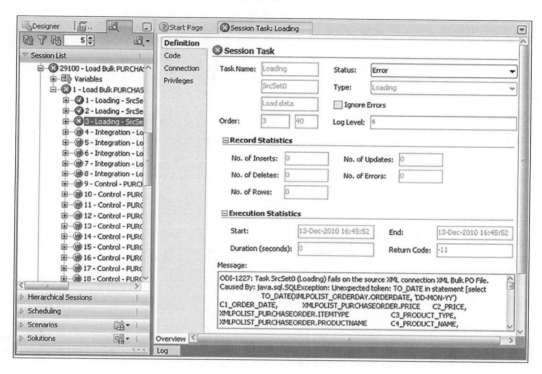

The previous screenshot shows a session that has failed. Drilling down into the session steps and opening up the failed session step reveals that the cause is the use of a TO_DATE function on an XML source data server (that is the in-memory engine). This is not altogether surprising because the mapping that uses this function should have been marked to be executed on the staging area, not the source — the source doesn't support this mapping syntax.

More detailed error investigation in Operator Navigator

What can you do if you have a less obvious error? The following screenshot shows an **Unexpected token** error (caused because we purposely selected the QUANTITY column twice):

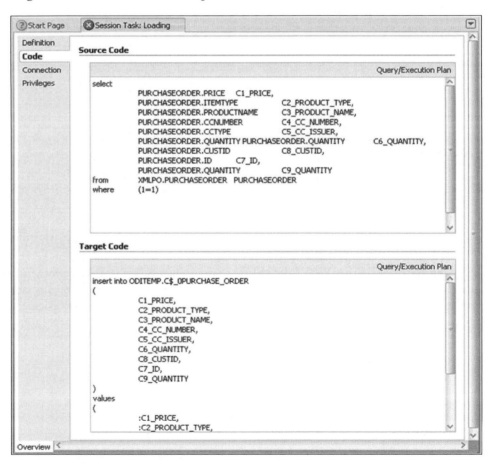

Clicking on the **Code** tab for the step reveals the actual code that was executed.

The original error message says the fault was detected on the source, so we know to check the code for that section. Sure enough we seem to have inadvertently dragged the PURCHASEORDER.QUANTITY column from our source datastore twice onto our target because it has a double entry (C6_QUANTITY and C9_QUANTITY) in the select statement.

That was an easy one to spot, but if something even more obscure occurs you can take advantage of an additional ODI capability. If you click on the **Query/Execution Plan** link you will see a SQL query window appear in which you can amend the code and execute the query to drill down into the true cause of any error and how to correct it.

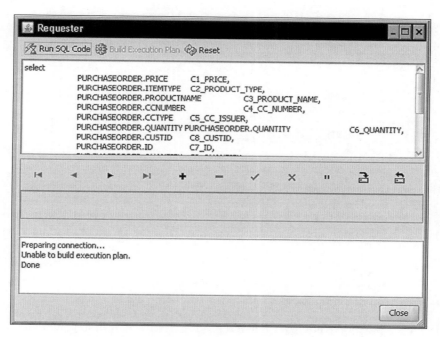

The execution plan cannot be built for the example query because there's a syntax error—which we already knew! If we were to remove the second reference to the PURCHASEORDER.QUANTITY column and click on **Run SQL Code** then we would see the returned records in the middle section of this dialog.

> Some errors can be detected even before execution by using the new ODI 11g *Simulation* feature in the ODI Studio. This feature sequentially generates all of the SQL statements that would be used during an actual execution of the specified interface.

If the error is a simple one to rectify in the SQL code (such as the one here) then you *can* change the code to be executed directly on the **Code** tab, save the session, and then restart the session (right-click on the session and choose **Restart**). Note that this should only be done during design-time unit testing as only the code in that specific session instance is changed.

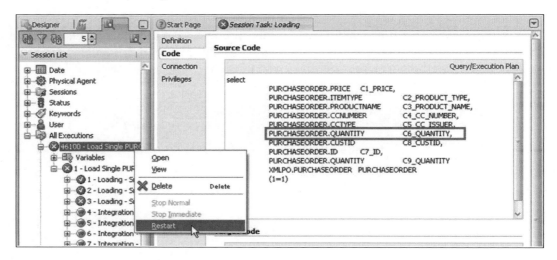

This approach generally works best if no other sessions have been run since the failure occurred. If the queries or session to be restarted rely on temporary tables that have been created in the early part of the scenario or interface execution, they will need to exist in the state when the failure occurred for the restart to work correctly.

> Although ODI provides this built-in SQL window, some external SQL tools like SQL*Plus provide better diagnostic messages — often highlighting the exact character position where a syntax error is found, so a good old cut and paste between tools is a not infrequent practice. Note that a cut and paste is not always possible without some additional editing since the source code at this point may contain some special characters or ODI variables.

Handling unexpected runtime errors

ODI Console, new with ODI 11*g*, is the tool that is the primary aid for diagnostics during runtime. ODI Console is a web-based application and it needs to be deployed to WebLogic Server in order to run. It can be accessed directly or via the Fusion Middleware Control element of Oracle Enterprise Manager that forms part of the Java EE installation of ODI 11*g*.

ODI Console is discussed in more depth in the next chapter, but it is useful here to see that it gives a similar view of the session execution log as the Operator Navigator in ODI Studio—albeit without the ability to use the SQL/Execution window or to alter session code (we're talking about a runtime environment here).

The drill-down is a little different from the Operator Navigator in that you highlight and view the parent session.

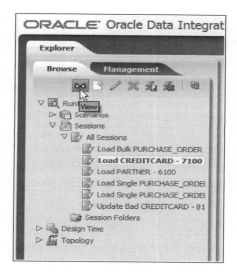

Then in the right-hand pane you scroll towards the bottom and click on the link on the desired session step.

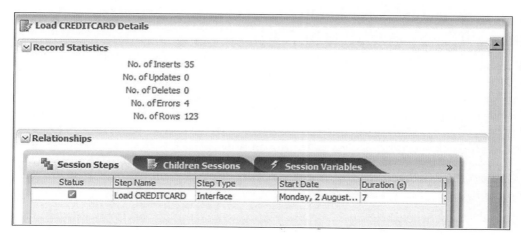

This in turn will show a list of each of the session step tasks (scroll to the bottom again).

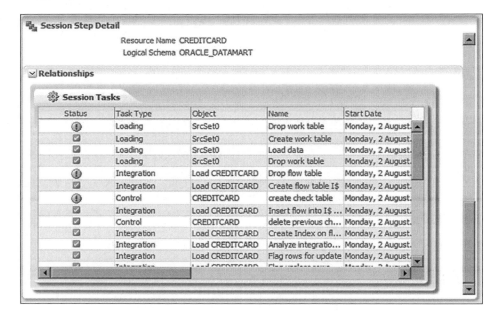

ODI Console also allows you to restart failed sessions. This is most likely to be of use when there has been some kind of temporary outage of a key source or target resource. In these situations a simple restart of the session will succeed, but it must be used with care in a production environment to ensure that unexpected results are not seen as a consequence. A session restart will most likely be subject to an organization's operational policies.

Handling operational errors

This category of error handling is covered in the next chapter, which is on management and monitoring. It involves the use of Fusion Middleware Control with the ODI plugin that is part of the Java EE installation components for ODI 11g. This allows the monitoring of ODI execution agents (both standalone and WebLogic-hosted) and also the availability of both Master and Work repositories. There is also a facility to view the log files for the various ODI platform components.

So rather than repeat ourselves, we'll leave further discussion of this topic to the next chapter.

Summary

In this chapter we've discussed two of the three main categories of error handling, namely, data errors and execution errors.

We saw that handling data errors forms part of a data quality policy and that rules governing data quality can be imposed through the use of ODI constraints, a Check Knowledge Module, and either Flow or Static Control (or indeed, both).

We also walked through the use of error recycling to demonstrate some of the capabilities of ODI 11g that can assist in this area of activity.

We also took a quick look at some of the design-time error diagnostic capabilities of ODI that can come in very useful during unit testing in an iterative development process.

12
Managing and Monitoring ODI Components

As we have seen throughout the book, Oracle Data Integrator is a robust and comprehensive platform for satisfying your data integration and data orchestration business and technical requirements. We will now turn our focus to ODI's management and monitoring capabilities—providing enterprise-ready task automation and rich visibility into your data and metadata.

The concepts and tasks covered in this chapter have three learning goals:

- Demonstrate the benefits and features of the built-in ODI Scheduler to manage and automate scenario execution

- Examine the capabilities and value of the **Enterprise Manager Fusion Middleware Control Console** integration for gaining visibility into the runtime infrastructure health of our data integration solution as well as key operational statistics

- Test drive the **ODI Console** web application which provides Data Lineage capabilities in addition to the ability to perform key functions of the thick client ODI Studio

Scheduling with Oracle Data Integrator

In this section, we illustrate by example how the out of the box ODI Scheduler user interface manages which scenarios are run at what scheduled time. ODI also provides a way to monitor the list of scenarios scheduled to run in the future. Schedule definitions support both simple (one time) and repetitive executions of a scenario. But you may ask, "What if my company has standardized on a third-party scheduling solution for automating tasks within my environment?"

Not to worry, we conclude this section with a discussion of options available for seamless integration of existing Scheduler solutions with ODI to satisfy the requirement of executing Scenarios or Load Plans on a scheduled basis.

Overview

Oracle Data Integrator satisfies the need for reliable and repeatable operations processes by providing an out of the box user interface for schedule management and automated execution of Scenarios or Load Plans. In addition, operations personnel are not locked into using the ODI Scheduler user interface for scheduling ODI tasks. ODI provides various facilities to enable third-party scheduling solutions to schedule and execute ODI tasks. ODI has a decoupled Scheduler architecture, separating scheduling data (Work Repository), schedule execution (Agent) and a programmable interface (web services, command line, and Java API) allowing third-party Schedulers to manage ODI runtime task execution.

The following figure illustrates the ODI Scheduler architecture:

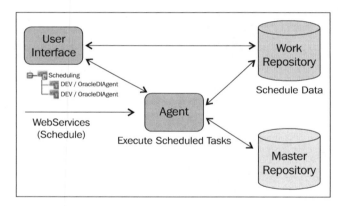

Before we illustrate the creation of scheduled tasks, it is important to understand what items can and cannot be scheduled as well as where schedule management resides within the user interface.

- When execution of ODI tasks are triggered outside the ODI Studio client software, what the Agent executes is an ODI **Scenario** or a **Load Plan**

- Unlike ODI 10*g* where there were separate agent types for schedule and non-schedule agents, ODI 11*g* has one and only one type of Agent—and it just happens to be able to schedule tasks

As project teams develop and validate ODI interfaces and packages during the development lifecycle, executable versions called scenarios are produced for release into production. The following ODI objects can be converted into a Scenario:

- Interface
- Package
- Procedure
- Variable

Load Plans are executable objects in ODI which help users orchestrate the execution of Scenarios, they were introduced in ODI 11.1.1.5.0. Load Plan steps can be executed in parallel or sequentially.

The best practice for a production Work repository is that only Scenarios or Load Plans are present, keeping the originating source objects only in pre-production Work repositories. The benefits of following this best practice process are:

- Eliminates changes/enhancements being made directly in production. ODI Studio does not show an interface mapping for an ODI interface or diagram for a package data workflow when opening a Scenario. Changes to the interface/package/procedure/variable must be made in another Work repository where the non-runtime only equivalents are present.

- Encourages the use of multiple environments during a data integration project lifecycle. To make a change to the runtime behavior of the Scenario in production, the change must be made in another environment that has more than just runtime versions deployed to the Work repository.

Automating Scenario generation

You may be asking yourself "Do I have to generate a scenario one at a time for each scenario I need in the production environment?" The good news is that the answer is no!

 ODI provides a tool for automating the generation of scenarios called **OdiGenerateAllScen**. Additional information on using OdiGenerateAllScen can be found in the ODI product documentation at http://docs.oracle.com/cd/E23943_01/integrate.1111/e12643/appendix_a.htm#CEGFHFIE.

It is also possible to generate or regenerate Scenarios using the Scenario generation wizard in ODI Studio at the Project or Folder levels within Designer.

Illustrating the schedule management user interface

To jumpstart your understanding of the ODI scheduling capabilities, we will illustrate an implementation of a commonly seen data integration scheduling requirement.

Creating a scheduled execution that will execute exactly once

In this illustration, an "exactly once" requirement is configured. The configuration maps to a one-time data load. In this example, we use the Load Sales Person interface we created in *Chapter 7, Working with Microsoft SQL Server*.

1. We create the Load Sales Person scenario from the **Load Sales Person** interface in Designer. We right click on the interface name and select **Generate Scenario**. We enter LOAD SALES PERSON AS SCENARIO as the scenario name and press **OK**.

2. Then we expand the tree control for the **Load Sales Person** interface. We see a node for **Scenarios** under **Load Sales Person**. We verify that an entry exists for **LOAD_SALES_PERSON_AS_SCENARIO Version 001** and expand the tree control for that entry.

3. We select and right click on the **Scheduling** node and select **New Scheduling**.

4. In the **Definition** tab, we make the following selections:
    ○ **Context:** Global
    ○ **Agent:** OracleDIAgent
    ○ Under the **Status** region of the finger tab dialog, we make the following modification:
        • **Active:** Selected
    ○ Under the **Executions** region of the finger tab dialog, we specify the following parameters:
        • **Simple:** Selected

- **Date**: We select today's date
- **Time**: We select a time within a few minutes of the present time

5. We select the **Execution Cycle** tab. Under the **Repetition** region, we select the None (Execute Once) radio button. No changes need to be made to the Constraints region of the dialog.

> **Creating a repeating scheduled execution**
>
> Under the Execution Cycle finger tab, we can also check **Many times** to create a repeating schedule. The maximum number of repetitions as well as the maximum cycle duration can be specified in this panel

6. We click on the save icon in the Designer Navigator icon toolbar and verify that a new scheduled entry appears under the **Scheduling** node of the **LOAD_SALES_PERSON_AS_SCENARIO Version 001** scenario.

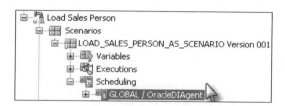

7. The schedule entry has been defined for the scenario, but is not yet visible to the OracleDIAgent agent. Schedule changes do not take effect immediately. After creating a schedule in ODI Studio, agents have their runtime schedule list updated during one of two events:

   ° A restart of the agent (stopping/starting the agent)

   ° The agent receives an update schedule request

8. We switch to Topology by selecting the Topology tab. We expand the **Physical Architecture** accordion view. Under **Agents**, we select and right-click on the **OracleDIAgent** agent, selecting **Update Schedule** on the pop-up menu.

9. A pop-up dialog appears. We click on the **Select All Work Repositories** checkbox and press the **OK** button. An **Information** dialog appears stating that the **Schedule update is complete**. Click on **OK**.

Quiz

True/False

If you want to stop a scenario execution scheduled for daily executions from executing a second time, one way to do that is stopping and restarting the ODI agent.

Answer: False. While daily execution of the scenario would not take place while the agent is stopped, all previously defined schedules within the valid start and stop times will be reloaded into the Agent and executed for valid scheduled times occurring after the restart of the Agent. An appropriate way to stop execution for a particular scenario that has one or more future executions scheduled would be to open the schedule nodes for that scenario and set them to inactive (**Status** region of the **Definition** tab). A red indicator is present on a schedule node that is presently set to inactive:

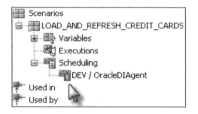

Using third-party schedulers

Situations can arise where using the built-in ODI 11*g* Scheduler is not an option (company-specific scheduling corporate standard or architecture directive). The ability of ODI to integrate with third-party schedulers is a known, understood, and addressed requirement. An external scheduler can use a command-line command or a web service interface to accomplish the task of executing a Scenario or a Load Plan.

Chapter 21, Running Integration Processes of the ODI Documentation describes in detail the use of a command line.

Boosting your productivity: Tips for entering remote scenario execution field names

Context: You may be tempted to enter the **Name:** of the execution Context in the ***Context** field. But the Context name shown in Topology Navigator is an alias for the Context code. The web service wants the Context code, which may not be the same as the text you entered for the **Name:** field when creating the Context in Topology Navigator. If you see a remote execution error stating invalid execution Context, go into Topology Navigator, expand the Context accordion view and open and view the Context in question. The field below the **Name:** field is the **Code:** field—make sure you enter the string matching the Context Code and not the Context Name. While they are usually the same, they do not have to be and has been observed as a source of execution errors.

Session Name: If an error message appears stating that the **ScenarioName** is the cause of the error (not found in Work repository), check for the correct use of the " _ " character rather than a blank character.

Scenario Version: If you get an error stating that the version does not exist in the Work repository, enter a three digit number rather than truncating leading zeros, that is, 001 rather than 1. The alternate entries of 1, 01, and 0001, all result in an error.

OdiUser: Do not confuse the Fusion Middleware Control Console userid with the OdiUser.

Fusion Middleware Console Control

Management and monitoring capabilities are required for virtually all enterprise class software projects. In addition, audit requirements have become increasingly important to businesses of all sizes.

ODI addresses management and monitoring requirements through integration with **Enterprise Manager Fusion Middleware Control Console (FMCC)**. The FMCC provides current visibility into the health and key performance and activity metrics for the ODI Agent, Master and Work repositories and integration with the ODI Console web application.

Taking a hands-on approach to the FMCC, the following FMCC features and capabilities are illustrated in this section:

- Illustrate how to launch and access the diverse and rich management and monitoring capabilities for an ODI domain
- Examine reports on the health, key performance, and activity metrics of the ODI runtime agent(s)
- Define once, control, and reconfigure anywhere
- Examine the ODI log files visibility and management within the FMCC

Launching and accessing the FMCC

The default landing page of the FMCC application can be accessed by entering the URL `http://<WebLogic Hostname>:port/em` in a web browser. The FMCC landing page can be used to quickly identify the health status (up/down) of the **Application Deployments** (including the ODI JEE agent), WebLogic domain, and ODI infrastructure. In the tree view navigation on the left, under **Application Deployments**, is a selectable link for **oraclediagent**—the deployed agent application on WebLogic. When selected, the Agent page shows everything you want to know about the JEE Agent runtime health, activity metrics, and published web services from the Agent (**OdiInvoke**) as well as a convenient ability to generate test web service invocations to **OdiInvoke**. More importantly the ODI infrastructure components are listed under the ODI folder including **Master Repository** under ODI with links to access the Work repositories and the various standalone or JEE agents deployed.

Domain

The named Domain page appears after clicking on the named domain entry under the **WebLogic Domain** folder in the **Fusion Middleware** region of the FMCC landing screen. Immediate and easy to locate information on the health of the admin server and core performance metrics are provided as well as information on **Clusters** and **Application Deployments**.

Administrative tasks available on the Domain page are available by selecting the WebLogic Domain menubar button located at the top left. Administrative tasks that can be performed in the FMCC web application directly from the Weblogic **Domain** drop-down in the upper left of the domain page include:

- Starting up or shutting down the Domain
- Port usage summary

- The ability to deploy/undeploy/redeploy an application
- Maintain security credentials/policies/roles
- Maintain JDBC sources

The percent of uptime, current status, and listen port of the WebLogic admin server are readily apparent.

It is possible to drill down on an ODI JEE agent deployment by clicking on its link (such as **oraclediagent** by default) under **Application Deployments** and take a look at the information and actions available when using FMCC to monitor and manage an agent.

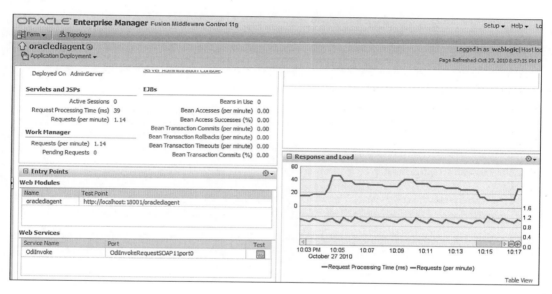

Agent

The Agent is at the heart of the ODI architecture, playing the key roles of a maestro and data movement conductor between data sources and targets and finishing the ODI code generation. While the ODI Agent is not a CPU intensive process, availability, network latency between the agent, sources and target, systems, as well as reasonable system and agent load volumes, are critical to success.

Of immediate interest on the deployed JEE agent page are **Requests (per minute)**, **Request Processing Time (ms)**, and available **Web Services (OdiInvoke)** with an accompanying **Test** button to test the web service.

Starting and stopping

In addition, the user has control to **Start Up** and **Shut Down** the Agent by selecting the **Application Deployment** drop-down in the upper left section and selecting **Control**.

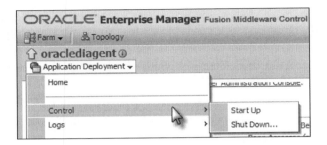

Performance summary

To display a graphical view of the Agent performance summary statistics by time, select **Application Deployment** under **oraclediagent**, and select **Performance Summary**.

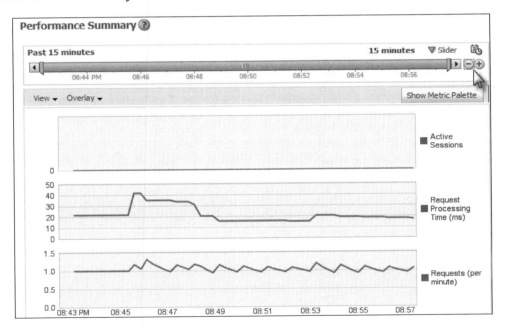

The duration of the **Performance Summary** graph can be increased or decreased by selecting the **-/+** zoom symbols at the upper right.

Log file visibility and aggregation

ODI Operator can have both real-time and historical consolidated views on multiple log files of interest by using the Fusion Middleware Control Console. The new consolidated log file viewer can access any deployed JEE Agent web application, WebLogic Server, ODI Console web application, and the FMCC web application log itself among others. This consolidated log view can help troubleshoot issues easily.

Visibility

When viewing the **Weblogic Domain** or **AdminServer** entries, the user can view and search log messages by selecting the **Logs | View Log Messages** entry from the WebLogic Application Server drop down at the top left of the screen. Additional and more comprehensive searches can also be performed by selecting **Broaden Target Scope** which provides the ability to view, search, and export resulting log file search result messages to a file. Selecting **Broaden Target Scope** provides a navigation entry point for consolidated log file viewing and searching across the hierarchies of manageable assets in the left hand tree view. Consolidated logs can also be viewed by selecting the **Farm** drop down and selecting **Logs | View Log Messages**.

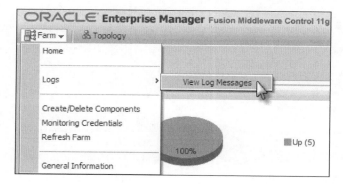

Aggregation

When selecting the **Farm | View Log Messages,** or selecting **Broaden Target Scope** from another view log file page within FMCC, the configurable search log page user interface is presented with a complete set of files to choose from when performing your search.

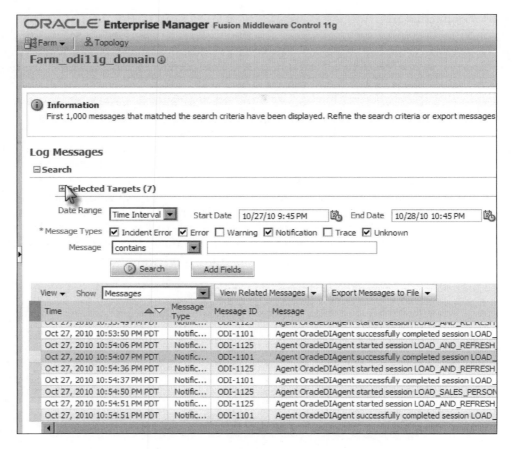

When pressing the **Search** button, the default logging configuration is executed for targets.

The ability to aggregate searches across many **Target Log Files** greatly improves the ODI users' productivity. Not only is the expansion of the **Selected Targets** useful for ensuring the proper entries are selected, the expanded dialog also has a much greater utility by itself. Here we have a well known landing pad for viewing the list of locations on disk for all of the ODI relevant **Selected Targets** on a given installation. Entire log files can also be viewed within FMCC.

Repository visibility

The FMCC also provides valuable and productive visibility into the data within the ODI Master and Work repositories. From the health of deployed agents to Session statistics, the FMCC frees ODI users from having to create custom one-off solutions for monitoring the health of their agents and having to bring up ODI Studio and Operator Navigator to view the results of a Session. The FMCC provides visibility into key physical assets of the ODI solution—the agents. In addition, given an agent, users can now view Load Plans executions and Session summary information.

Session statistics

Summary and detailed Session statistics are available in the FMCC. In addition, a well thought out capability for searching the contents of Session history is available. To get to the Session statistics search dialog, follow the given steps:

1. Select **MASTER REPOSITORY** under the Farm ODI folder:

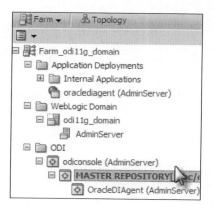

2. From the **Master Repository** drop-down, select **Search Sessions**

3. Enter your search criteria and press **Search** or simply press **Search** to see all the Session history.

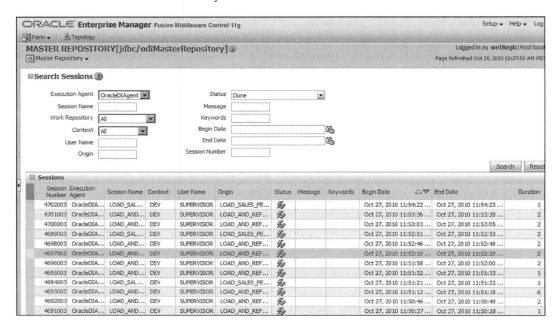

To view the details of a session record, click on the specific session number in the first column (**Session Number**) and the session details appear.

Oracle Data Integrator Console

Oracle Data Integrator Console provides remote management capabilities of key ODI components and objects. But ODI Console goes beyond the functionality offered in ODI Studio in two important areas: Data Lineage and Flow Map. Taking a hands-on approach to the FMCC, the following ODI Console features and capabilities are illustrated in this section:

- How to launch and access ODI Console
- Data Lineage
- Flow Maps

Launching and accessing ODI Console

The ODI Console web application is deployed on a WebLogic application server and its default landing page can be accessed by entering the URL associated with the context root of the ODI Console web application. To launch ODI Console, follow the given steps:

1. Open a web browser and enter `http://myhost:port/odiconsole`.
2. Select the repository you wish to connect to from the **Repository** drop down.
3. Enter the **User Id** and **Password** credentials for the repository and click on **Sign In**.

Data Lineage

Data Lineage offers the capabilities to look at an end to end view of data flows from a specific datastore point of view. These views cross the traditional Model and Interface views offered in Designer. Data Lineage also offers the end user drill down capabilities as well as the ability to easily and accurately assess impact. To access the Data Lineage functionality, follow the given steps:

1. Launch ODI Console in your web browser.
2. Log in using the appropriate Work repository.
3. With the **Browse** tab selected, a user can click on the expansion icon to the left of **Design Time**, and then click on the expansion icon to the left of **Models**. Here we see both Flow Map and Data Lineage nodes.
4. Click on **Data Lineage** to highlight the entry, then move up to select the View icon in the **Browse** tab icon toolbar. A **Data Lineage** tab will appear in the tabbed dialog workspace on the right side of the user interface.

[The View icon is the one that looks like a pair of sunglasses.]

In the **Options** region, you will need to select:

○ **Model**
○ **Sub-Model** and
○ **Datastore**

5. Additional options such as the ability to display **Interfaces** in the **Lineage** graph are also available

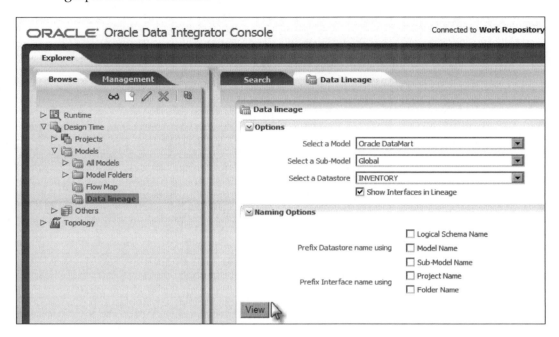

6. As the number of sources, models, interfaces, packages, and targets increase over time, having a Data Lineage reporting function producing varying granularity of detailed diagrams showing our data integration solution relationships and dependencies is invaluable to quickly and productively understand the as-is solution and perform impact analysis.

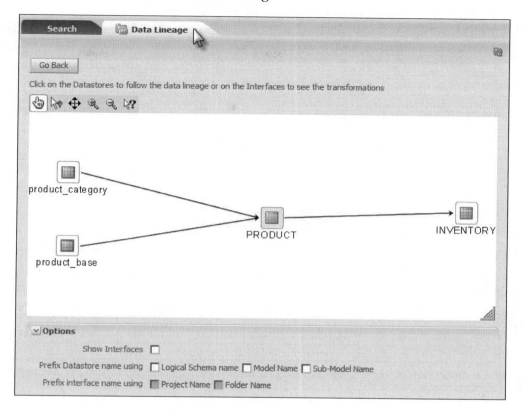

7. Press View to view the Data Lineage:

The resulting diagram offers the opportunity to include a number of optional content items in the Data Lineage reports including **Interfaces**, **Logical Schema**, and **Model** names.

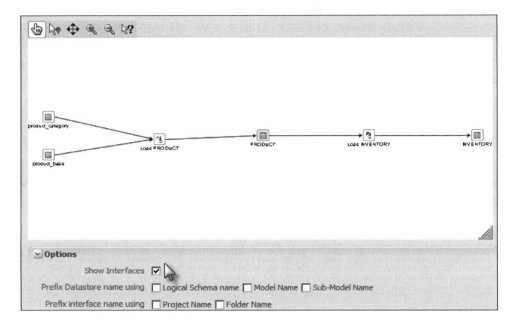

Click on **Show Interfaces** to display interfaces in the figure. Drilldown capabilities within the Data Lineage reports are also supported.

Flow Map

Where Data Lineage is focused on providing visibility into the relationships, dependencies, and data flow from or to a single datastore, the Flow Map feature is Model-centric and broader in scope by reporting on additional ODI key constructs as well as varying the granularity of detail of the Model-centric dependency reports. Granularity of detail in the Flow Map graphical reports can be controlled by:

- Restricting reported dependencies to only certain ODI projects
- Tailoring the granularity of detail of the Flow Map by selecting one item from each of the following two groups:

    ○ Models, Sub-Models, or Datastores

    ○ Projects, Folder, Packages, or Interfaces

A Flow Map representing the relationship between Datastore and Interface objects for only a project or two is similar to a Data Lineage report that includes interfaces, but may reflect more than one Datastore. The ability to drill down on Models, Projects, and Interfaces is similar to Data Lineage reports, though each ODI object type has its own representation of information presented on the drill down.

Summary

Management and monitoring are two critical non-functional requirements for an enterprise class application. As illustrated in this chapter, Oracle Data Integrator provides key capabilities in these areas. You should now be more knowledgeable and comfortable using the management and monitoring capabilities of ODI.

In this chapter we examined the following topics:

- Execution scheduling and ODI, including how to view and use the built-in ODI Scheduler for creating one-time and recurring data integration tasks. The options for integrating with third-party schedulers was also covered in detail.

- A thorough look at how to launch and use the Oracle Fusion Middleware Control Console for visibility into the health, status, and key performance statistics of the Oracle Data Integrator runtime infrastructure.

- Learning how to launch the new Oracle Data Integrator Console web application and learning how to use both the Data Lineage and Flow Map features—features that can dramatically improve the productivity of developers, testers, and business analysts on your data integration project teams.

13
Concluding Remarks

Congratulations! If you went through the different chapters, you are well on your way to becoming a productive Oracle Data Integrator developer and data integration project team member. ODI is one of the most comprehensive and popular data integration products in the industry, so you have added an in-demand entry to your skill set portfolio and resume.

By investing your time in this book, you have become well-versed and proficient in using the ODI Studio and Agent functionalities and have gained valuable expertise in creating data integration mappings and workflows. The authors of this book have dozens of years of accumulated experience working with Oracle Data Integrator on a daily basis, helping you avoid some of the frequently seen bumps along the road when first learning the product by providing a generous number of tips and hints within the various chapters. Our goal was not to simply provide a cursory or introductory understanding of ODI, but rather to give you a jumpstart in productivity as soon as your first data integration project starts. You now have the knowledge of working with Oracle, Microsoft SQL Server, MySQL, flat files, and XML files, as both sources and targets, as well as using all the different ODI objects and concepts. Finally, you should have developed confidence in working with the data integration project aspects—from defining sources and targets, to creating mappings and data workflows, to Agent execution, testing, troubleshooting, management, monitoring, Data Lineage, and impact analysis.

So what's next? Our first recommendation is to gets hands-on with Oracle Data Integrator as soon as possible and start using it frequently. Other sources of material to help you internalize Oracle Data Integrator and data integration concepts are:

- The ODI product forum on Oracle Technology Network (`http://forums.oracle.com/forums/forum.jspa?forumID=374`)

- My Oracle Support (`https://support.oracle.com/`), which provides an extensive knowledge base about Oracle Data Integrator

- Oracle Data Integration blog (`http://blogs.oracle.com/dataintegration/`)

- A couple of blogs covering ODI: BI Quotient (`http://www.business-intelligence-quotient.com/`), More to Life than this (`http://john-goodwin.blogspot.com/`), and ODI Experts (`http://www.odiexperts.com/`)

- Oracle University (`http://education.oracle.com`—look under **Middleware Training** then **Data Integration**)

- We should also mention several books from Packt Publishing that we find are often complementary when working with customers on their data integration initiatives including *Oracle SQL Developer 2.1*, *Oracle GoldenGate 11g Implementer's guide*, and *Getting Started With Oracle SOA Suite 11g R1 – A Hands-On Tutorial*

Finally, it is worth repeating some of the themes mentioned in the book. Use ODI over home-grown SQL coding for your data transfer and data enrichment and transformation activities—let the ODI Knowledge Modules do the heavy lifting SQL generation work for you. You now have the knowledge and confidence to "just say no" to the often seen default approach of manual coding implementations. Consider using Oracle Data Integrator and Oracle GoldenGate together when real-time data access of a relational database source is required. For cases where the amount of real-time data is smaller and changes are inherently event-driven, consider ODI Data Services to provide real-time data integration and shared remote access to your source of truth data in your target models. Lastly, have your SOA business processes delegate bulk and large data operations to Oracle Data Integrator through web services.

Build your skills and career with confidence and courage with Oracle Data Integrator.

Index

O

variables, to alter workflows
   Load Plans 82
   packages 80
visibility 339

W

WebLogic Domain menubar button 336
WebLogic Server 339
work repository 17

X

XML
   about 263
   introducing 263-265
XML files
   handling 96-100

XML files, with ODI
   background 268
   data, integrating from single
      Purchase Order 270-272
   models, creating from XML file 270
   overview 269
   Purchase Order, integrating from
      XML file 269
   requisites 268
   scope 269
   simple Purchase Order file, integrating 274
   single order interface flow logistics 272, 273
XML reverse engineering 104

Thank you for buying
Getting Started with Oracle Data Integrator 11*g*: A Hands-On Tutorial

About Packt Publishing

Packt, pronounced 'packed', published its first book "Mastering phpMyAdmin for Effective MySQL Management" in April 2004 and subsequently continued to specialize in publishing highly focused books on specific technologies and solutions.

Our books and publications share the experiences of your fellow IT professionals in adapting and customizing today's systems, applications, and frameworks. Our solution based books give you the knowledge and power to customize the software and technologies you're using to get the job done. Packt books are more specific and less general than the IT books you have seen in the past. Our unique business model allows us to bring you more focused information, giving you more of what you need to know, and less of what you don't.

Packt is a modern, yet unique publishing company, which focuses on producing quality, cutting-edge books for communities of developers, administrators, and newbies alike. For more information, please visit our website: www.packtpub.com.

About Packt Enterprise

In 2010, Packt launched two new brands, Packt Enterprise and Packt Open Source, in order to continue its focus on specialization. This book is part of the Packt Enterprise brand, home to books published on enterprise software – software created by major vendors, including (but not limited to) IBM, Microsoft and Oracle, often for use in other corporations. Its titles will offer information relevant to a range of users of this software, including administrators, developers, architects, and end users.

Writing for Packt

We welcome all inquiries from people who are interested in authoring. Book proposals should be sent to author@packtpub.com. If your book idea is still at an early stage and you would like to discuss it first before writing a formal book proposal, contact us; one of our commissioning editors will get in touch with you.

We're not just looking for published authors; if you have strong technical skills but no writing experience, our experienced editors can help you develop a writing career, or simply get some additional reward for your expertise.

Oracle SOA Suite 11*g* R1 Developer's Guide

ISBN: 978-1-84968-018-9   Paperback: 720 pages

Develop Service-Oriented Architecture Solutions with the Oracle SOA Suite

1. A hands-on, best-practice guide to using and applying the Oracle SOA Suite in the delivery of real-world SOA applications

2. Detailed coverage of the Oracle Service Bus, BPEL PM, Rules, Human Workflow, Event Delivery Network, and Business Activity Monitoring

3. Master the best way to use and combine each of these different components in the implementation of a SOA solution

Oracle 11*g* Streams Implementer's Guide

ISBN: 978-1-847199-70-6   Paperback: 352 pages

Design, implement, and maintain a distributed environment with Oracle Streams

1. Implement Oracle Streams to manage and coordinate the resources, information, and functions of a distributed system

2. Get to grips with in-depth explanations of the components that make up Oracle Streams, and how they work together

3. Learn design considerations that help identify and avoid Oracle Streams obstacles – before you get caught in them

Please check **www.PacktPub.com** for information on our titles

Oracle 10g/11g Data and Database Management Utilities

ISBN: 978-1-847196-28-6   Paperback: 432 pages

Master twelve must-use utilities to optimize the efficiency, management, and performance of your daily database tasks

1. Optimize time-consuming tasks efficiently using the Oracle database utilities

2. Perform data loads on the fly and replace the functionality of the old export and import utilities using Data Pump or SQL*Loader

3. Boost database defenses with Oracle Wallet Manager and Security

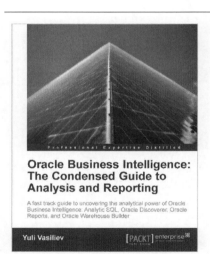

Oracle Business Intelligence : The Condensed Guide to Analysis and Reporting

ISBN: 978-1-84968-118-6   Paperback: 184 pages

A fast track guide to uncovering the analytical power of Oracle Business Intelligence: Analytic SQL, Oracle Discoverer, Oracle Reports, and Oracle Warehouse Builder

1. Install, configure, and deploy the components included in Oracle Business Intelligence Suite (SE)

2. Gain a comprehensive overview of components and features of the Oracle Business Intelligence package

Please check **www.PacktPub.com** for information on our titles

Printed in Great Britain
by Amazon.co.uk, Ltd.,
Marston Gate.